KICK
KENNEDY

ALSO BY BARBARA LEAMING

Jacqueline Bouvier Kennedy Onassis: The Untold Story

Churchill Defiant: Fighting On, 1945–1955

Jack Kennedy: The Education of a Statesman

Mrs. Kennedy: The Missing History of the Kennedy Years

Marilyn Monroe

Katharine Hepburn

Bette Davis

If This Was Happiness: A Biography of Rita Hayworth

Orson Welles: A Biography

Polanski: A Biography, the Filmmaker as Voyeur

KICK KENNEDY

THE CHARMED LIFE
AND TRAGIC DEATH OF THE
FAVORITE KENNEDY DAUGHTER

Barbara Leaming

THOMAS DUNNE BOOKS

ST. MARTIN'S PRESS 📖 NEW YORK

THOMAS DUNNE BOOKS.

An imprint of St. Martin's Press.

KICK KENNEDY: THE CHARMED LIFE AND TRAGIC DEATH OF THE FAVORITE KENNEDY DAUGHTER.

www.thomasdunnebooks.com

www.stmartins.com

The Library of Congress Cataloging-in-Publication Data is available upon request.

ISBN 978-1-250-07131-6 (hardcover)
ISBN 978-1-4668-8243-0 (e-book)

Our books may be purchased in bulk for promotional, educational, or business use.
Please contact the Macmillan Corporate and Premium Sales Department at 1-800-221-7945,
extension 5442, or by e-mail at MacmillanSpecialMarkets@macmillan.com.

First Edition: April 2016

KICK
KENNEDY

One

————————————

Outside, the moorlands were sheathed in darkness, the vast acreage of the park empty save for animals roaming in the night. Inside the golden stone palace, we two were alone together in a library crammed with well-loved books, tables littered with strange and often precious objects, and a long scarlet sofa bearing the traces of many naps by its owner. It was nearly midnight. It had been an intense evening, full of wide-ranging conversation, which had ended with a drive through the floodlit gardens surrounding the house.

Now, for a long moment, the two of us sat in silence in the low light of the room. Two leather chairs had been pulled round to face each other. The hands of the tall, emaciated figure sitting opposite me played nervously over the handle of his walking stick, before he put it aside.

At the age of eighty-two he was crippled with arthritis, and the hour in the damp just now had visibly pained him. But he had made it clear that he was not ready for the night to end. He had ushered me into this room and closed the door as if to indicate that there was some purpose not yet fulfilled.

The silence suddenly seemed loud, and then, without warning, one long, bony hand reached out and grabbed my wrist with shocking strength, and the old, nearly blind duke began to tell me a story.

. . .

I fancied her. I wanted to claim her for myself." This was how the duke began his tale.

She was just starting down the stairs when he saw her first. He had been standing at the bottom of the steps with the other boys. They were all impatiently waiting in the Great Hall for the girls to come down from their rooms and join them for dinner.

It was Friday evening, April 15, 1938, at Cliveden, the Italianate palace on the River Thames, in Buckinghamshire, owned by Lord and Lady Astor. Usually, house parties there were mixed affairs comprised of adults and young people, but on the present occasion, Easter weekend, it was exclusively the friends of the Astors' two youngest sons, Jakie and Michael, who had been asked to stay, though various adults would arrive for meals.

Lord Andrew Cavendish, eighteen-year-old grandson of the 9th Duke of Devonshire, suddenly broke off from the assembled group. Long, skinny arms and legs flying, a messy mop of hair flopping over his forehead, Andrew darted up the stairs toward the petite figure who had just appeared. He had spotted something about her that, he later insisted, he simply had never encountered in a girl previously. The moment she made her entrance, it was as if there was no one else in the cavernous room.

Every eye had turned to her—but it was only Andrew who had acted.

He was used to being aggressive. Indeed, by rights he should not even have been included in a house party, since he was not only the youngest of the boys, but also the only one of the group who had yet to matriculate at university. He was laughingly referred to by some as "the boy who couldn't wait to grow up." A year earlier he had begun to insinuate himself at parties to which his older brother had been invited.

Andrew's charm, wit, and exuberance made it impossible for most people to resist his efforts to be included. His "constipated older brother," as Jakie Astor jestingly and not a little cruelly described William, Earl of Burlington, most certainly did resist, however. Billy Burlington, as he was known, was frequently made miserable by Andrew's intrusive presence, and he often took it upon himself to check what he saw as the second son's rambunctious behavior. But Billy, aged twenty, was not present on this particular weekend, for the boisterous tone at Cliveden was decidedly not to his taste. More often than not, he pointedly avoided the scene there.

Tonight, therefore, Andrew was most happily on his own. There was no restraining hand to prevent him from dashing up those stairs. The girl he was rushing toward was, if truth be told, actually quite plain in appearance. Her hair was a shade of "mousy brown" and verged on being frizzy. Her shoulders were also unfortunate, set much too high, and her neck was far too short. In height, she was not quite five feet three, and her figure was, at that point anyway, "on the lumpy side." The British girls much envied their American counterparts' long, shapely legs. Yet, as would later become apparent, this particular American girl was obsessed with the conviction that her legs—American though they undeniably were—were too heavy.

Andrew would long remember that his opening gambit had been to say something funny to her (though he could not recall exactly what), and that her buoyant laughter had instantly made one forget her physical flaws.

All he had been able to think of, he later said, was that he had never before seen a girl who radiated "such vitality."

Her name, when Andrew got that far, was Kathleen Kennedy, but she said that everyone called her "Kick," and from then on she was never anything but "Kick" to those who encountered her in England. She was, Andrew had realized by this time, the eighteen-year-old daughter of the newly arrived U.S. Ambassador to the Court of St James's. Joseph P. Kennedy Sr. had descended upon London with an unprecedented blast of self-generated publicity. The diplomat had offered up stories centered not merely upon himself but upon the fact that he and his wife, Rose, were the parents of nine children. To date, however, only Kick and the four youngest had arrived in England. Since at this point Kick was the only one of the offspring who was of an age to partake in London social life, a good deal of the early publicity had concentrated on her.

Kick had traveled to London with a purpose. When her father was appointed to the ambassadorship by President Franklin D. Roosevelt, both parents decided to arrange for her to be presented at Court, in conjunction with the London Season. The Season consisted of a round of parties, dinners, and dances that took place each spring and early summer, as the debutantes were brought out in a matrimonial market designed to secure them suitable husbands. Such were the young men who, with startling rapidity, would guide them from the cosseted isolation of country houses in England or Scotland to their new lives as married women.

Kick, however, was decidedly not in London in search of a marriage partner. There was no intention on the Kennedys' part to emulate wealthy Americans of the past who, with the objective of securing a title for their daughters, had married them off to impoverished peers. Kick planned to stay in England for no more than six months before returning to the U.S., where her London debut would add luster to this granddaughter of a Boston-Irish saloon keeper as she looked for an American husband—a Roman Catholic, of course, though one with a higher social status than that enjoyed by her parents. Indeed, at the time Kick left the U.S. for Britain, she had been in the process of being courted by precisely one such fellow, J. Peter Grace, the twenty-five-year-old heir to the W. R. Grace fortune, who meant to propose to Ambassador Kennedy's daughter the following year.

In any case, the London Season had been about to begin in earnest when Kick received an invitation to Cliveden. Nancy Astor, who was herself an American, liked to take care of compatriots who found themselves, as she had once been, strangers to a world so different from their own. No sooner had Lady Astor met the new American ambassador at a dinner party in London than she had proposed including his daughter in the Easter weekend festivities.

In anticipation of Kick's arrival, Lady Astor worried that the newcomer might prove too shy and too stiff for her sons' rather wild set of friends. That was the reason why, just behind Kick on the staircase in the Great Hall that evening, there hovered a shy, dark-haired girl with delicate features and the palest of porcelain white skin. Lady Jean Ogilvy, the nineteen-year-old daughter of the Earl of Airlie, had been raised at Cortachy Castle in Scotland and had been brought out in the 1937 London Season. Joseph P. Kennedy's predecessor in the ambassadorship, Robert Bingham, had hosted a dance in Jean's honor at the American Embassy residence in Prince's Gate on the occasion of her coming out. Now Nancy Astor had assigned Jean the bedroom next to Kick's, with the directive: "I've got this little American girl. You have to look after her." Kick had indeed seemed "rather lost" at first. Still, as Jean laughingly remembered many years later, it became instantly apparent, even as she endeavored to carry out her appointed role, that her high-mettled new charge "didn't need any looking after!"

For Kick Kennedy, England was but the latest "gift" in a long series of treats presented to her by her adoring father. She had come to England, and to Cliveden in particular, because of Joe Kennedy. And she assumed that, precisely for that reason, both would prove to be happy experiences. Heretofore, "Darling Daddy" had been the one who could always be counted on to provide her with a life full of adventures, excitement, and surprises. He had given her screenings of the latest movies before they were officially released, tickets to Broadway shows for herself and her friends, dinners in the best restaurants, and all the pretty dresses that a girl could want. He arranged for her to ski in Switzerland during her school break. He set up meetings with influential men to assist her in unfamiliar cities. He paid for her travels and foreign schooling, and gave her extra money when she asked for it. He let her sip Shirley Temples with her two elder brothers, Joe Junior and Jack, in Palm Beach night-clubs. And when she wished the rules to be altered in her favor, he had even provided special perks to the Sacred Heart nuns who administered the convent school in Connecticut that she'd attended since the age of thirteen. Most of all, the old man had instilled in her the conviction that whenever anything went wrong, whenever some unforeseen obstacle materialized in her path, he could be counted on to "fix" things. As a consequence, Kick expected life to be wonderful, each chapter more de-lightful than the one that had come before.

To Jean Ogilvy, Kick had started down those steps at Cliveden with "unshakable self-confidence." Kick's only complaint about England thus far was that since she had arrived a few weeks previously, the boys had all seemed rather dull and humorless, at least compared with her favor-ite brother Jack's set at home. But that certainly seemed about to change when she spotted the gangly, exceedingly good-humored fellow racing up the steps. From the moment Andrew Cavendish addressed her, the words tumbling out of his mouth so swiftly that they were barely if at all comprehensible, Kick appeared to sense that life was once again meet-ing her expectations after all.

For a long moment, the three young people stood in place on the stair-case, like figures in a frieze: proper, nervous Jean a few steps above Kick and eager, ebullient Andrew a step or two below. As ample as Kick's experience of life had been to date, for all of her travels and for all of the people she had encountered, nothing in her past had quite prepared her for the particular world to which Jean and Andrew were about to intro-duce her.

This was the world of the aristocratic cousinhood, a world that more often than not remained hermetically sealed against outsiders. Its mem-bers shared feelings, books, manners, habits, history—and most of them, blood. In their rarefied milieu, cousin married cousin for generation after generation, until the web of interrelationships was so tangled that every-one seemed to be related to everyone else many times over. Yet for all of the apparent sameness, for all of the like-mindedness that seemed to have been bred into them, there were also important nuances that distinguished them from one another, critical differences bearing on such matters as politics and religion that, imperceptible though they might be to an outsider, were often the cause of tremendous conflict and pain. Jean was the ideal guide to this world, as she had had so little experience of anything else. To her the aristocratic cousinhood was, really, the only world.

That evening on a staircase in a great house overlooking the River Thames, an extraordinary story was about to begin. Kick Kennedy was poised to enter a centuries-old society of which she as yet had little understanding, a world in which, however improbably, she was at length to play an important—to some minds, emblematic—role. Among the surviving members of the tribe, her story would continue to resonate, to be passionately, even obsessively, discussed and debated, long after the Little American Girl herself was dead.

For the moment, however, as she laughed and bantered with Andrew, whom she seemed not entirely to comprehend, and who was himself not always quite certain of what she was saying, all that appeared to matter was that the young nobleman wished to claim her for his own. By the time they reached the bottom of the stairs, however, with Jean in avid pursuit, Andrew realized that he was to have no further opportunity to advance that claim, at least not that night. Almost without transition, Kick was soon conversing easily with the other, somewhat older males waiting to go in to dinner.

Among these were nineteen-year-old Jakie Astor, an irrepressible jokester, as well as Andrew's great friend; twenty-two-year-old Michael Astor, the incipient ladies' man in the group, as well as a major crush of Jean Ogilvy's; and David Ormsby-Gore, nearly twenty years of age, who had been brought up virtually as a brother to Andrew, their mothers, the granddaughters of the Victorian-era colossus Prime Minister Lord Salisbury, being sisters.

Kick possessed qualities that these young men had rarely if ever seen in a girl. The girls they knew, the eighteen-year-olds who were brought to London by their families from rural England and Scotland to be presented at Court and to make their social debut, tended to be silent and nervous when they encountered boys for the first time. They were girls who simply were not used to being around young males other than their brothers, and they made their discomfiture clear in everything they did and said.

Kick was notably different. She did not hang back shyly or demurely. On the contrary, she instantly propelled herself into the fray, laughing at the boys' jokes, making teasing remarks of her own, and cackling with delight when, half in gaiety, half in gravity, Jakie Astor complained that her accent made it impossible for him to understand so much as a word that she was saying. The newcomer was willing to laugh at herself—her mistakes, her gaucheries, and even her physical flaws—in a way that was simply unknown among the English girls. Andrew later described that willingness (which, he pointed out, Kick shared with her brother Jack, but with no other Kennedy family member) as "the essence of charm."

She was, moreover, a strangely blended character whose personal contradictions were of immense appeal to the boys in this particular set. On the one hand, Kick was clearly more outgoing and at ease than the girls to whom they were accustomed. She had grown up in the often raucous, at times violent, company of two older brothers, the eldest, Joe Junior, and the second son, Jack. She had traveled with them, accompanied them to nightclubs, been adopted as a mascot by Jack's entourage of mischievous male friends. Racy talk, cabaret gossip, knowing references to Hollywood movies and Broadway shows—all these were as nature to her.

Paradoxically, Kick might also be said to have had a cloistered upbringing, owing to the doctrinaire Roman Catholicism of her mother, to whom she was devoted. Kick had attended convent schools, both in the U.S. and in France. At eighteen years of age, she had been long and deeply inculcated with Roman Catholic principles. Kick would no more consider missing Mass on Sundays and holy days than she would failing to drop to her knees and utter her prayers before she went to bed at night. In contrast to her older brothers, both of whom were sexually active, Kick was nothing if not innocent. Her brothers—Jack especially, careless though he might be of the sensitivities of a girlfriend— worked hard at preserving Kick's innocence, which was as important to the brothers and to their father as it was to Rose Kennedy.

That Easter weekend of 1938, Kick's unique combination of innocence and experience proved irresistible to the Astor boys and their young friends: "country-member bad boys," as Andrew later characterized them, by which he meant fellows who, however wildly they might talk and behave, would, at this point in their lives anyway, probably have been terrified had a truly worldly American girl appeared among them.

The scene in the Great Hall was cut short by a summons to dinner. Meals at Cliveden tended to be chaotic affairs, with conversations conducted not merely with one's dinner partners, but often literally shouted up, down, and across the table. Andrew and David, particularly, had the reputation of marathon talkers. Through their mothers, both boys were descendants of the Cecils, one of the great Protestant families of England, known through the generations for their acute minds and distinctive sparring manner of speech.

Capable like their forebears of producing more words in a minute than most other people can in five, Andrew and David typically raced from topic to topic, with barely a pause for breath. Once the duo had launched into one of these breakneck conversations, even their cousins often found it impossible to tell which fellow was speaking at a particular moment, so completely did their words and voices overlap and merge into one another. But rather than slow their pace, they often began to jabber even more quickly, as though struggling to keep up with the thoughts and images careening through their brains. At times, Andrew and David appeared to speak simultaneously, causing observers to question whether they were even attempting to listen to each other.

On a given occasion, their talk was likely to cover topics ranging

from the bets they had placed with the Newmarket bookies, whose rak-
ishly tilted felt hats and other elements of attire they were known to
emulate; to the latest debates in the House of Commons, which they
monitored with the same avidity that American boys followed baseball;
to all the latest and choicest gossip of London Society, of which Andrew
was a particular connoisseur.

In this antic atmosphere, Kick sparkled. It was not just that she was
voluble. It was that she loved talking as much as they did, and that her
speech was as unique and flavorful as the boys'. There was her Boston
twang, of course. There were the slangy phrases such as "Oh, kid, what's
the story?" with which she spiced her conversation. But most of all, there
was her way of talking on and on, regardless of whether or not she was
quite making sense, that the boys found matchlessly endearing and entertaining.

Kick's chatter, as she herself referred to it, was a social weapon that
she had honed over time. It had long been the custom of Joseph P. Kennedy Sr. to use his influence in the various milieux among which he
moved—business, finance, politics, religion, entertainment—on behalf
of his children. He thought nothing of requesting that busy people
take the time to smooth the way for his offspring. Almost always, the
individuals whom old Joe reached out to proved eager to ingratiate
themselves with him. Kick discovered that no matter how naive and
nonsensical her talk, her father's associates all responded as though her
every word were a nugget of wit and a source of delight.

That experience, oft repeated, led Kick to become at once conscious
and confident of her effects. Mixing self-possession and self-mockery,
the girl who came to Cliveden that Easter weekend acted as though there
were never any doubt that, so long as she kept on talking and laughing,
she would be universally liked and admired, as always.

Still, Kick had not yet played her full hand—far from it. The following day, with the much-anticipated arrival of the most ambitious, as
well as the noisiest, member of the set, David's twenty-year-old Oxford

roommate, Hugh Fraser, the tenor of the conversation shifted drastically. As chance would have it, from then on all that the fellows seemed to want to discuss were topics that Kick had previously heard much about at home.

In 1933, shortly after Adolf Hitler became German chancellor, the Oxford Union, the university debating society known as a training ground for future British prime ministers and parliamentarians, had voted in favor of a motion that in the event of a war they would "in no circumstances" fight in defense of King and Country. The vote reflected the mood of a nation that recoiled from the possibility of another world conflict at a time when memories of the slaughter of the Great War (1914–1918) remained vivid.

Winston Churchill, the former First Lord of the Admiralty who since the previous year had been arguing in the House of Commons for rearmament measures aimed at preventing a new war with the Germans, did not doubt that were war to be declared, young Britain would do its duty. Churchill was concerned, however, that the King and Country resolution might influence the Germans and others to believe that "a decadent, degenerate Britain" would indeed refuse to fight, and he worried that that miscalculation could result in another world war, the very opposite of what the "foolish boys" of Oxford had intended.

Five years later, Kick's first visit to Cliveden was occurring during the same month that Hugh Fraser, in collaboration with another member of the set, Julian Amery, was leading the fight at the Oxford Union to reverse the "ever-shameful" King and Country resolution, an undertaking that would not come to fruition till the following year, when Hugh was himself president of the Union. Just now, he and Julian were making the case for conscription at a moment when the question of Britain's willingness to fight another war, should it prove necessary to do so, could scarcely have seemed more timely.

In 1936, Hitler's armies had invaded the Rhineland, after which Churchill had predicted that the Germans would next target Austria. But when, during the two years that followed, Hitler failed to make another move, a state of denial appeared to set in among Britain's governing class, many of whom wanted to believe that Churchill—that self-glorifying warmonger, as they saw him—had simply been wrong and that the Nazis' territorial ambitions had been sated by the Rhineland episode.

In March 1938, however, a little over a week after Kick arrived in London, German troops overran Austria. Britain recognized the conquest within a matter of days but continued relations with Germany as though nothing had occurred. In the event that Hitler moved against his widely anticipated next target, Czechoslovakia, the French had a treaty obligation to come to the aid of the Czechs. Britain, for its part, was bound to France in the event that the latter went to war against Germany. But what in fact would Britain do?

Churchill argued that the British needed to state plainly their irrevocable commitment to join France in the defense of Czechoslovakia. British prime minister Neville Chamberlain, who yet had hope of coming to friendly terms with the dictators of Germany and Italy, preferred to keep the Germans and the rest of the world in suspense about British intentions. Hugh Fraser's Saturday, April 16, 1938, appearance at Cliveden, coming as it did at a time when national attention was focused on his efforts at the Oxford Union, plunged the Astor brothers and their young guests into the very center of the controversy.

Since the time of the Rhineland invasion, the boys in this group had been persuaded that war was inevitable, despite anything that certain of their parents might say and insist. That expectation infused the boys' lives with a special intensity. Never doubting that before long they would be called upon to fight, and perhaps to die, they believed that they were "entitled" to enjoy themselves in the precious months and years that remained to them.

As Andrew would later wryly acknowledge, he and the others seized upon the coming war as an "excuse" to drink more and drive faster than they might otherwise have done. Their record of spectacular car crashes became legend. At the time Kick first encountered him, David Ormsby-

Gore boasted a new set of false teeth, which, Jean explained to her, was the consequence of his having crashed into the rear of a truck when he was driving at a speed of ninety-eight miles per hour on his way back to Oxford from the Newmarket races. Jakie Astor, who had been a passenger in David's car—along with Hugh Fraser and another friend of theirs, Peter Wood—was left with a prominent dentlike facial scar. Both boys wore their injuries like medals. Far from chastening the young men in the set, this accident and others like it seemed only to encourage them to carouse the more vehemently. They rarely managed to forget the coming war, however, and certainly not when Hugh Fraser was about.

Hardly would Hugh and David, both of whom had protuberant noses, begin talking than they would, in the parlance of the set, be "nose-to-nose" about the perilous situation in Europe. At the start of these frenetic discussions, which were of compelling interest to all of the boys, the girls in the group tended to peel away, being more concerned with, in Jean's phrase, "the next dance and what we were going to wear." So, that Easter weekend of 1938, there was a good deal of fascination among both sexes when Kick, rather than go off with Jean, chose to remain behind with Hugh, David, and the other fellows. The previous evening, Kick had dazzled and delighted the group with her chatter. On the present occasion, she astonished them by her eagerness to listen.

Rather than a stratagem on her part, her visible enjoyment of the boys' talk, then and later, was sincere. Kick had grown up in the company of a brother, Jack, who had read many of the same English books these young men had; who, like them, had avidly followed Winston Churchill's campaign in the House of Commons for British rearmament; and who had tracked the original King and Country debate and its aftermath in the pages of *The New York Times*. In the wake of the 1933 Oxford Union resolution, Jack—who at the time had been a sickly, bookish sixteen-year-old prep school student in Connecticut—had concluded that the British, whose traditions of honor and duty he had previously come to revere, had grown "decadent." He had often addressed these and related themes in the course of political discussions at the family table in Hyannis Port and elsewhere, which were also attended by Joe Junior, their father . . . and Kick, though as a girl she was thought to be without the possibility of a future in politics. Seeking to train and test his sons, the eldest of whom he was determined would be U.S. president one day, old Joe Kennedy saw this give-and-take as a crucial part of their political education. The patriarch encouraged all three children to interrupt him at any point, to ask questions, to offer their opinions, and even to challenge him.

Hence Kick's readiness with Hugh, David, and the other English boys not just to listen, but also at moments to gamely interject questions and declarations of her own. The young grandees were enchanted. For the remainder of the weekend, the young people of both sexes played tennis and croquet, rode horses in the woods, and boated on the Thames. Still, it had been quickly established that whenever the urgent talk of international events resumed, Kick, alone among the females, would linger conspicuously with the fellows.

On Monday morning, the country house weekend that Kick later described to Nancy Astor as "the best thing that ever happened to me" concluded. As a consequence of that weekend, Kick wrote, "All the loneliness I had for America has disappeared because now England seems so very jolly." Kick returned to a London that remained largely shut down for the holiday. She was scheduled to go to Paris presently on a shopping expedition with her mother. By the time Kick came back from France, Jean Ogilvy would herself have left for Cortachy Castle, where she was due to remain for two weeks.

Unwilling to wait that long to continue the fun, Kick again did something that Jean or the other English girls would never have considered doing. In Kick's position, Jean would have regarded it as a matter of etiquette that one did not ask people out to lunch after having encountered them but a single time. Thus the shiver of surprise and delight that Jean experienced when she picked up the telephone at her family's London home to hear Kick excitedly proposing that she join her for lunch that very afternoon at the American Embassy residence in Prince's Gate.

Much as Jean longed to go, she felt that she must decline because she had her father with her in London. But obstacles that seemed insurmountable to Jean were as nothing to the Little American Girl.

"I've got my dad, too," Kick rejoined, before going on to suggest that Jean simply bring Lord Airlie with her.

Two

O n a quiet Monday afternoon in London, in April of 1938, a
rather unlikely foursome were enjoying a leisurely lunch
in the large dining room at the American Embassy residence in Prince's Gate, near Hyde Park. At intervals, the two teenaged
girls in this ebullient party, Kick Kennedy and Jean Ogilvy, would mis-
chievously, laughingly, rush off to yet again crank up the gramophone
on which a recording of the popular American song "Franklin D. Roosevelt Jones" had been playing "over and over" throughout the course
of the meal.

Whether or not it had been the girls' intention, the insistent music
competed with the voices of their fathers, one the recently arrived U.S.
Ambassador to the Court of St James's, and the other the patriarch of a
family of ancient Scottish lineage who, in his capacity as the Queen's
Lord Chamberlain, oversaw the monarch's household. As both men, Joe
Kennedy and Joe Airlie, had the same first name, their adoring daughters

would forever fondly and lightheartedly refer to the occasion of their meeting as "the lunch of the two Joes."

Watching Kick's tall, redheaded father, who had a booming laugh, a loud voice, and a large fund of slangy phrases, Jean could not but be struck by the qualities of energy and directness that he shared with his daughter. Joe Kennedy was a man who simply charged forward in life. He went around obstacles, precisely as Kick had done when she arranged this very lunch; and he seemed to accomplish it all with a delightful outpouring of jokes and a "twinkle" in his vivid blue eyes.

Just as Kick had enchanted the young people at Cliveden by how different she was from the girls of the set, so too her opinionated, outspoken father contrasted markedly with other diplomats, notably with his predecessor, Robert Bingham, whom Lord Airlie and his wife had known well and had often visited, sometimes in this very dining room. But, as their daughter would point out many years later, whereas Lord and Lady Airlie might have encountered Robert Bingham socially even if he had not been the American ambassador in London, they almost certainly would never otherwise have met Joe Kennedy, who was of a lower social class than his predecessor and was—to Jean's sense— possessed of a personal "coarseness" that seemed highly unusual in a diplomat.

Indeed, it had been Kennedy's own intense consciousness of matters of class in American society that had led him to covet the London posting in the first place. Fueled by no little amount of savage indignation due to a history of social slights and snubs, Kennedy hoped to assuage and avenge some of that hurt, as well as to elevate himself and his family socially. He had sought the ambassadorship by way of compensation for his key political support of Franklin Roosevelt in the 1936 presidential election.

Strange to say, the very background and personal qualities that had provoked a good deal of controversy in Washington when Kennedy was given the embassy in London would, at least at first, make him seem a refreshing change to many British aristocrats. Most particularly, they shared his belief in the wisdom of coming to terms with the European dictators, and admired his willingness to speak his mind about that controversial topic whether or not the administration in Washington agreed with him on every point. Though not all aristocrats supported the policy of appeasement, many were eager to make an ally of the Reich. The record of casualties sustained during the Great War had been especially high among Britain's patrician elite, which regarded itself as having sacrificed the flower of a generation. A broad swath of aristocrats further believed that Nazi Germany, by its very existence on the map, provided an indispensable bulwark against Soviet Russia, which they, like Kennedy, saw as the far greater threat.

The two Joes, therefore, had been getting on very well indeed when Kick suggested that while their fathers happily talked on, she take Jean to meet her six-year-old brother, Teddy, who was the Kennedy family's much-spoiled and beloved baby. Heretofore, Kick's impending presentation at Court—alongside her older sister, Rosemary, aged nineteen, whom she described to Jean as "a little backward"—had been regarded as the event that would officially launch her in London Society. But, already, with her triumph at the country house weekend at Lady Astor's, and with her having consolidated the friendship with Jean at "the lunch of the two Joes," Kick had in effect launched herself far more successfully than any Court presentation could possibly have done.

As soon as she and Jean were back in London following their sojourns in France and Scotland, respectively, Jean began to include her in lunches with leading debs, who were constantly in and out of one another's houses, strategizing about their next moves in the matrimonial market, planning their costumes, and gossiping about the young nobles with whom they had danced, or failed to dance, the night before. Notable among this group was Jean's cousin, Lord Redesdale's daughter Deborah Mitford, known as "Debo," who lived in Rutland Gate, just around the corner from Kick; Gina Wernher, the "frightfully beautiful" and immensely rich granddaughter of a Russian grand duke; and

Jean's younger sister Margaret, whom Debo had indelibly dubbed "Maggot."

Accordingly, by the eleventh of May, when the actual presentation took place, Kick was already so thoroughly immersed in the world of the cousinhood that an air almost of anticlimax crept into her diary entry, which noted with a certain disappointment and disillusionment how quickly she had walked past King George and Queen Elizabeth before the much-anticipated ceremony was at an end. Of far greater significance to the narrative of Kick's social emergence was her visit three days later, in the company of her parents, to Blenheim Palace in Oxfordshire.

After dinner at the English Baroque residence of the Marlborough dukes, four "drunken youths from Oxford," as Kick described them in a diary entry, suddenly appeared on the scene. Two of the fellows— Hugh Fraser and Jakie Astor—she had of course previously met at Cliveden. The other two boys were quite new to her. On the present occasion, twenty-year-old Dawyck Haig, the 2nd Earl Haig, son of the late commander of the British Expeditionary Force in the Great War, was so inebriated that he managed to break a statue when he flung a champagne bottle in its direction. But it was Kick's introduction to the fourth rabble-rouser, Lord Robert Cecil, the twenty-one-year-old future head of one of England's premier Protestant dynasties, the house of Cecil, that would at length prove to be of the greatest consequence.

Tall, darkly good-looking, supremely entertaining, and often scandalously ill-behaved, Robert was the grandson of the Marquess of Salisbury and the son of Lord Cranborne, a leader of the Conservative opposition to Prime Minister Neville Chamberlain's policy of appeasement. Widely regarded as one of the two most eligible bachelors in London, Robert had previously demonstrated a taste for the "forbidden fruit" of Catholic girls in the persons of Hugh Fraser's sister Veronica Fraser and of Winston Churchill's niece Clarissa Churchill.

Robert was a great favorite of his cousin Jean Ogilvy, who, then and later, loved few things better in life than to recount his exploits with a mixture of admiration and alarm. Because of Robert's prodigious drinking, Jean was forbidden to drive with him anywhere. Lord Airlie, when he supplied his car for her outings with Robert, had to arrange for not one but two chauffeurs, due to Robert's habit of remaining out so late that more often than not a second shift was required. Lady Airlie, exceptionally strict with her daughters, was known to sit along the ballroom edges watching Jean through a lorgnette lest she violate the cardinal rule of never dancing more than two dances with the same young man. On one particular evening that became legend among the members of the set, Robert Cecil, gliding past with Jean in his arms, suddenly produced a lorgnette of his own, through which he satirically peered back at Lady Airlie, to the mother's outrage and the young people's exhilaration.

Kick had an opportunity to meet her rapidly widening circle of Oxford admirers again a few days hence. Ambassador Kennedy took her along with him to Oxford, where there was to be a reception in his honor during Eights Week, the occasion of the annual intercollegiate rowing races. As she had done at Cliveden, Kick impressed the boys with her difference from the other girls they knew when she made a point of actually listening to her father's address. One undergraduate member of the cousinhood who soon confessed to being infatuated with her was twenty-one-year-old Tony Loughborough, heir to his grandfather the Earl of Rosslyn.

By the time Kick materialized at Oxford, Tony had already heard much about her from his mother, who had been a guest at Blenheim Palace when the Kennedys were there. Tony was quick to pursue Ambassador Kennedy's daughter, whom he presently treated to her first outing at a glamorous London nightclub, Ciro's. By and by, he perceived that Kick, however fond of him in turn, was interested solely in their being close friends and nothing more. In years past, Kick had displayed a gift for adroitly enlisting as "pals" those of her brother Jack's friends who insisted that they had fallen in love with her—and at length she managed to do so with Tony, who would long remain devoted to her.

Meanwhile, Tony faced a good deal of competition for her attentions.

Viscount Duncannon, the heir to the Earl of Bessborough, had made early claims, taking her off to dinner at his parents' residence, as well as escorting her to various parties. Lord John Stanley, grandson and heir to the Earl of Derby, had met Kick at Blenheim Palace and afterward spent Derby Day at Epsom in her buoyant company. One notable absence from Kick's dance card during this period was the name of Lord Andrew Cavendish, from whom there had been no follow-up in the aftermath of their meeting at Cliveden. Andrew had disappeared for a reason. His grandfather, Victor, 9th Duke of Devonshire, had died on the sixth of May. Upon Duke Victor's demise, Andrew's father became the 10th Duke, and Andrew's older brother Billy Burlington had become the Marquess of Hartington, and was thereafter known as Billy Hartington. A period of mourning had ensued for the Cavendish family, at the conclusion of which Andrew Cavendish, as he continued to be called, had been shipped off to Lyons to study French.

At the whirligig of parties, balls, and dinners that comprised the 1938 London Season, Kick was often frustrated by the code that governed the young people's behavior. To Jean Ogilvy had fallen the task to—in Debo Mitford's words—introduce Kick "to her English contemporaries and to the unwritten rules and nuances of social life." Still, nothing that Jean said by way of explanation seemed capable of assuaging Kick's puzzlement at a young man's being prohibited to ask one to dance unless there had previously been a formal introduction. Kick also failed to comprehend why the notion of a boy's cutting in on another fellow on the dance floor seemed so utterly to horrify her new English friends. No matter how many times she was informed that this or that was simply the custom of the country, Kick's diaries and letters attest to the fact that she found many of the rules absurd. She wanted things to move. She lived for fluidity.

Sometimes, however, she acknowledged the need to bow to traditions she did not like or understand. At the beginning of June, Kick and her sister Rosemary were to be feted at a coming-out party of their own at Prince's Gate. Some eighty people were expected at dinner, with about three hundred more scheduled to join them afterward for the dancing. Kick admitted that she needed help with the seating arrangements at her own table for eight, but she mistook the problem of whom to include, and whom to place exactly where, to be a product of what she described in her diary as the numerous "petty jealousies" that existed in London. In reality, decisions of this nature were routinely based on matters of precedence that, however mysterious to her and her mother, were second nature to Jean Ogilvy. Delegated to help make critical decisions about the formation of the main table, Jean began by seating herself and Debo there. To Kick's right, in the position of highest honor, she placed Prince Frederick of Prussia. Viscount Duncannon she set on Kick's left. She further anointed Lord John Stanley and Lord Robert Cecil to be part of this premier grouping.

That night—while Bert Ambrose's band played, the American nightclub entertainer Harry Richman sang, and young couples danced on the pavement outside in the early morning hours to the tune of "Moonlight in Manhattan"—Robert seemed taken anew with Kick. Whether on account of the young nobleman's interest or merely by way of reciprocation, not long afterward she received an invitation from his grandmother Lady Alice, the Marchioness of Salisbury, to a young people's house party at Hatfield House, the family seat in Hertfordshire—a party that was to transform Kick into something much more than simply a source of delight and diversion to the cousinhood.

For nearly four centuries, the Cecils of Hatfield House had been advising monarchs and in other ways exerting critical behind-the-scenes influence on their nation's political life. They were noted for their gifts of vision and strategy, but also for their willingness, when the Cecil stock became, as the phrase was, exhausted, to endeavor to refresh and revitalize their blue blood by an infusion of red. At such times, instead of marrying aristocrats they chose their partners from other, presumably tougher and more vigorous strata of society. According to the family narrative, in the fullness of time the breed was thereby strengthened, and power and preeminence regained. At Hatfield House, Queen Victoria's three-time prime minister, the 3rd Marquess of Salisbury—great-grandfather of Robert Cecil on the one hand and of the Cavendish brothers, Billy and Andrew, on the other—was believed to have been the magnificent product of this replenishing process.

Kick, when she arrived at Hatfield House on Friday, June 17, noted with astonishment the number of Catholic guests—four, including herself—in a household known for its anti-Catholic animus. Veronica Fraser was there with her mother, Lady Lovat, who, in light of Robert's reputation, had refused to allow her to come to Hatfield alone. Robert, however, had arranged to circumvent Lady Lovat's ever-watchful presence by placing Veronica in a tiny room with a secret egress via a closet, through which she could steal as soon as her mother had fallen asleep in the adjoining, much larger bedroom. Also present that weekend was another beautiful Catholic girl, Clarissa Churchill, on whom Robert had danced attendance the previous year, until his mother, Lady Cranborne, intervened. For Lady Cranborne, the Catholic issue was then much in play, her twenty-two-year-old brother Richard having lately eloped with another Catholic beauty, Pamela Lloyd Thomas, to the monumental anguish of his and Lady Cranborne's father, old Lord "Dick" Cavendish.

In the course of the house party, the tensions surrounding what was thought to be a group of conniving Catholic girls that had targeted the great Protestant families of England, supposedly with an eye toward making those venerable houses Catholic, would at length find expression in the rough treatment to which Kick was subjected—some of it at the instigation of no less a figure than Robert's grandmother.

Kick's weekend began happily enough, however, when, that evening, all the young people attended a dance at a neighboring house. The only complication was that by the time Robert and his guests returned, Hatfield had been closed for the night. They had a good deal of trouble getting in, and even then they had to find their way to their respective rooms in utter darkness.

Saturday began with tennis, a sport that Kick approached—as she approached all sports, in fact—with ferocity. She, like her siblings, had

learned to play hard from a father whose maxim was, "We want win-
ners, we don't want losers around here." Kennedys did not play for fun;
they played to win. Whether the activity be tennis, football, or sailing,
they regarded victory as a matter of life and death.

Robert Cecil had seen Kick play tennis just a few days before when
he had unexpectedly turned up at Cliveden, where she had been a mid-
week guest of Jakie and Michael Astor. For some of the other young
people at Hatfield, however, this was a first opportunity to watch all of
that fierceness and aggression erupt from so tiny a girl. If her size had
led any of them to assume that she was as delicate as she was petite, the
morning's exhibition surely dissipated all such preconceptions.

But whereas her performance in the course of that first Easter weekend at Lady Astor's had endeared her to the Astor boys and the other
fellows, this time she seemed to have provoked a rather different response.
For Kick, things turned ugly after dinner, when, as she noted with alarm
in her diary, "John Stanley got rather rough," squirting a water siphon
at her. In her place, another girl might have burst into tears, but it was
also a dictum of her father's that "Kennedys don't cry." Accordingly, at
least in front of her host and fellow guests, she made a point of treating
the incident as just another of the young nobleman's jolly jokes.

Afterward, Kick saw fit to retire at an early hour. But when she went
upstairs, she discovered that her enormous bed in the Oliver Cromwell
bedroom had been short-sheeted as a prank, making it impossible
for her to extend her legs beyond the middle of the bed. Still loath to
exhibit any distress, Kick calmly searched out the one young man in
the house on whose sympathy she knew she could depend absolutely.
Tony Loughborough helped Kick to refold and rearrange the sheets as
if the practical joke had never occurred in the first place.

The harassment continued the next evening, Sunday the nineteenth
of June, when, going up to dress for dinner, Kick found that all of her
left shoes had vanished. She thereupon squeezed into two mismatched
shoes—one white and the other black—and limped downstairs to the
dining room. Bullying was not a new phenomenon to Kick. After all,

she had grown up in a household where the hot-tempered oldest boy routinely beat up the smaller, weaker second son, who had learned early on that for dignity's sake it was best to pretend afterward that the brutality had never taken place. So, too, at Hatfield House, Kick acted as if nothing were wrong and laughed at herself and her plight, though secretly she was disconcerted and not a little horrified when she discovered that it was her host who had taken her shoes and his grandmother who had suggested that he harass her in this manner.

Kick's refusal to crumble made a vivid impression on the members of the aristocratic cousinhood, both those who had been present that weekend and those, far greater in number, who heard about the episode later. Heretofore, she had been known and much admired for her high spirits. As a consequence of her eventful stay at Hatfield House, she also began to acquire a reputation for being tough. In effect, Robert Cecil and his paternal grandmother had tested her, and Kick had passed the test brilliantly.

After two months in London, Kick had met nearly all of the members of the group of young people to which Jean had set about to introduce her. At this point, however, one crucial bit of the puzzle remained to be put in place before the picture could be said to be complete. Kick had yet to encounter the one member of the cousinhood to whom Jean was closest.

On June 24, 1938, Kick and Jean spent much of the day together watching the tennis matches at Wimbledon. Afterward, they attended a small dinner party hosted by Lord and Lady Airlie, following which the guests were to go on to a large dance that the Speaker of the House of Commons, Edward FitzRoy, was giving in honor of his granddaughters, Anne and Mary, at the Palace of Westminster. It was on the occasion of the Airlie dinner party that David Ormsby-Gore introduced Kick to his cousin Billy Hartington, whose future grandeur caused him to be known as the other of London's two most eligible bachelors, beside Robert Cecil.

At six foot four, Billy, then a student of history at Trinity College,

Cambridge, towered over Kick, who was his dinner partner that night. Handsome, with a pale complexion, an intriguing half smile, and a quiescent manner that Jean affectionately described as "rather sleepy," Billy was a large man who at that point gave the impression of not quite having grown into his body yet. Physically, indeed, in almost every respect, Billy bore little resemblance to his younger brother Andrew Cavendish, who was absent from the dinner party, but whom Kick of course had met previously, at Cliveden.

Though both Cavendish brothers were tall, Billy was bigger and broader than the slim second son. Andrew was dark-haired, Billy fair. Andrew was highly strung, Billy exuded an air of calm. Andrew was energetic to the point at times of seeming hyperactive, Billy so languid and lazy that he once refused a cup of coffee, because, as he protested to his mother, "I can't be bothered to drink it." Andrew talked at the breakneck speed associated with their mother's family, the Cecils; Billy spoke slowly and deliberately. Andrew was outgoing, Billy reserved and not a little worried that girls wished to be with him solely because of all that he stood to one day inherit. Where the second son desperately envied Billy his status as their father's heir, Billy was no less jealous of Andrew's greater ease with members of the opposite sex.

Billy, who prized conversation above all other activities, had derived from Lady Alice Salisbury, his maternal grandmother, the tic of rubbing the palms of his hands together in keen anticipation of what grandparent and grandson alike delightedly referred to as "a good talk"—which, from the outset, was precisely what Jean observed Billy to be savoring in his first encounter with Kick. That evening at the Airlie dinner table, Billy and Kick talked and jested and talked some more. The two young people were absorbed in each other throughout dinner. It was as if their other dinner partners—indeed, the rest of the guests—had ceased to exist.

Both Billy and Kick were visibly distressed when it came time for the group to go on to the FitzRoy dance. An additional issue was that, rather than proceed with the others, Kick was scheduled to participate in another of the ceaseless photo opportunities arranged by her publicity-mad father. She was, she noted pointedly in her diary, "forced" to return to Prince's Gate. David Ormsby-Gore rescued the situation by volunteering to pick her up there and take her to the dance after she had attended to her publicity chores. When at length David materialized at the embassy residence, it was of no small significance that he was accompanied by Billy Hartington. Ordinarily, Billy was not one to take action in this manner; it was more like him to wait for others to come to him. After that first encounter with Kick, however, nothing in his life would ever again be quite the same.

Many years later, Andrew would perhaps come closer than anyone to grasping Billy's relationship with Kick. "It was," Andrew would say, "difficult for each to imagine the existence of the other. They were so utterly different. They adored being with one another because each was a constant surprise to the other. What were they going to find out about this person? What was this person going to do next?"

At the Palace of Westminster that first night, the music and dancing went on till daybreak. For most of the young people at the time, the principal drama at the FitzRoy dance concerned not Kick Kennedy, but rather Debo Mitford. To the outrage of her mother, Lady Redesdale, Debo violated the rules by dancing every dance with her great friend Mark Howard of Castle Howard. Her feelings for Mark were by no means romantic. On the contrary, it was Andrew Cavendish in whom Debo was by this point exclusively interested. Having been seated next to an apparently quite fascinated Andrew at a dinner party earlier in the Season—as it happened, shortly before Andrew met Kick—Debo had anxiously looked for him at every subsequent dance and party that she attended. This evening, her consummate disappointment over Andrew's absence had, by her own account, led to the display with Mark Howard.

Kick, meanwhile, spent as much time as possible at the Palace of Westminster with Billy. When Kick wrote about the evening afterward in her diary, the word "romantic" appeared there for the first time. And in the scrapbook she maintained separately, she preserved a first press photograph of him, dashing in winged collar and black tie, as he danced with the Speaker's granddaughter, Mary.

A week later, Kick and Billy were both included in the July 1, 1938, coming-of-age celebrations for Billy's cousin Charlie Lansdowne at Bowood House in Wiltshire. Immeasurably complicating the situation was the fact that both Andrew Cavendish and Debo Mitford were present at the ball as well. There had long been an undercurrent of tension between the Cavendish brothers, not least because of a custom observed by the British aristocracy, the purpose of which was to keep the family estates intact. According to the unwritten law of primogeniture, the first-born male child could look forward to inheriting everything upon his father's death, whereas the second son was entitled to expect nothing. It was not a question of who was better suited to lead the family; it was simply and strictly a matter of birth order.

The only way for a second son to advance to the primary position was by the death of his older brother. Charlie Lansdowne, who was being feted on the present occasion, bore the title of Marquess of Lansdowne because his elder brother had died at the age of twenty, three years before the death of their father, the 6th Marquess, in 1936. Another example of a second son who had catapulted to the number one position was David Ormsby-Gore, also present at Charlie's coming of age, who, though he had grave reservations about his fitness for the new role and responsibilities, became his father Lord Harlech's heir upon the death of an older brother, Gerard Ormsby-Gore, in an automobile accident in 1935.

Not surprisingly, the institution of primogeniture often led to feelings of acute bitterness and resentment on the part of those who had, as Andrew Cavendish liked to say, drawn the short straw in life. In Andrew's own case the family tensions were exacerbated by what he perceived to be their parents' greater love for Billy. When the firstborn son was an infant he had had to be placed in an incubator, and for a time it had seemed as if he might not live. As a consequence of their nearly having lost him, his father and mother, Edward and Mary, known as

Eddy and Moucher, respectively, had always loved him with what his uncle the future prime minister Harold Macmillan later described as "more than ordinary affection."

At length, the tendency of both parents to dote on Billy had had a deleterious effect on Andrew. Recognizing his upset, Eddy and Moucher strove to reassure him of their affections. Nonetheless, Andrew seemed always to interpret their special feeling for his brother to mean that he was himself somehow unlovable. Andrew further resented the fact that both his father and mother encouraged Billy's efforts to manage the second son in public, as when Billy sought to check Andrew's often rambunctious behavior at the country house weekends and other social events that they both attended.

A lifetime of fraught personal relations between the Cavendish brothers formed the backdrop to Andrew's discovery that, in his absence, Billy had met and become besotted with the girl whom the second son had previously had it in mind to claim for himself. Under the circumstances, was Andrew likely to simply step back? He had certainly never seemed at all inclined to defer to Billy in the past.

In the lore of the set, two oft-spoken-of episodes encapsulated the many: There was the time when Billy had asked a group of young people to spend the weekend at Compton Place, his family's house near the seaside village of Eastbourne. Andrew, known to covet whatever his brother had, promptly invited all the same young people back the next weekend for a house party of his own—without Billy.

And there was the time when, during a country house weekend at Rossdhu, the Scottish family estate of the brothers' friend Ivar Colquhoun, Billy had indignantly escorted Andrew, whom he accused of being drunk, from the house. Andrew, finding that Billy had gone so far as to lock him out, climbed up a drainpipe and catapulted himself back in through the window of the drawing room where all of the young people were gathered. Jean Ogilvy, who had been present on both occasions, later fondly compared the younger Cavendish boy to a small dog who is forever trying to "outdo" a big dog.

By the time Charlie Lansdowne's coming of age had drawn to a close, it therefore remained an open question as to just how matters were going to play out among the elite quartet comprised of Kick Kennedy, Andrew Cavendish, Billy Hartington, and Debo Mitford.

Might the small dog yet take some unexpected action to outdo the larger one?

Kick, of course, had had a great deal of experience with highly competitive and contentious relations between her own two elder brothers, Joe Junior and Jack. But whereas the unwritten law of primogeniture had presented a seemingly insurmountable obstacle to Andrew Cavendish, Jack Kennedy, at least theoretically, had faced no such roadblock. Sickly, scrawny, and altogether lacking in their father's approbation though Jack had been, he had long and quietly proceeded in life as though he might yet dislodge Joe Junior from his position of preeminence. Not without justification, Jack regarded himself as cleverer and wilier than his leadenly self-serious and therefore easily satirized and provoked older brother. Frustratingly, however, nothing Jack had done to date had managed to alter old Joe Kennedy's belief in the firstborn son's innate superiority. As Kick would later remark, in the Kennedy household it had been "heresy" to so much as suggest that Jack was better in any way than the anointed older brother. Nonetheless, throughout her girlhood, Kick had repeatedly and unabashedly made exactly that claim, confident that her status as what Rose Kennedy would later call old Joe's "favorite of all the children" would permit her to get away with her preference for the underdog in the fraternal struggle.

Suddenly, that enduring struggle was transplanted to London when both Joe Junior and Jack arrived from America in the company of Ambassador Kennedy, who had gone over to collect them, on July 4, 1938. Before long, both Kennedy brothers were cutting conspicuous figures on the London scene. Joe Junior—"the Big One," as the English debs referred to him—was widely touted by his father as the more brilliant and promising of the brothers, a young man destined to become U.S. president one day. Young Joe certainly looked the part; he seemed more poised and mature than his twenty-two years might have led one to anticipate. In contrast to his outward air of "gravitas," however, he was in truth replete with anxiety and insecurity, ever fearful as he was of failing to satisfy the patriarch's expectations. Also in contrast to his distinguished public demeanor, young Joe soon developed a reputation among the girls of the set for what two of them, Fiona Gore and Jean Ogilvy, described many years later as roughness and aggressiveness. In an episode that did Joe Junior's reputation in London no favors, when Gina Wernher fell ill and went off to the country to recuperate, the Big One frightened and horrified her and her duenna by turning up unexpectedly at the hotel in mad pursuit.

Jack, on the other hand, was regarded by most of the debs as the more appealing and more attractive of the Kennedy brothers by far. His exceedingly boyish appearance and manner caused some members of the set to assume that he was Kick's younger brother, when he was in fact more than two years her senior. Whereas in the U.S., Kick had been adopted as a mascot by Jack's adoring claque of friends, upon his arrival in London it quickly became apparent to him that she was no one's mascot anymore, having swiftly established herself at the very center of her select new English group. Henceforward, Jack's identity in London would be as Kick Kennedy's brother, rather than the other way around.

Meanwhile, Joe Junior, in keeping with the preconceptions established by his father, entered into an important friendship with Hugh Fraser. As the most ambitious and promising member of the set, Hugh, often spoken of as a possible future British prime minister, seemed very much Joe Junior's compeer. Jack, for his part, gravitated to less promising and less ambitious fellows, such as David Ormsby-Gore and Tony Loughborough. Nonetheless, the assumption that it was the elder Kennedy brother who was destined for political preeminence was challenged on at least one occasion—and by someone other than Kick, who had long been alone in taking such a contrarian view. After observing Jack Kennedy at a dance, Lady Redesdale was heard to declare, "I would not be surprised if that young man becomes President of the United States."

Not everyone was equally taken with the second son, however. Lady Redesdale's daughter, Debo Mitford—who in later years would become a close friend of President John F. Kennedy's—danced with him at the July 13, 1938, ball presided over by Lady Mountbatten at her London penthouse in honor of her niece Sally Norton. Debo dismissed Jack Kennedy afterward in her diary as "rather boring but nice."

At the time, of course, no young man seemed quite as fascinating to Debo as that other much-thwarted second son, Andrew Cavendish. And never perhaps had Andrew seemed more effectively thwarted than on the night of Sally Norton's party, to which Billy had made a point of asking to escort Kick.

Earlier in the evening, Billy had come to collect her at the American Embassy residence in anticipation of taking her to a smaller, preliminary dinner party hosted by the King's brother and sister-in-law, the Duke and Duchess of Kent. When Billy arrived at the embassy residence, he had been accompanied by his aunt, Adele Astaire Cavendish. The sister and former dancing partner of Fred Astaire, and now the wife of Eddy Devonshire's alcoholic younger brother Lord Charles Cavendish, Adele also had an invitation to dine with the Kents. At length, insisting that she knew which residence was theirs, she ushered her nephew and his date into the wrong house. Kick, as was her nature, thought the entire incident hilarious—and, following her lead, so did Billy, though in other company he almost certainly would have been plunged into a fit of agitation at his theatrical and often controversial aunt's mistake. Fortuitously, that air of hilarity and relaxation established the tone for the young people's first real date, which continued at the Mountbatten penthouse, where guests danced on a large balcony that gave long views of the city below.

The romantic evening was but a prelude to an invitation from the Duchess of Devonshire asking Kick to attend a house party at Compton Place. The occasion was to be one of many parties timed to coincide with the annual Goodwood races, which served as the finale to the London Season. Kick was eager to accept, though she, her mother, and the other Kennedy children—with the exception of Rosemary, who was going to Ireland—were scheduled to leave London on the twenty-second of July to spend the rest of the summer in Cannes, where old Joe had taken a house. The event at Compton Place was not due to begin until the twenty-fifth.

Though Rose Kennedy had her reservations about allowing Kick to remain behind with her father in order to attend the house party at the duke's, Kick did at length manage to secure permission. The day after Rose and the other Kennedy siblings embarked for the South of France, Kick went off for the weekend to Cliveden. Meanwhile, it was agreed that on Monday, Jakie Astor would collect her at the embassy and drive her to Compton Place, to which he too had been invited, along with, among others, Robert Cecil; Andrew's best friend, Tom Egerton; Debo Mitford; and Dawyck Haig's sister Rene, who till then had been Billy's acknowledged "favorite" of all the girls in the set. Tellingly perhaps, Kick had altogether forgotten that her American suitor, Peter Grace, was also due at the embassy residence, he and she having previously made informal arrangements to be together during his summer vacation. She would have been in Cannes that day in any case, but when Peter appeared at Prince's Gate on the twenty-fifth, he found her waiting not for him, but rather for Jakie.

Later that day, Kick had her first glimpse of the gray stucco-faced Elizabethan Jacobean house where, over the course of a decade, she was to experience some of the most joyous, as well as some of the saddest, days and nights of her life. There would come a time in the not so remote future when Compton Place, which was ever redolent of the duke's pungent Turkish cigarettes, would by turns beckon to Kick as a sanctuary from her misery and sense of personal isolation, and repel her on account of the excruciating memories it threatened to trigger. For now, however, it was the locale where matters of the heart seemed to quietly arrange themselves at last, with Billy and Kick, on the one hand, and Andrew and Debo, on the other, operating as established couples—Andrew having uncharacteristically, and by his own account reluctantly but unavoidably, acquiesced to his brother's claim to Kick.

Andrew might have paired off with Debo in any case, but he would long be irked by his mother's having invited Kick as Billy's guest. His mother's invitation had signaled to Andrew that it was time for him to step back.

The Duchess of Devonshire, whom Kick first encountered at Compton Place, was to become one of the most important figures in her life, a woman who would over the years sympathize with her, love her, inspire her, comfort her, and, in the end, bury her when her own mother did not. At Hatfield House, Lady Alice Salisbury had tested Kick, who by her response had amply demonstrated the prized red blood that coursed in her veins. At Compton Place, Lady Alice's daughter had a chance to observe the phenomenon for herself. That the duchess very much approved of what she saw would be suggested by the stream of invitations Kick received from her in the months that followed.

After her stay at Compton Place, Kick was due to join her mother and siblings in Cannes, but before she left England she and Billy arranged to meet again on September 21, on the occasion of Jean Ogilvy's twentieth birthday celebration at Cortachy Castle, during what was known as the Scottish Season. Kick had begun her British sojourn with the intention of going home after six months. She now meant to stay indefinitely—if, that is, her father did not insist on sending her home due to the looming threat of war.

For all that spring and summer, the international tensions that had been so passionately spoken of in the course of Kick's life-changing first country house weekend, at Lady Astor's, had been steadily worsening. The London Season of 1938 overlapped with the mounting Czech crisis. Hitler, persuaded—precisely as Hugh Fraser, echoing Churchill, had warned he would be—that the British were unprepared to fight, had been moving inexorably toward the seizure of Czechoslovakia. Chamberlain in the meantime had put intense pressure on the Czechs to acquiesce to German demands of self-determination for the approximately three and a half million Sudeten German residents along the northern, western, and southern borders of Czechoslovakia. On the day Kick flew to the South of France with her father, a British emissary arrived in

Prague with instructions from Chamberlain to prepare the Czechs for
the handover of the Sudetenland to Hitler.

In the anxious weeks that followed, while Kick swam and sunbathed
with her family, word reached the British Foreign Office that Hitler had
already made up his mind to seize all of Czechoslovakia in September,
a report that was soon bolstered by sightings of German troop move-
ments between Nuremberg and the Czech frontier. By mid-August, the
Nazis had amassed over one and a half million troops. Kick, meanwhile,
accompanied Jack on a side trip to Austria, in the course of which her
brother hoped to assess the impact of the German occupation, as well
as to derive some sense of what might be in store for the Czechs.

In early September, as Kick shopped for clothes in Paris with her
mother, the world nervously awaited Hitler's address to the annual party
rally at Nuremberg, a speech in which it was widely anticipated he would
clarify his intentions with regard to Czechoslovakia. Hitler's ranting
September 12, 1938, performance, broadcast internationally, was not
reassuring. By turns insulting the Czech state and demanding self-
determination for the German-speaking minority, Hitler made it clear
that he was ready to intervene.

On the fifteenth of September, Chamberlain flew to Germany in
hopes that the Fuehrer might yet be appeased. In Berchtesgaden, the
British prime minister discovered that Hitler had escalated his de-
mands. He was no longer insisting simply on autonomy for the Sudeten
Germans, but rather on the full annexation of all Sudeten areas to the
Reich.

Four days later, when Kick arrived at Cortachy Castle, overlooking
the River South Esk in Angus, Scotland, it seemed as if Europe might
be about to erupt in another war.

"We listened to the radio for news flashes," Kick wrote in her diary
that day, referring to herself, Jean Ogilvy, and the other young people
who were just arriving for Jean's birthday party, which was set to take
place two days hence. "The international situation grows increasingly
worse."

Three

On the evening of September 21, 1938, Kick found her assigned place in the dining room of the cream-colored castle, which had been used as a hunting lodge in the fourteenth century by Robert the Bruce, King of Scotland, and had been enlarged numerous times since. The dining room's extensive windows overlooked what had come to be known as the American Garden, a reference to the ornate plantings that had been brought over from the U.S. Among the other young people who were just then finding their places at Lord Airlie's dinner table on the occasion of his daughter Jean's twentieth birthday dinner were her sister Maggot, Ivar Colquhoun, and Rene Haig.

When all were seated, two chairs remained conspicuously empty.

Billy Hartington and David Ormsby-Gore had been due to begin the long drive up early that morning. For most people, the trip would likely take about twelve hours. But with David at the wheel, it had been expected that the boys would require considerably less time.

Which was just as well, for Jean perceived that Kick had been keenly anticipating her reunion with Billy for far longer than merely the two days she had already been in residence. Indeed, Kick appeared to have regarded her time in the South of France as but a necessary interlude before their next encounter. She was a good deal thinner than when Jean or the others had last seen her, and she had acquired a mannerism of emphasizing her newly svelte waist by delightedly spanning it with both hands, a gesture she could not possibly have managed before. Kick insisted that the substantial weight loss had been the consequence of its having been so warm in the South of France that she had had no appetite for weeks. Jean, who noticed that Kick seemed not to have regained her appetite at Cortachy, guessed that like countless young women in love before and since, she had in fact been dieting madly in anticipation of seeing her young man again.

So when that young man proved to be late in making his appearance, and worse, when Lord Airlie angrily decreed that the birthday festivities begin without Billy and David, Kick was as distressed as Jean was embarrassed. Lady Airlie was the parent known to be gruff and difficult with her daughters, as well as with their friends. The curly-haired, colorfully kilted Lord Airlie tended to be good-humored, and was much beloved by the young people in the cousinhood. Yet when, partway through the meal, the butler came in to inform Lord Airlie that the missing guests had arrived at last, he was instructed to tell Billy and David that they were too late for dinner, then show them to their rooms. These orders notwithstanding, the butler later brought up plenty of food for both young travelers, at Kick's and Jean's frantically whispered behest.

As the girls understood, Lord Airlie's wrath was less a reflection of any rigid insistence on his part upon promptness or proper attire than of how affected he was by the terrible tension of the moment, the British government having been engaged in days of discussion and debate about Hitler's demands at the Fuehrer's meeting with Chamberlain at Berchtesgaden. *garten*

Unlike Joe Kennedy, who, to the horror of certain of his Harvard classmates, had managed to evade military service in the last war, Joe

Airlie had fought bravely in the trenches. He bore the scar of a wound
to his leg, and he had been awarded the high honor of a Military Cross.
Joe Kennedy wanted Britain to come to terms with Hitler because,
among other reasons, he feared another war might wipe out his personal
fortune and impede his plans for assuring the political futures of his eldest sons, particularly of young Joe. In any case, Ambassador Kennedy
did not think the decadent, depleted British capable of fighting, let alone
winning, a new military conflict with the Germans. As always with Joe
Kennedy, matters of honor and principle were simply not factors in his
calculations.

    Joe Airlie, though he too supported the policy of appeasement, was
another matter altogether. He was acutely sensitive to the questions of
honor and duty raised by the Czech crisis. He had met Hitler and—
unlike some aristocrats who professed to admire the Fuehrer—he
found the German's policies and politics abhorrent. Nonetheless, as one
who had personally endured the agony of the last war, he could not bear
the prospect of that agony being visited upon the next generation. Lord
Airlie's fit of temper when Billy and David arrived late expressed his
monumental upset at the prospect that these two childishly undisciplined
young men, as he viewed them, might soon be leaving a Scottish shooting party, where grouse were the targets, for the fields of death where
they themselves would provide targets for the Germans.

    While Jean's father reacted to the prevailing anxiety with irascibil-
ity, Kick responded by striving to concentrate on the pleasures of the
moment now that she and Billy had been reunited at last. To watch them
together that week—as Kick sat directly behind Billy while he shot
grouse each afternoon; as she and he enjoyed noontime picnics and
moonlight walks on the moors; as, dressed in evening clothes, they
danced to records played on Jean's old windup gramophone—was to observe a young couple who were unmistakably in love.

    To Kick's dismay, however, it was impossible to shut out the dramatic
international developments that were threatening to snatch Billy away
from her at the very moment when she and he were really just discover-

ing each other. She who had previously enchanted the boys of the aristocratic cousinhood by her readiness to listen to their animated talk of politics and world affairs was suddenly and conspicuously a good deal less than enthusiastic about those topics.

On Friday, the twenty-third of September, Kick wrote to Jack's friend Lem Billings in America: "All you can hear or talk about at this point is the future war which is bound to come. Am so darn sick of it." At the time she voiced that sentiment, Chamberlain had returned for a second round of discussions with Hitler, this time in the Rhineland town of Bad Godesberg. Again, the Fuehrer drastically augmented his demands. He stipulated that if the Czechs failed to vacate the Sudetenland by September 28, German troops would march into the disputed territories on the first of the month. Though in Bad Godesberg he had objected to Hitler's terms, Chamberlain, when he returned to London, urged his cabinet to accept them.

Lord Airlie, meanwhile, persisted in going out every morning with the boys to shoot, a voluminous plaid wrapped round his broad shoulders against the chill. On one occasion during this nerve-jangling period, the older man snapped when the fellows began to pepper one another with shotgun pellets. Immediately he ordered all of them into the cars and back to the castle. "You are all dangerous and you are coming home!" Lord Airlie shouted, saddened, as he was later heard to grumble, that these young fools might soon find themselves on an actual battlefield for which they were in no way prepared.

On Sunday the twenty-fifth of September, the day after Chamberlain returned to London with Hitler's ultimatum, the young people at Cortachy drove some eight miles to Airlie Castle, the home of Jean's grandmother, the Dowager Countess of Airlie, who was a sister of Lady Alice Salisbury. Accompanying them now were Robert Cecil and Debo Mitford, who had joined the party in the meantime, and whose presence in the group highlighted how very divided the country in general, and the upper class in particular, remained with regard to the policy of appeasement.

Robert's father, Lord Cranborne, was an outspoken antagonist of the
European dictators on the one hand and of the British appeasers on the
other. By contrast, two of Debo's sisters were fanatical supporters of
the Reich. Unity Mitford, a close personal friend of Hitler's, had been
a member of the dictator's entourage at the Nuremberg party rally. In
Germany, Unity was threatening to take her own life in the event that
the country of her birth went to war against her beloved Fuehrer. Another Mitford sister, Diana, had secretly married the founder of the
British Union of Fascists, Sir Oswald Mosley, at the home of Nazi pro-
paganda chief Joseph Goebbels, where the wedding guests had included Hitler himself. Not all of the Mitford sisters, however, favored
the Nazis. Two, Nancy and Jessica, embraced socialism and commu-
nism, respectively. Debo, the youngest Mitford girl, professed to be
uninterested in the politics of the day. Other patrician families were
divided as well, though none perhaps as spectacularly as the Mitfords.
In Billy's household, for instance, the Duke of Devonshire, who served
as Chamberlain's Under-Secretary of State for the Colonies, supported
appeasement. The duchess privately preferred the views of her brother
Lord Cranborne, though publicly she deferred to her husband's opinion
on the matter.

Centuries-old Airlie Castle was said to be haunted, and Granny
Airlie, a dramatic figure who favored outdated ankle-length skirts and
elaborate, wide-brimmed "picture hats," did her best to encourage her
young visitors' talk of ghosts. She was full of stories of young people's
hair having suddenly turned gray on the premises and of the appalling
fate that had befallen past visitors who dared walk down to the river at
night. But, as Debo would point out many years afterward, even in this
romantic setting, where history and legend were so deeply woven into
the fabric of daily life, some of the young people could not help but act
out the acute anxieties connected with the threat of imminent war. The
determined silliness and laughter appeared to go too far at times. Once,
swaying jerkily and erratically as they crossed the river on a suspension
bridge, the merrymakers succeeded in accidentally catapulting Jean into

the rushing waters, so that she had to spend the rest of the day in one of the dowager countess's kilts while her own garments dried.

That evening at Cortachy, where the radio reports from London were nothing if not alarming, the boys seemed to reach an apex of wildness. Ivar Colquhoun sprayed the drawing room with a fire extinguisher, and Jakie Astor, who had now joined the party, insisted very late at night on going downstairs to fetch some more alcohol. Drunkenly gathering not just a bottle or two, but rather Lord Airlie's entire drinks tray in his arms, Jakie headed up the wide wooden staircase—whereupon he slipped, loudly smashing every item on the tray to pieces.

On Kick's final day at Cortachy Castle, the twenty-sixth of September, she and Billy attended the races in Hamilton, where they had a few last hours together. The couple made a date to see a play in London on the thirtieth, the day she was scheduled to return from Scotland. Still, as she and Billy parted, Hitler's deadline loomed, along with the possibility that by the time of their anticipated reunion, London might already be in flames. Chamberlain, who had encountered staunch opposition from within his cabinet, had been left with little choice but to notify Hitler that should France, in keeping with her treaty obligations to the Czechs, enter into hostilities with Germany, Britain would feel obliged to support her.

Finally, Kick set off, rather gloomily, to spend a few more days in another Scottish household, where, the following night, she listened to a despairing radio address by the prime minister. In a weary-sounding voice, Chamberlain well nigh confessed to having failed in his peacemaking efforts, though he stressed that he would not hesitate to make a third trip to Germany if he believed it would do any good.

In London, meanwhile, trenches were being dug, antiaircraft guns deployed, and gas masks handed out in anticipation of a feared aerial assault, to take place as early as the twenty-eighth, which had come to be known popularly as Black Wednesday. That morning, Ambassador Joseph P. Kennedy called his wife, who was on a golf holiday in Scotland at the Gleneagles Hotel. Old Joe instructed Rose to return to Prince's

Gate at once in anticipation of preparing to return to the U.S. with the children in the event of war.

As it happened, that same day Kick went to the Perth races, where she met up again with Jean Ogilvy, who was now accompanied by a second wave of Cortachy houseguests, including Andrew Cavendish, Tony Loughborough, and Charlie Lansdowne, as well as Debo Mitford and Robert Cecil, who had stayed on from the previous week. Suddenly, an unexpected shaft of light pierced through the general foreboding, when Chamberlain, in the midst of an address to the House of Commons, reported that he had just had a message from Hitler, agreeing to postpone his mobilization for twenty-four hours, and proposing to meet with the leaders of Britain, France, and Italy the next day. In the House, Chamberlain's announcement was met with silence at first, then a roar of cheers. So, too, at Perth, the young people in Kick's group were jubilant, leading her to write in her diary: "I have never seen such happiness." Following the races Kick and her friends went on to a cocktail party, where, Jean remembered, Munich and the war were the only topics of conversation.

That night, Kick boarded a train for London, uncertain about what the morrow might bring—would there be peace or war? She arrived in London "to find peace and everyone deliriously happy." In the wake of Chamberlain's triumphant declaration to the British people that he had brought back with him from Munich "peace with honor" and "peace for our time," Kick and Billy went off for an evening of theater and further celebrations at the Café de Paris with David Ormsby-Gore and other friends.

For Billy and his circle, however, as for many others, the euphoria did not last long. Three days hence, Billy and Kick, along with David Ormsby-Gore and Tom Egerton, went to stay at Churchdale Hall, the duke's house in Ashford-in-the-Water, which they planned to use as a base for expeditions to the Nottingham races. Andrew Cavendish, accompanied by Debo Mitford, was already in residence at Churchdale, where the duchess was to serve as the young people's chaperone, the duke being in London at the time in connection with his governmental duties. Kick was soon noting in her diary that she and Billy talked for hours every night. And no wonder: Her October 3, 1938, arrival at Billy's childhood home coincided with the opening, at the Palace of Westminster in London, of a furious debate about the wisdom of the prime minister's deal with Hitler. Duff Cooper, Winston Churchill, Anthony Eden—all denounced what they saw as Chamberlain's betrayal of the Czechs, as well as his wishful thinking that Hitler would keep his word about this being the last of his territorial demands.

Every beat of the proceedings was minutely analyzed and assessed by the Cavendish boys and their guests at Churchdale Hall. One speech, though, seems to have had particular resonance for the group. Lord Cranborne, the duchess's brother, set out to dismantle Chamberlain's claims to have obtained peace with honor. "Peace he certainly brought back to us, and there is not one of us who will not wish to thank him with a full heart for that priceless gift . . . But where is honor? I have looked and looked and I cannot see it. It seems to me to be a wicked mockery to describe by so noble a name the agreement which has been reached. The peace of Europe has in fact been saved —and we had better face it—only by throwing to the wolves a little country whose courage and dignity in the face of almost intolerable provocation has been a revelation and an inspiration to us all."

Cranborne was equally dismissive of Chamberlain's assertion that he had secured peace for our time. Hitler, Cranborne pointed out in acid tones, had failed to keep earlier promises with regard to Austria and Czechoslovakia. "These precedents do not justify us in abandoning our anxiety."

So, the question of whether there might yet be war persisted in looming over Billy and Kick on the one hand, and Andrew and Debo on the other, when, in the course of the house party, the two couples visited nearby Chatsworth, the family seat of the Devonshire dukes. Though Eddy Devonshire and his family were not due to take up residence at the ducal palace until Christmastime, Billy seemed unable to wait to show Kick all that would one day be his. The great house—for the family always referred to it as "the house"—had been built in its original form by Sir William Cavendish and his wife, Bess of Hardwick, after their marriage in 1547. Now, much altered, enlarged, and enriched by the generations since, Chatsworth, its yellow stone facade glittering in the sunlight, had achieved a completely unique, and somehow magical, romantic perfection. Beyond its doors were 175 rooms and miles of corridors filled with the treasures accumulated over centuries: astonishing collections of paintings, drawings, manuscripts, books, minerals, furniture, and jewels. The house itself was situated in a thousand acres of parkland, and within the park there was a garden covering more than a hundred acres.

In the midst of wandering along garden paths lined with mysterious rock arrangements and towering trees, Kick, with her sense of fun, seemed to take special delight in the famous Squirting Tree, as it had been dubbed by the future Queen Victoria when she first happened upon it at thirteen years of age. Activated by a wheel hidden behind some adjacent rocks, the metal branches of what looked to be a willow tree squirted water on unsuspecting passersby. The Squirting Tree was a trick, a practical joke. But as Andrew would darkly reflect many years afterward, it was the future that was destined to play tricks on these four unsuspecting young people—tricks that neither couple had anticipated on that laughter-filled autumn day in 1938.

On the sixth of October, Kick and Debo headed back to London, and Billy and Andrew went on to Cambridge, where the elder brother was in his last year and the second son entered his first term. That same day, despite the attacks on the Munich Agreement that had riveted the young people's attention, a motion supporting Chamberlain's actions—"That this House approves the policy of His Majesty's Government by which war was averted in the recent crisis and supports their efforts to secure a lasting peace"—passed by an emphatic vote of 366 to 144. Nonetheless, the words of the critics who questioned the morality and efficacy of the prime minister's deal with Hitler had opened a national debate that would go on for months to come—until, in Andrew's formulation, shame over what Chamberlain had done at Munich finally trumped fear.

Kick, in the meantime, no longer faced the imminent threat of being sent back to the U.S. because of war—and of thereby being separated from Billy. Initially, there was some talk at Prince's Gate of her attending a school in England, now that she had decided to abandon her original plan of remaining for no more than six months. The problem, as her mother soon perceived, was that the English girls who had become Kick's friends did not generally go on to college after they had made their debut. Instead, more often than not they returned to their parents' country homes until London social life resumed at the time of the so-called Little Season, or they remained in the city and occupied themselves with charity work. In October, Kick, along with another of the popular debs of the 1938 London Season, Jane Kenyon-Slaney, volunteered at a day nursery for poor children.

Kick had a good deal more freedom about seeing her young man unchaperoned than, say, a friend such as Debo Mitford enjoyed with hers. In the waning days of October, therefore, it was no particular problem for Kick to travel to Cambridge in the company of Jane Kenyon-Slaney for an excursion to the Newmarket races with Billy and tea afterward in his rooms at Trinity College. Despite her freedom of movement, however, on this and other occasions her relationship with Billy remained innocent. That night, when the girls missed their train, Billy sent them back to London in a chauffeured car.

By the following month, Billy was ready to signal his romance with Kick to his relatives, unlikely though they were to be pleased. On November 23, 1938, members of the houses of Cecil and Cavendish convened at the Savoy in London for a coming-of-age party in honor of Richard Cavendish, who had previously scandalized his relatives by marrying the Catholic Pamela Lloyd Thomas. To the families' further horror, since the time of Richard's elopement two grandsons of Lord Salisbury, Robert Cecil and David Ormsby-Gore, had formed romantic attachments to Catholics, Veronica Fraser and Sissie Lloyd Thomas

(Pam's sister), respectively. It was in this context that the appearance at the Savoy of another of Lord Salisbury's grandsons, Billy Hartington, in the company of a new Catholic interloper drew so many stares of agitation and alarm. When in her diary afterward Kick alluded to the wide disapproval with which she had been met, she struck a note of amused defiance: "All Billy's relatives sitting about getting an eyeful."

If the Cecil and Cavendish relatives were aghast at Kick Kennedy's presence on Billy's arm that night, there was one family member who was in fact exceedingly pleased. Kick's visit to Churchdale Hall had consolidated the duchess's sense that, despite the formidable religious difficulties, she would be the perfect partner for Billy. To the duchess's perception, Kick possessed the life force that seemed at times to be woefully wanting in him. Sailing into an event such as this with Kick on his arm was so utterly unlike Billy, who was, in Jean Ogilvy's phrase, "normally reticent." On this and other occasions, Kick's effect on the future duke was positive and palpable. That Eddy Devonshire had a virulent hatred of all Catholics did not impede the duchess. Though she deferred to her husband about politics, she had no intention of giving in to him on the issue of what woman would be best for their son. Ironically, Kick's refusal to be cowed by the collective dismay of Billy's relatives was a demonstration of precisely the strength that had attracted the duchess to her. Then and later, had Kick proven to be rather less tough, she would not have served the duchess's purpose quite so well.

The duchess could hardly have made her support for Kick clearer than she did two weeks later, on the occasion of the December 9, 1938, family dinner that the Devonshires hosted at their art-filled London home, Carlton Gardens, on the eve of Billy's twenty-first birthday. As Chatsworth was still in the process of being readied for them to move in, the duke and duchess put off Billy's official grand-scale coming-of-age celebration until the summer. In the meantime, many of the same Cecils and Cavendishes who had previously been appalled to see Kick and Billy together at Richard Cavendish's party at the Savoy reconvened at Carlton Gardens, where further horror was in store. In an audacious symbolic gesture, the duchess had placed Kick to Billy's right—in the position of honor. For Billy's relatives, there could be no mistaking what Kick's position at the table meant. The seating was a tacit acknowledgment of the place that she now had assumed in Billy's heart. Of no less importance was the fact that Kick would never have been given the position of honor without the duchess's approval.

In the course of the evening, Kick was again intensely conscious of the displeasure with which Billy's relationship with her was met by a broad swath of his family. There were "dirty looks," as Kick described them in her diary, from various notables, including Billy's paternal grandmother, the formidable and rather frightening Evelyn, Dowager Duchess of Devonshire, who was known in the family as Duchess Evie or Granny Evie.

Due to accompany her mother and siblings to St. Moritz, Switzerland, for a Christmastime ski holiday, Kick was much with Billy in the aftermath of his birthday dinner: Late that very night, we catch sight of them at the 400 Club. The following day, Billy's actual birthday, they are at the racetrack, before they go on to a country house weekend at Mountfield, where they play "mad games on the lawn" with their host, Tom Egerton, as well as with David, Sissie, Andrew, and other companions. At a December 13, 1938, dance in London, Kick and Billy spend the better part of the evening talking exclusively to each other, apart from everyone else. And the following night, she breaks a previously arranged date with another fellow to go out with Billy. Meanwhile, Jean Ogilvy has returned to London from Scotland, and the friends have several long lunches where they talk of little else but Billy.

Before Kick left for the holiday, she and Billy had one final afternoon together, the twenty-first of December, shopping in a snowy London. Accompanied by Tom Egerton, they went on to Ciro's, where the headwaiter came out to warn Billy that the duke was inside. Billy's father might have been the last person Kick wanted to encounter that evening, aware as she was of his disdain for Catholics in general and for her in particular. Billy, however, seemed unfazed by the prospect of encountering the duke, and they went in. At one point, the duke came over to Billy's table to talk a bit. He was, as always, exceedingly polite to Kick, but somehow his extreme disapproval of the relationship was palpable nonetheless.

That night, when Kick parted from Billy, she'd had a vivid reminder that no matter how very much in love he might be, if they were to have a future together he would in the end have to be willing to defy his father. Several weeks previously he had braved the disapproval of various relatives when he entered the Savoy with Kick on his arm; later, he had been palpably pleased by his mother's decision to seat Kick to his right at his birthday celebration in Carlton Gardens; and tonight, he had disregarded the warning of the headwaiter at Ciro's. Still, as she confessed to Jean Ogilvy, she wondered whether he would ask her to marry him— not because she doubted that he wanted to, but rather because she had no idea whether in the end he would be prepared to cause such monumental anguish to the duke.

The cataclysm, of course, would not all be on the side of Billy's family. Presently, when Kick arrived in St. Moritz to spend three weeks in her mother's company while her father visited the U.S., she confronted what was sure to be the other half of the problem: the inevitable opposition of the Kennedy family, especially of Rose Kennedy, to the very notion of marriage to a Protestant. To this point, Kick had mostly been dealing with the displeasure of Billy's relatives, who—at the Savoy, Carlton Gardens, and elsewhere—had been directly confronted with evidence of his relationship with a Catholic girl. Rose Kennedy, for her part, had yet to really grasp the danger. Five months previously, Rose had exhibited some resistance to Kick's wish to postpone her departure for the South of France in order to accept the duchess's invitation to a country house weekend at Compton Place. In the end, however, Mrs. Kennedy had given her reluctant consent. If, in the interim, she had made no particular effort to prevent Kick from spending so much time with Billy, perhaps it was because the aristocratic cousinhood's tendency to move and play very much as a group made it possible for

Mrs. Kennedy not to perceive the speed with which her daughter's relationship with a Protestant male was progressing. But Kick well knew what was happening, and as she had told Jean Ogilvy on several occasions, she dreaded the explosion that was sure to ensue when her mother perceived it as well.

Importantly, it was not simply, or even principally, Rose's *opposition* that Kick dreaded. She knew that her involvement with Billy had the potential of causing great *pain* to her mother. And for Kick, who had long operated within the Kennedy family as the beleaguered Rose's principal protector and defender, that prospect was almost as difficult to contemplate as that of being forced to break off with Billy. Rose lived with a husband who was not only compulsively unfaithful, but who went so far as to parade certain of his women in front of her; and she lived with sons, Joe Junior and Jack, who thought nothing of mocking and disparaging a parent they found cold and at times absurd. Kick adamantly refused to join her elder brothers in this harsh treatment of Rose. On one occasion, not long before the family had been transplanted to England, she had made a great scene when old Joe Kennedy brought one of his many girlfriends to the family table at Cape Cod. Risking the rage of the father she adored, Kick had indignantly objected to the mistress's presence.

Rose, for her part, had long endeavored to armor herself against the potential for embarrassment. Even when Joe paraded his girlfriends in front of her, she simply "acted as if they didn't exist," in the phrase of his friend Arthur Krock. But Rose had not always seemed so weirdly at peace with her circumstances. In 1930, at the time of her pregnancy with Kick, she had gone so far as to attempt to flee from her husband. Heavy with child, she had sought sanctuary in the household of her father, who soon insisted that she return to Joe Kennedy and to the children she had left behind with him. Before she obediently returned, she attended a Roman Catholic retreat overseen by the Boston diocese, where, with newfound fervor, she embraced the religious practices that would thereafter help to numb herself against the enduring anguish of her marriage.

Never perhaps was the haze of denial in which Rose dwelt more oddly manifest than in England, where the U.S. ambassador's publicity people relentlessly billed the Kennedys as a model family, even as he persisted in openly and unashamedly betraying his wife.

The opinion of the world meant much to Rose Kennedy, who, however improbably, chose to regard her family as exemplary Catholics whose behavior set a standard for others to follow. She was particularly keen to have the approbation of those people whom she regarded as her social superiors in elite Catholic America, families such as the James F. McDonnells of New York City, whose daughters, Anne and Charlotte, had been classmates of Kick's when she attended a convent school in Connecticut. The McDonnells visited the Kennedys in St. Moritz that holiday season. In the course of their stay, Charlotte McDonnell wrote a poem about her friend Kick's romantic dramas, which included references to the fellows whom Kick had previously spurned, such as Peter Grace, and to the one young man whose next move she was then so eagerly awaiting: "Such is Kick! God's gift to Billy!!!/Will he . . . won't he? won't he??/Billy . . ." With Charlotte so aware of Kick's feelings, it was perhaps only a matter of time before Rose Kennedy learned of them as well, with all of the domestic fireworks that were sure to follow her discovery.

Meanwhile, it was a source of distress to Kick that her Swiss sojourn made it impossible for her to attend an event that Billy had been keenly anticipating for some time. On the seventh and eighth of January 1939, Billy's cousins and friends descended upon Derbyshire on the occasion of his first young people's house party at Chatsworth. Immediately, Billy had taken possession of the quarters known as the State Dressing Room, which gave long views of the Emperor Fountain, the Cascade, and the vast landscape that would one day be among his possessions. The cousins remarked among themselves that his choice of accommodation spoke volumes about his love for the good things that fortune promised him, and about his love of personal comfort; Billy had claimed for himself a room with its own private bath, leaving his guests to line up for what was at that time the only other working bathroom in the ducal palace.

Jean Ogilvy would later remember Billy's party as having been great fun, despite the inconvenience. She also recalled it as a time when, precisely because they were at Chatsworth, her beloved Cavendish cousin was forcefully confronted with the duties that he would one day inherit along with all of those possessions, duties that were religious as well as secular. Among these duties, for instance, was the appointment of various Protestant clergymen, which as Billy's sister Anne pointed out, he felt he would be unable to perform if he had a son of a different faith. And if that son were indeed a Catholic, how could the boy, when he became duke one day, possibly interview and say whom he would have as a clergyman in a Protestant parish? So, at a moment when Kick, in St. Moritz, was confronting the impact that marriage to a Protestant would have on her family, Billy, in Derbyshire, faced tough questions of his own about how marriage to a Catholic might impact on his ability to perform his bounden duty as a Devonshire duke.

Despite questions on both sides, as soon as Kick and Billy went out to dinner on the night of her return to London, January 13, 1939, they immediately resumed the easy, playful rhythms of their relationship. However much the religious issue continued to loom, this was still an exceedingly happy time for them. In the weeks that followed, they saw each other constantly. There were more dinners in London, trips to the races at Newmarket and elsewhere, and dinner parties in his rooms at Cambridge, where he served pâté de foie gras from Fortnum & Mason in London. Billy's charm was becoming more obvious to all as he acquired the ability to laugh at himself when Kick enumerated the absurdities and pomposities of "the Marquess," as she at once satirically and fondly referred to him. She teased him about his excessive concern for his appearance; about his tendency to boss his younger brother around; about his upset when she wanted to snatch up a souvenir ashtray after dinner in a Spanish restaurant, as she would have thought nothing of doing in the company of her elder brothers in Palm Beach. He in turn pointedly refrained from teasing Kick when, pretending that she had not become aware of the etiquette in such matters only recently, she grandly labeled a hostess "nouveau riche" for writing out her dinner guests' titles in full on their place cards.

Those who saw Kick and Billy laughing and jesting, as they liked to do, could not but suspect that she was very much his for the taking. Still, the question that Charlotte McDonnell had posed—"Will he . . . won't he?"—remained emphatically in play. So much so, in fact, that despite Kick and Billy's status as an established couple, other prospective suitors, headed by Hugh Fraser, Tony Loughborough, and William Douglas-Home, had not yet abandoned all hope with regard to her.

In the meantime, romantic developments among other members of the set were alternately encouraging and discouraging to Kick's own hopes. The February 1939 marriage of the couple's close friends, Ann de Trafford and Derek Parker Bowles, seemed to suggest that the religious obstacles could be overcome. Ann was Catholic, Derek Protestant. Nonetheless, they had been married in a Catholic church—the Brompton Oratory. That, Kick noted pointedly in her diary, would not have been permitted in the U.S. Moreover, one of the ushers at the Catholic wedding ceremony had been none other than Billy Hartington—another hopeful sign.

By contrast, the experience of a second couple in their group had been a good deal less happy. Lord Salisbury had asked his grandson, Robert Cecil, to bring Veronica Fraser to see him in London. That day, the head of the house of Cecil explained to Veronica why the family's position as leaders of the Anglican community stood in the way of Robert's marrying her. Rather than ask Veronica to abandon her faith, Lord Salisbury gently requested that both young people wait a year and refrain as much as possible from seeing each other during that period. Such was the austere, silvery-white-haired old man's authority that the lovers agreed to do as he asked. Lord Salisbury, of course, was Billy's grandfather as well. The precedent of his intervention in Robert Cecil's life suggested the possibility that he might soon take similar action to sun-

der his Cavendish grandson from Kick. Among the young members
of the aristocratic cousinhood who had lately embarked on romances
with Catholic girls, Robert's position was closest to Billy's, in that
both fellows were in line to become the heads of illustrious Protestant
houses. If the often rowdy and rebellious Robert had capitulated to
their grandfather, was Billy, whose nature was so much milder than
his cousin's, not likely to do the same?

More and more, Kick's marathon talks with Billy when she and he
wandered off together at a party or a dance seemed to assume a graver
tone. They found themselves chatting "about life," which, as their friends
came to understand, was their code phrase for imagining possible futures
as a couple. What sort of life might they have together in the event that
the religious obstacles could be overcome? What might he and she accomplish as Duke and Duchess of Devonshire? At Chatsworth, Billy had
become absorbed in the collection of letters written by the eighteenth-
century Devonshire duchess Georgiana, who had dazzled the London
of her era. In particular, it was Georgiana the political hostess who fascinated Billy, and whom he began to see as a model for the influential
figure Kick might become one day as his wife.

Before long, however, the future seemed more uncertain than ever.
On March 15, 1939, Kick was still in Rome with her family following
the coronation, three days previously, of Pope Pius XII when German
troops marched into Czechoslovakia, in violation of the terms of the Munich Agreement. No one in Britain, not even at length the prime minister himself, could go on pretending that Hitler was to be trusted. The
Fuehrer, by his actions, had proven that Cooper, Churchill, Eden, Cranborne, and other government critics had been right to decry the prime
minister's gullibility at Munich. Even Chamberlain's most stalwart
supporters began to abandon him. In Eastbourne, on the sixteenth of
November, the Duke of Devonshire, a minister just below cabinet rank,
declared apropos of the fall of Prague: "The Prime Minister is striving
manfully, but warm supporter though I am, I am bound to confess that
his policy is not bearing fruit, and is not meeting with the reception which

we hoped it would." To some ears, that last phrase seemed almost comical in its understatement.

Though Chamberlain initially resisted admitting to failure, on March 17, 1939, he delivered a radio address in which he confessed that his foreign policy was now in tatters. Hitler, the British prime minister conceded, was no longer to be believed. "If it is so easy to discover good reasons for ignoring assurances so solemnly and repeatedly given, what reliance can we place upon any other assurances that come from the same source?" Chamberlain went on to ask whether the conquest of Czechoslovakia was the last attack upon a small state or whether it was to be followed by others.

The same day that Chamberlain made those remarks, Ambassador Joseph P. Kennedy, back from Rome, returned to his London post to discover a political climate that had been radically transformed. Previously, his views had harmonized with those of many Britons, who, like him, preferred to make a deal with the European dictators rather than have to undertake another war. While old Joe had been away in Rome, however, a massive shift in public opinion had occurred. Britain seemed united at last in its sense of shame over what the prime minister had done in pursuit of peace. In Andrew Cavendish's phrase, shame had "taken the safety catch off the hunting rifle," and Britain, reluctant though it had long been, was finally ready to again confront the Germans.

By this time, a year had passed since Kick's first English country house weekend, at Lady Astor's, around the time of Hugh Fraser's and Julian Amery's efforts to reverse the Oxford Union's notorious King and Country resolution. The boys' defeat, that spring of 1938, had been a reflection of the power that the argument for appeasement continued to exert on the nation. Now again, in 1939, both young men returned to the charge at the debating society. This time, however, they were making their case for conscription in the wake of the fall of Prague.

In keeping with the national symbolism of the debate, more than a thousand spectators filled every last inch of floor space, the windowsills, and even the presidential dais, and many more had to be refused admission at the front door. Hugh Fraser asked Julian Amery to propose the motion, "In view of this country's commitments and the gravity of the general situation in Europe, this house welcomes conscription." Julian Amery thereupon made the case that after eight years of fatal mistakes in British foreign policy, it had become clear that "only a policy of power can save the situation." He argued that peace could not be preserved till the dictators were persuaded that they could be beaten in war. Similar arguments had been made in the past, but they read very differently in the wake of recent events. It was not just British foreign policy that Hugh Fraser and Julian Amery sought to alter; it was the image of British decay that the King and Country resolution had helped create. Following a debate that lasted into the night, the 1933 decision not to fight for King and Country was overturned.

Six months previously, Kick had rejoiced when Chamberlain seemed to have averted a new war, thereby assuaging her fears in the aftermath of Cortachy that she would soon have to return to the U.S., and that Billy would be sent off to fight. Since then, however, the phrases "peace with honor" and "peace for our time" had been revealed as nothing more than illusion and wishful thinking. In recent weeks, Britain had begun to live within a time lock, waiting anxiously for the moment when Hitler acted against his presumed next target, Poland. Whatever personal decisions Kick and Billy were to make had to take place within that breathing space of as-yet-undetermined length.

But first, Billy wanted to speak to her of his feelings about the ideals that he ardently believed to have been betrayed at Munich. It was not simply whether or not the British prime minister's foreign policy had been efficacious that preoccupied Billy; it was whether or not it had been moral. At a moment when Joseph P. Kennedy was insisting that a war with Nazi Germany would be suicidal for the British and that even now London would be wise to look to its own interest and make additional concessions to Hitler, Billy sought to convey a very different perspective to the ambassador's daughter. He undertook to make Kick understand the traditions of honor and duty that, in his view, had been egregiously betrayed at Munich, traditions that, he maintained, had long made Britain great. Since the time of Kick's first meeting with Billy, much had, and would long be, made, and justly so, about all that she was capable of doing for him. Yet it is also the case that Kick drew substance from Billy, whose values and ideals were unlike anything she had ever had a chance to absorb from her father. In the course of their many long talks during this period, Billy by slow degrees bequeathed to Kick a way of looking at the world that, more and more, would open a substantial, often painful breach between herself and her family.

Already, that breach had disclosed itself on the occasion of a dinner party that Kick gave at Prince's Gate, which was attended by Billy Hartington, David Ormsby-Gore, Jean Ogilvy, Fiona Gore, and other members of their set. Following the meal, the group repaired to a screening room, where Kick's father showed them a movie about the Great War. As images of slaughter in the trenches began to play, Ambassador Kennedy suddenly leapt in front of the screen. Pointing to the pictures of soldiers being mown down by gunfire, he warned Billy and the other young men, "That's what you'll be looking like in a month or two!"

Both Fiona and Jean would long remember the moment when Kick, angered and embarrassed by her father's performance, undertook to distance herself from him. "You mustn't pay attention to him," Kick assured Billy, who was seated beside her at the screening. "He just doesn't understand the English as I do." Kick understood, as her father apparently did not, that for Billy and the others, fighting was a matter of honor and that they well knew the price that they as soldiers might someday be required to pay. Lord Airlie, even when he had scolded the boys for peppering each other with shotgun pellets, had never doubted that in the end they would perform as duty required of them; Joe Kennedy, by contrast, long persisted in the belief that the British might yet be persuaded that it was not in their interest to take on the Germans.

The year before, at Cliveden, Kick's willingness to tag along when Hugh Fraser, David Ormsby-Gore, and the other boys spoke of the coming war had set her apart from the English girls, who were then far more interested in discussing the 1938 London Season. In a mark of how much had changed in a year, by the time of the 1939 Season those very same girls were avidly speaking among themselves about the imminence and inevitability of war. A sense that the boys would soon be going off to fight influenced not just Kick and Billy, but others in their circle, to, in Jean Ogilvy's phrase, "grow up more quickly" than they would other- wise have done, and "not to waste a minute."

Adding to the sense of radical upheaval were predictions that the aris- tocratic way of life as it had been known to date was likely to be among the casualties of the coming conflict. The misguided optimism with which the patrician elite had faced the onset of the Great War was no- where in evidence now. In some of London's great houses, the strange spectacle of festivities taking place amidst packing crates and furnish- ings covered in white sheets suggested a stage set in the process of be- ing frantically disassembled before the play itself had quite ended. Were these houses being closed for the duration of the war—or for good? Not a few revelers were convinced it would be the latter. Many were the la- ments that the splendor of the 1939 Season would never be repeated. "I have seen much, traveled far, and am accustomed to splendor, but there has never been anything like tonight," wrote the Conservative MP Chips Channon of the ball held on July 7, 1939, at Blenheim Palace for Sarah Spencer-Churchill, the daughter of the Duke of Marlborough. ". . . Shall we ever see the like again?"

For Kick, who was also at Blenheim, the Season's grandest eve- ning resonated in a rather different way. That night, Veronica Fraser made her appearance on the arm not of the young man she loved, but of Julian Amery—their pairing in compliance with Lord Salisbury's request that she and Robert Cecil refrain as much as possible from seeing each other.

In this fraught atmosphere, Billy made his move at last. Though the government had introduced conscription, sending out a clear signal to the Germans that Britain was serious about defending Poland against

an invasion, Billy had no intention of waiting to be called up. He planned
to join the Army as soon as he was done at Cambridge. In any case, were
war to be declared, old Joe Kennedy would undoubtedly send his family
back to the U.S. at once. When Kick and Billy spoke of this eventual-
ity, they concluded that there was only one way she would be allowed
to remain in England. He thereupon spoke explicitly to his father of his
wish to marry Kick. The duke, reminding Billy of his future responsibilities, made it clear that it was out of the question that Kick should become his wife. Casting his argument in such a way as to carry great
weight with his son, Eddy Devonshire portrayed the need to take a Protestant bride as a matter of duty.

Though his actual twenty-first birthday had been celebrated in
December 1938, preparations were now under way for Billy's coming-of-
age celebration at Chatsworth. No one can have known that this August
1939 extravaganza, extending over several days, would prove to be the last
great party before the war. At the previous, much smaller party in Carlton
Gardens, the duchess had seated Kick in the position of honor, to Billy's
right. Eight months later, the duke need not have feared a similar public
gesture of endorsement from his wife. Rose Kennedy, no longer oblivious to Kick's romantic attachment to a Protestant nobleman, forbade
her to be among the more than 2,500 guests who were to descend upon
Chatsworth to celebrate the majority of the son and heir. Kick, required
to remain with her family in the South of France, missed Billy's party.

At the ducal palace, she was perhaps the more conspicuous by her absence from the festivities. On the present occasion, Billy's Cecil and Cavendish relations had no opportunity to subject her to the "dirty looks" of
which she had complained in the past, but they could and did persist in
talking about her—and about the threat that she and other Catholic inter-
lopers were believed to pose to the Protestant dynasties. One overheard
snippet of conversation would long be cited by Billy's contemporaries as
encapsulating the anxiety that had gripped their parents' and grandparents' generations. Pesky Lord Dick Cavendish, whose son had previously eloped with a Catholic, and Lady Alice Salisbury, three of whose

grandsons, including Billy, were feared about to do the same, had been seated together talking, when suddenly Lord Dick was heard to loudly and agitatedly proclaim: "These Catholic girls are a menace!"

A little more than a week after the party at Chatsworth that Andrew Cavendish compared to the Duchess of Richmond's ball before the Battle of Waterloo, Hitler signed a nonaggression pact with the Soviet Union that appeared to clear the way for the conquest of Poland. The following day, Billy Hartington officially entered the Coldstream Guards. Parliament, meanwhile, was recalled, the fleet ordered to its war stations, and a treaty signed formalizing commitments given several months before that Britain would defend the Poles against a German onslaught. Ambassador Joseph P. Kennedy directed all U.S. citizens who did not have essential business in Britain to leave immediately. He also instructed Rose Kennedy to vacate the family house in the South of France and come to London, in anticipation of traveling home. Within days of Kick's return to Prince's Gate, Hitler's troops swept across the Polish frontier and German warplanes began to unload their bombs on military as well as civilian targets in Poland.

On Sunday morning, September 3, 1939, Britain warned the Germans to pull back. When Hitler failed to provide the necessary assurances, Chamberlain went on the radio to announce that Britain was "now at war with Germany." Flanked by her brothers Jack and young Joe, Kick thereupon raced to the Palace of Westminster, where the prime minister was due to address the House of Commons. In this very setting, Kick had once danced with Billy at the Speaker's party for his granddaughters. That prior occasion, hours after she and Billy first met, had marked the beginning of their romance. There was reason to fear that today's events might signal its end. Despite Kick's tearful pleas and protests to be allowed to remain in London, her father ruled that she was to return to America at once with her mother and siblings.

As Kick would later reflect, she had really always expected to marry Billy, "Some day—somehow." She consented to go home in 1939, intent on finding a way back to him.

Four

On September 12, 1939, Kick, along with Rose, Eunice, and Bobby sailed from Southampton on the SS *Washington*. The other children—with the exception of Rosemary, who was being allowed to stay behind with the old man because she seemed to have thrived in her convent school—were to follow separately. The SS *Washington*, the flagship of the United States Lines, carried, among other passengers, 1,487 U.S. citizens, the greatest number of Americans to flee Europe on any vessel since the declaration of war. Due to acute overcrowding, many voyagers had to sleep on cots in the swimming pool area, the exercise room, the post office, the lounge, and other public spaces. Since the German torpedo attack on the British liner the *Athenia* a week and a half earlier, which had left twenty-eight American passengers dead, Ambassador Kennedy had been pounding the State Department to send more American ships to England for the use of all U.S. citizens who wished to escape.

Kennedy's decision to leak his complaints to the press led skeptics in

Washington to view him not as the hero he constantly portrayed himself as, but rather as a self-serving publicity seeker. However one regarded his motives, there could be no denying that he had successfully attached himself in the popular imagination to the general theme of the mass evacuation of Americans on the eve of cataclysm. Some travelers on the liner *Washington* claimed to feel a little safer making the six-day transatlantic crossing in the company of Ambassador Kennedy's wife and children, whose presence they saw as protection against a potential German strike. Whether because the name "Kennedy" appeared on the passenger list or, more likely, simply because the liner *Washington* was a U.S.-flagged vessel, the voyage, blessed with fine weather, proved to be a safe one.

As the ship was about to dock in New York, Kick wrote to her father of her disbelief that eighteen months could have passed since she had been sailing in the opposite direction. The time she had spent in England seemed to her already "like a beautiful dream." Though Kick's father had had to wrest her away from London, and though the months and years that followed would be punctuated by her dogged efforts to be reunited with Billy, she persisted in treating her English sojourn as a gift like all of the others that old Joe had showered upon her in the past. "Thanks a lot Daddy," she wrote on the eighteenth of September, "for giving me one of the greatest experiences anyone could have had. I know it will have a great effect on everything I do from herein."

Indeed it would, and often in ways that would prove far from delightful to Ambassador Kennedy.

No sooner was Kick back in the U.S. than much of her former existence struck her as severely wanting. She had anticipated that things at home would have changed in her absence, as she knew herself to have changed. Instead, she wistfully told her father in a letter written after she had been back at the family home in Bronxville, New York, for a week: "Everything is just the same." That was perhaps especially true of her old beau, Peter Grace, with whom Kick had already attended a polo match and a stage play in the course of that first week. Peter was as devoted to her as ever, but she could not but feel that she had outgrown him. Rejected by the college that had been her first choice, Sarah Lawrence in Bronxville, Kick began classes instead at Finch, a junior college on the Upper East Side of Manhattan, where she made it clear that she saw herself as merely "killing time" until she managed to get back to London.

Meanwhile, she spent many weekends in Cambridge, Massachusetts, where Jack and Joe Junior were enrolled at Harvard, the former embarking on his undergraduate senior honors thesis and the latter pursuing a law degree. Other weekends, her brothers came to New York, where she made the rounds of nightspots with them and their friends. Torby Macdonald, Lem Billings, and other members of Jack's claque danced attendance on her, and she was ardently courted by Zeke Coleman, George Mead, and other prospective new beaux. In Palm Beach, as in Boston and New York, Kick often turned up at fashionable events in the company of her siblings. She attended a society luncheon at the Bath and Tennis Club with Jack; a swimming party at the Seminole Club with Eunice and Pat; a private dinner dance at the Everglades Club with Jack and Eunice. But all of it paled in contrast to her memories of London.

It has been said that there are certain modes of life that, once they have been experienced, make it almost impossible to be content in any other situation. Residing in Manhattan in circumstances that many other girls doubtless envied, Kick could not but ruefully reflect that had she married Billy and had there been no war, she would have been inhabiting "a castle and not a 3 room apartment." But England had provisioned her with something even more important, something intangible, something that she had been able to bring back with her to the U.S. In England, she explained to Lem Billings, she had emerged at last as, in his paraphrase, "a person in her own right, not just a Kennedy girl." This new sense of herself, apparently, was not something that Kick intended to relinquish without a struggle.

All the while, the letters flew back and forth between Kick on the one side and Billy and various members of the aristocratic cousinhood on the other. The previous autumn Kick had been in Scotland for the Perth races. Now Jean Ogilvy sent word that their group had again gathered at Cortachy Castle. Andrew had been there with Debo Mitford. Billy had also been in attendance, but, sadly, without the girl to whom he persisted in considering himself informally engaged. That, even after Kick had returned to the U.S., Chatsworth continued to perceive her as a threat was suggested by the duke's ongoing laments about his son's romance. Following a lengthy September 23, 1939, conversation with Eddy Devonshire at a luncheon at the Spanish Embassy in London, Chips Channon recorded in his diary: "He is obdurate about his son Billy Hartington's engagement to Miss Kennedy; he will not budge; the Kennedy alliance is not to his liking; he has an anti-catholic mania, and has forbidden the match."

Nancy Astor wrote to Kick of a house party at Cliveden at which Billy, in a departure from his usual pointed avoidance of those raucous occasions, astonished everyone by suddenly joining Andrew, Jakie, and the rest. "They bemoaned your absence," Lady Astor reported in an apparent effort to banish any fears on Kick's part that she might already have been forgotten. "They tried to be cheerful and succeeded in part, but it was very difficult." At other times, Kick's old friends reacted with palpable delight to the merest mention of her name. In a subsequent letter, Nancy Astor noted that when her niece Dinah Brand heard Kick alluded to in conversation, the girl's "face lighted up and her little ears stood straight on end like a rabbit's." So the connection with Britain that Kick still felt, the abiding belief that it was, in Jean Ogilvy's phrase, where her real life and real friends were, was not just the product of a young person's fanciful imagination. The cousinhood persisted in feeling that she belonged there as well.

Immeasurably exacerbating Kick's frustration during this period was that the imminent bombing cited by her father as the reason she must leave London at once had failed to materialize. At a moment when Britain had been tensely geared up to defend itself; when there had been predictions of more than two hundred thousand British air raid casualties during the war's first twenty-four hours alone; when countless additional hospital beds had been readied, and the mass evacuation of women and children from London and other cities undertaken, a strange, unsettling sense of anticlimax had ensued.

On the assumption that London and Paris, having vindicated their honor by the declaration of war, would be relieved to be spared the need to do any actual fighting, Hitler proposed a peace settlement that required them to accept German hegemony in East and Central Europe. The Nazi leader calculated that the immediate, brutal, and overwhelming destruction of Poland would persuade the British and the French to back down. During the maddening months of stalemate and stasis known by turns as the Twilight War, the Bore War (a pun on the Boer War), and the Phony War, a jest made the rounds in London that Hitler was seeking to bore the British people into peace. Meanwhile, the prolonged passivity seemed to have a corrosive effect on British morale.

In any case, as far as Kick was concerned her father had sent her home for no good reason. To make matters worse, unlike many Britons, Kick's patrician friends in London were finding this curious interlude anything but monotonous and dispiriting. Their mothers' having fled to the countryside in anticipation of an early aerial assault, the girls, in particular, were suddenly enjoying a good deal more fun and freedom than ever before. Former debs, on their own now, worked by day and spent as many evenings as possible with their uniformed young men in the very nightclubs they'd previously frequented only when they had managed to elude their chaperones.

Finally, the ambassador's return to the U.S. on home leave in the late autumn provided Kick with an opportunity to pitch her father in person about her wish to be allowed to spend her summer vacation with him at Prince's Gate. For obvious reasons, she cast the idea of another London visit not in terms of any reunion with Billy, but rather of her eagerness to see old friends in general. This subterfuge had the very great advantage of being true, as far as it went.

Ambassador Kennedy arrived in the U.S. at a pivotal moment in his tumultuous personal and political saga. He carried with him a sealed private message from Nancy Astor to her close friend, Philip Lothian, the British ambassador in Washington. Formerly a proponent of the policy of appeasement, Lady Astor was now a staunch supporter of the war, and she regarded Joe Kennedy's opposition to U.S. participation as "scandalous." Noting humorously that she hoped the American ambassador did not take the opportunity to open her letter to Lothian, she reported on Kennedy's defeatist attitude and on his view that the continuation of the European war would be disastrous for the financial markets. She made it clear that as a consequence of these and similar attitudes on Kennedy's part, people in Britain had begun to fear him. It is evident from her letter that in spite of all this, she persisted in her immense personal affection for Joe Kennedy and in her belief that he had otherwise been a splendid ambassador. Nonetheless, she warned Philip Lothian to watch him closely in Washington.

None of what Nancy Astor had to say about Joe Kennedy was unfamiliar to Philip Lothian, who had had previous, decidedly less benign, communications on the matter from officials at the British Foreign Office, where there was the feeling that a complaint about the U.S. ambassador, possibly even a request that he be recalled, might soon need to be made. It had been one thing for Kennedy to speak in such a manner prior to the British declaration of war, but it was quite another for him to persist in doing so now. Lothian, a former German sympathizer who had entirely revised his views on Hitler after the occupation of Prague, had made it his mission to drive home to the Americans that Britain's survival was crucial to U.S. security. Kennedy, when he conferred with Lothian during his home visit, was careful not to express any of his controversial opinions. Presently, however, Lothian sent word to Lady Astor that Kennedy apparently had shown no such reluctance with various others in Washington. Still, up to that point Kennedy's remarks, to figures that included President Roosevelt, had been uttered in private.

As Christmas drew near, Ambassador Kennedy, joined by Jack and

Joe Junior, visited the East Boston church, Our Lady of the Assumption, where in ancient times old Joe had been an altar boy. On the present occasion, he gave an impromptu speech that, however he may have intended his comments to be construed, amounted to his first public address since the inception of the European war. Openly and unabashedly, Joe Kennedy urged that the U.S. refrain from getting involved. "As you love America," Kennedy declared, "don't let anything that comes out of any country in this world make you believe that you can make the situation one whit better by getting into the war. There's no place in the fight for us. It's going to be bad enough as it is." Kennedy, who was usually a good deal more astute about public relations matters, appears to have been oddly oblivious to the prospect that his remarks would be disseminated in the British press. Nor, as he went off to Palm Beach to spend the holiday with Rose and the children, did he yet have any inkling of the calamitous impact that accounts of the speech were already having on his reputation in Britain, where his comments were widely regarded as anti-British.

Joe Kennedy's home leave extended through late February, during which time he again met with Franklin Roosevelt, conferred with doctors in Boston about the state of his health, recuperated from a serious stomach disorder—and considered Kick's proposal of a summertime trip to London. There was talk that Jack might accompany his sister abroad, and even that Rose and the rest of the Kennedy children might come over as well.

Meanwhile, the news of Sissie Lloyd Thomas's February 9, 1940, marriage to David Ormsby-Gore, with Billy Hartington serving as David's best man, at the Roman Catholic Church of St. James's, Spanish Place, fueled Kick's hopes that she and Billy might similarly be able to overcome the religious obstacles. In stark contrast, the love affair of Robert Cecil and Veronica Fraser had finally concluded in great sadness, when Robert's mother put an official end to it. Robert had previously told Veronica that when the relationship ended he would send her a family brooch or locket with the inscription, "It's better to have loved and lost than never to have loved at all." Convinced that Lady Cranborne had indeed broken things off, Veronica waited for a package, a letter, or even a card from him. But she waited in vain—Cecils, she later reflected, being taught from early on to always be cautious and to avoid committing themselves in writing.

Whether Kick's fate when she reached London at last would be more like Sissie's or Veronica's remained to be seen. In any case, Joe Kennedy sailed on the liner *Manhattan* with his daughter's pleas that she be allowed to come over, on her own or in the company of other family members, still fresh in his ears. In the belief that her father seemed inclined to agree to a visit, Kick wrote at once to Billy and others in Britain to confidently announce that she would be with them again before long. She spoke too soon, for the situation that confronted Ambassador Kennedy when he arrived in London on March 9, 1940, instantly changed everything.

The brash American diplomat who had been so popular when he first took up his post two years previously was surprised and appalled to discover that in his absence from London he had been transformed into a pariah. There was much public anger about his remarks at the East Boston church. There was resentment that at such a critical point in British history he had chosen to remain out of the country for several months; there was indignation that when at length he did return he had failed to bring his wife and children; and there was anxiety that he would use what was thought to be his great influence at the White House to press for a negotiated peace. In fact, Joe Kennedy was far from the trusted counselor to Roosevelt that many Britons believed him to be. The President, while publicly pledging that the U.S. would never enter this war, had rejected Joe Kennedy's repeated urgings that Washington broker a peace settlement with the Nazis. Roosevelt had gone so far as to initiate a secret correspondence with Churchill, a maneuver that Kennedy saw as a deliberate affront. More and more, Kennedy would find that he was being ignored, bypassed, and otherwise marginalized by a White House that thought it best to work around rather than through its own ambassador. At the moment, however, it was his low standing in Britain that seemed to concern Kennedy most when he ruled on Kick's request.

On March 14, 1940, the ambassador wrote to notify Rose of his change of heart about any sort of family visit. He spoke of his desire to spare his children exposure to the negativity about the U.S. in general and to himself in particular that now seemed to prevail in Britain. But it is clear from his comments that the father's principal concern was the impact that such sentiment threatened to have on Kick. He knew of her immense affection for her British friends, and of the warm feeling they had shown for her in turn.

And now, he worried that were she to be reunited with them, the nasty political arguments that were likely to break out might spoil her happy memories. As if the old man meant to counter in advance Kick's inevitable assurances that she understood the British so much better than he, and that there really was nothing to worry about, Joe asked Rose to convey a remark recently heard from the lips of one prominent member of Kick's set.

On a visit to Cliveden, to which he had brought an armload of gifts of Lady Astor's favorite chocolate and chewing gum, old Joe had also happened to encounter Jakie Astor. At a moment when the British were known to be very keen to involve America in the European war, Jakie purported to take a contrarian view. Always ready with a barbed witticism, he insisted that he was actually rather pleased that the Americans had chosen to stay out. The British, Jakie continued, were eager to win this war on their own—"without America taking credit for it." Joe Kennedy offered Jakie Astor's comments as a specimen of the anti-American sentiment that he feared would upset his daughter.

Kick, for her part, saw nothing very disturbing or daunting in any of it. She was confident that her British friends knew that she did not share her father's views on the war. When over time she kept on pressing to be allowed to come over, the old man responded with a new argument. He pointed out that these days there was really nothing for young people in London to do "but spend practically every night in a night club." That particular prospect, it need hardly be said, did not seem so objectionable to Kick.

Her father, however, remained adamant. He refused to be influenced even by a message from Jack in which the second son shrewdly appealed to old Joe's self-interest. Knowing how dependent on public perception his father was, Jack maintained that Kick's London vacation would benefit the Kennedy family overall by showing that they had not merely left Britain because things had become unpleasant there. Kick, though she refused to abandon hope, finally wrote to let Billy know that she probably would not be able to come over after all. When she sent off that message, she had no idea that by the time it reached him he would be far from Britain.

On April 9, 1940, what Churchill characterized as the trance in which the British and the French had been agonizingly suspended for eight months was abruptly broken when Hitler invaded Denmark and Norway. A week later, Joe Kennedy offered a new rationale for why Kick could not possibly return to London anytime soon. All the young fellows, he grimly reported, were being "shuttled off to war."

So, at least for now, events in Europe seemed to have derailed Kick's campaign to be reunited with Billy. The next letter she had from him confirmed the futility of her hopes of seeing him again anytime soon. Billy wrote from the Maginot Line in France, where he was with the British Expeditionary Force, waiting along with the rest of humankind to see what Hitler's next move would be.

In the early hours of May 10, 1940, German forces, moving by land and air, overran Belgium, Holland, and Luxembourg. Belgium, abandoning its long-insisted-upon neutrality, removed border barriers so as to permit the entry of the British Expeditionary Force. Among the hundreds of thousands of advancing soldiers, Billy and his Coldstream Guards regiment were soon passing into Belgium, to the joyous greetings of a slew of girls, who rushed up to garland the troops and their rifles with lilacs.

Press coverage in the U.S. initially emphasized the clockwork efficiency of the British onslaught, confirming a sense that prevailed among not a few Americans at the time that Britain and France together would handily manage to turn back the Germans without the U.S. needing to get involved. Adding to the tone of optimism were the newspaper descriptions of perfect spring weather and nearly cloudless blue skies, and of joyously singing, newly energized British troops to whom the summons to action had proven, in the phrase of *The New York Times*'s correspondent, "a psychological tonic" after the long months of waiting and training since war had been declared.

Meanwhile, that same day in London, Neville Chamberlain was left with little choice but to tender his resignation as a consequence of wide dismay with his administration's botched efforts to rescue Norway. He handed over to Winston Churchill, who soon faced a devastating series of setbacks. German tanks broke through the supposedly impregnable Maginot Line. The Battle of Flanders took a disastrous turn for the British, who began to retreat into France. Overall, the Allies were stunned by the ferocity and unstoppability of the Nazi war machine. Official opinion in London held that it was only a matter of time before Hitler struck at Britain.

On Sunday evening, May 19, 1940, Churchill delivered the first radio address of his premiership. His intended audience consisted of three distinct groups. He aimed to steel the British people for the monumental struggle that lay ahead. He meant to put the Germans on notice that Britain was prepared to fight to the death. And he hoped to persuade the Americans that this was their fight as well and that the time had arrived that they really must join in.

Churchill spoke of the tremendous battle then raging in France and Flanders; of the remarkable combination of air bombing and heavily armored tanks that had permitted Hitler to break through the French defenses; and of the alarm and confusion that the Germans had managed to spread in the course of their attack. He admitted that it would be foolish to disguise the gravity of the hour, but insisted that it would be still more foolish to lose heart and courage. "Our task is not only to win the battle, but to win the war," he went on. "After this battle in France abates its force there will come the battle for our island, for all that Britain is and all that Britain means—that will be the struggle."

For Kick, Churchill's address had special resonance, frantically worried as she was not just about the fate of Britain's vast fighting force in general, but about one young soldier in particular. Churchill in his remarks articulated values of honor and courage that she had often heard Billy speak of as well. The broadcast gave voice to the British self-concept that meant so much to Billy, and it put in sharp perspective the claims of money and property that her father had frequently offered as reasons for the U.S. to stay out of this war. Financial interests, Churchill emphasized, were "nothing compared with the struggle for life and honor, for right and freedom, to which we have vowed ourselves."

The day after the text of the speech had been published in *The New York Times* and other newspapers, Kick wrote a letter to her father that left no doubt that her sympathies remained firmly with the British. Echoing Churchill's phrasing in the broadcast, she noted: "I still keep telling everyone that the British lose the battles but win the wars." Kick went on to report that a student vote had been taken the previous week at Finch as to whether the U.S. ought to go into the war. "I and another girl were the two yeses," she wrote. "All the rest voted no." Usually careful about showing her parents how much she still felt for Billy, she exhibited no such restraint now. In the aftermath of Churchill's public acknowledgment of the acute danger in which the British Expeditionary Force then found itself, Kick's words to her father fairly screamed from the page: "Is Billy alright?"

Kick was by no means the only one frantic to find out about him. At a time when the Germans had driven a wedge between the outmaneuvered British and French armies; when the British Expeditionary Force found itself trapped in a Nazi-devised "sack"; when Allied casualty statistics were running high; and when there was a feeling within the British camp that "nothing but a miracle" could save the Expeditionary Force from annihilation, Billy's parents and siblings also longed for news. But none was to be had. Eddy and Moucher Devonshire had simply stopped hearing from their son. Churchill, speaking in the House of Commons on May 23, 1940, reported that German armor, having reached the English Channel, had entered into fierce fighting with Allied soldiers in the area of Boulogne, some thirty miles from the shores of England. Looking ahead to what he feared might soon emerge as the greatest military disaster in his nation's history, Churchill warned the House to prepare for "hard and heavy tidings." In a clear sign that the government anticipated an imminent attack on Britain, orders went out for the arrest of Sir Oswald Mosley and other homegrown fascists who might prove all too ready to welcome and aid the Nazi invaders.

Meanwhile, efforts were under way to evacuate the British Expeditionary Force and to return as many men as possible for the defense of the island. However they could manage it, British troops, under orders to pull back, fought their way to the coast, where myriad vessels small and large waited at Dunkirk amid relentless attack from bomb-dropping, machine gun–firing German planes that were sometimes more than a hundred strong in formation. Hitler's misjudgment that air power alone could prevent the men of the British Expeditionary Force from escaping, and that he could thus judiciously withhold German armor for later use, proved critical to the success of the British rescue operation. Where once it had been hoped in London that perhaps 20,000 or even 30,000 British soldiers might be extracted, instead some 335,000 troops came home, to national jubilation.

But among the tired, tattered, often traumatized soldiers who poured out of bullet-pocked fishing boats, motorboats, steamboats, sailboats, pleasure boats, and other motley craft, many of the men vowing to soon be ready for "another go at Jerry," there was no sign of Billy. More than a week after Kick had implored her father to learn what he could about Billy's fate, no report of his safety or survival had yet reached her. No British friend could joyously contact her to say that Billy had come home with the other soldiers, because in fact he had not. Was he dead?

Wounded? A German prisoner? There was no information one way or the other. An estimated six thousand British troops had yet to be accounted for when Lord Gort, commander in chief of the British Expeditionary Force, returned to London on June 2, 1940, on Churchill's orders. Gort came home most reluctantly, even angrily, pledging, like so many returnees before him, to go back and meet the Germans again— "and the next time victory will be with us."

Two days later, Billy remained among the missing to whom Churchill briefly paid collective tribute when he addressed the House of Commons in a landmark speech that history would remember for its promise that rather than surrender to the German invaders, Britain would fight on the beaches, fight on the landing grounds, fight in the fields and in the streets, fight in the hills, and if necessary fight on alone. "We shall defend our island, whatever the cost may be." In the U.S. there was public rejoicing at the dramatic rescue and return of all those British fighting men, and there was much impassioned response to Churchill's oratory— but still Kick had had no word about Billy.

Like the young American woman he had once forbidden his son to marry, Eddy Devonshire found it hard to fully participate in the general celebrations. In the course of a house party at Cliveden the weekend after Churchill's speech, the duke strove to conceal his anguish and anxiety from Lady Astor and her other guests. Despite his best efforts to be stoic, there could be no mistaking his "drawn, miserable" countenance, and the country house weekend proved to be a somber one for all in attendance.

Still, as Nancy Astor was to discover, the duke had lately been given reason to hope that Billy might yet be all right. Eddy Devonshire had learned that Billy had in fact been temporarily left behind in Flanders because of his ability to speak French. Up to that point, anyway, Billy had not been killed or captured. It was what happened in the days that followed that remained agonizingly unknown. Repeatedly his parents wrote to him in France, and repeatedly their letters were returned undelivered. After the gathering at Cliveden, the duke traveled north to

Churchdale Hall, hoping that good news might soon reach him there. By the following weekend, however, he and the duchess had yet to hear anything from or about their son.

In the weeks since Jean Ogilvy had last heard from Billy, she had been struggling desperately not to think about the premonition she had had when he was first sent to Belgium: the certainty that the cousin she adored would be killed in the opening days of combat. It had seemed to her not just a dreadful thing to think, but also very odd. She and Billy were both still so young. People their age did not die. At first, she had been immensely relieved when no bad news had reached her. But then, she learned that Billy had gone missing. Had she been right after all? Could it be possible that she would never see or speak with him again?

Jean had been living with those and related questions for weeks when, on the afternoon of June 18, 1940—the day after the fall of France, and the very day Churchill returned to the House of Commons to announce that the Battle of Britain was about to begin—she heard a knock at her front door in London.

When she opened the door, in walked Billy.

His appearance, she would long remember, was jarringly unlike that of the evacuees she had seen in news photographs: men who had not washed in days; men with scraggly, mud-and-blood-encrusted beards; men whose uniforms were ragged and begrimed; men who were missing one or both boots. Billy was attired in meticulously clean and freshly pressed battle dress, his hair carefully combed, his pale skin visibly scrubbed. At that moment, he looked precisely like the man she had last seen months earlier, the Billy who had gone off to war. Kick's question to her father—"Is Billy alright?"—seemed finally to have an answer.

But things were not as simple as they initially appeared. For as soon as Billy was indoors, as soon as he was sure that he and Jean were alone and unobserved, it became evident that he was far from all right. To Jean's astonishment, her Cavendish cousin suddenly exploded in emotion of a kind and an intensity that seemed utterly out of character. She had never seen Billy like this before. And she would observe him to burst out in a comparable manner on only one subsequent occasion, in 1943.

Now, palpably upset, almost in tears, Billy would not, perhaps could not, stop talking. Detail after ghastly detail of his ordeal poured out. Billy told her he had seen terrible things. Worst of all, he said, had been that the horrors never stopped. "They just attacked and attacked." And all he could do was keep running. "We ran away!" he said over and over. "We ran and we ran!" At length, he had commandeered a Baby Austin automobile and had managed to get out of France via St. Nazaire.

Billy spoke of his sense of guilt at having survived when so many others—not just soldiers, but also fleeing French families, innocent men, women, and children—had been killed. Instead of relief that he was safely home at last, all that Billy seemed to care about was how and when he could get back to Europe and complete the job that had been left undone. The next time, he felt certain, the British would get it right. The next time, they would not run. The next time, they would vanquish the forces of evil that had come at them so unexpectedly and overwhelmingly.

Indeed, the German army had set out not just to fight their Allied antagonists in the Battle of Flanders, but also to terrorize them. Hitler's Stuka dive bombers were designed to overpower and unnerve by their extreme proximity to their targets, and by the eardrum-shattering, anxiety-provoking noise produced by special sirens known as the Trumpets of Jericho that were affixed to the legs of the aircraft. The merciless machine gunning of vast numbers of refugees appalled and disconcerted the enemy army with the massacres' sheer sadism and gleeful flouting of the codes of warfare. This too was part of the Nazis' strategy of terror. If they treated innocent civilians so, what would they do to captured Allied troops?

When the British Expeditionary Force came home, not a few returnees were visibly shell-shocked, trembling and staring blankly, the result of having been hunted like animals for days and nights on end, then ceaselessly menaced with bombs and bullets when they reached Dunkirk and later when they attempted to cross the English Channel.

Lest the sight of these physically and psychologically shattered warriors, and the import of the dark tales they had to tell, affect public morale and even incite mass panic on the eve of the German invasion, some traumatized troops were confined to barracks prior to being sent off on leave. Other soldiers were ordered to disclose as little as possible to family and friends about the nightmare they had just lived through in France.

On the day Billy visited his cousin, his impeccable attire was a gesture toward concealing and suppressing all that he had just experienced. Still, in the course of his conversation with Jean, he seemed to make no effort to hide the fact that his whole world had just been upended. He whose life had been shaped since birth by centuries-old rules had encountered a savage enemy for whom there appeared to be no rules. He who had gone off to war motivated by ideals of honor and justice had witnessed the mass killing of French refugees, fields littered with eviscerated corpses and detached body parts, images of unfathomable cruelty and malevolence that seemed to call everything he'd thought and believed into question.

He who had been so lazy and languid had suddenly had to flee for his life, always moving, always tensely watchful, sleepless and hungry, chased without letup by armored tanks and screaming, diving planes. He who, unlike his brother, had been slow to grow up had been abruptly and irrevocably deprived of his innocence in the war zone. He to whom anything like real anger had previously been almost an alien emotion had become consumed with rage at the slaughter of fellow soldiers and innocent civilians, atrocities he had been agonizingly powerless to prevent, deaths he felt strangely compelled to now avenge.

Billy and other veterans of the Battle of Flanders rejoined their units and began intensive preparations for the Battle of Britain. In the meantime, whenever Billy was in London he seemed more than ever to seek Jean out. It was as if he had disclosed to her an aspect of himself that from then on needed to be scrupulously hidden from most other people, but at least Jean knew that it was there. He and his Ogilvy cousin had always been exceptionally close, but their talk that first day formed the basis of a vital new bond.

On June 28, 1940, ten days after that conversation, Billy invited Jean to tea at his family's home in Carlton House Terrace. Following the declaration of war against Germany, the most valuable paintings and furniture had been removed from the white stucco-faced residence on a cul-de-sac in St. James's and sent up to Chatsworth for safekeeping. But the London house itself, quite wonderful in its own right, still contained many beautiful things, and Billy told Jean that he wanted to give her a tour of the remaining treasures.

When Jean arrived that afternoon, he seemed to make a point of being very much like the Billy of old, showing her about proudly, pausing every now and again to enthusiastically recite the history of this or that marvelous object. But it seemed to Jean that there was something a little forced, something heartbreakingly sad about the performance. It was, she reflected many years afterward, as if Billy were struggling to recapture, perhaps even to remind himself of, the person he had been before his encounter with evil and killing had changed him forever.

In important ways, the young man whom Kick had left behind in 1939 had ceased to exist.

Five

———

In Hyannis Port, the anxiety of the past few weeks conferred a new sense of urgency to Kick's campaign to secure her father's permission to go to London. If the obstacles had been formidable before, they were well nigh insurmountable now. Between July and September, the Luftwaffe pounded the Royal Air Force in an effort to establish air superiority in preparation for a German invasion of the British mainland.

Meanwhile, life at the Kennedy residence appeared to go on much as before. A visitor to the household at the time, Jack's friend Charles "Chuck" Spalding, later recalled a typical afternoon there: Jack autographing copies of the recently published book version of his Harvard senior honors thesis, *Why England Slept,* about the Conservative politician Stanley Baldwin, Neville Chamberlain, Munich, and the policy of appeasement; Joe Junior holding forth on his Russian travels; Rose Kennedy conferring on the telephone with a priest; Pat recounting how a German aircraft had crashed in the proximity of Ambassador Kennedy's country home near Windsor; Bobby attempting to persuade his brothers and sisters to play charades; and all the young people suddenly choosing up sides for a game of touch football, with Kick "calling the huddle" for the team on which the delighted guest soon found himself.

Also that vacation season, Kick, usually with Jack at her side, cut a ubiquitous figure on the major East Coast social circuits in Newport and Long Island. At Bailey's Beach, an elite club in Newport, she was so often observed dressed in tennis whites, racket in hand, that she came to be regarded as something of a regular there. Other than the sight of her at Cape Cod knitting a scarf for Billy, to all outward appearances Kick seemed to have compliantly and contentedly settled in to the sort of existence that her parents had hoped she would embrace when she returned to the U.S. the previous autumn.

But the picture was deceptive, for all that summer of 1940, far from having given up on finding her way back to Billy and England, she had merely been waiting for her opening.

It came at last in the form of a letter from her father that was delivered in Hyannis Port on the sixth of August. Actually, several letters from Prince's Gate arrived that day, one for each of the Kennedy children then in residence at the Cape, including Rosemary, who had been sent home in May for safety's sake. In his message to Kick, Joe Kennedy reported on the activities of the Astor family and other of her London friends. But it was the ambassador's long letter to Rose Kennedy—who, as was her custom, passed it around to all the children—that provided Kick with the opportunity to approach him anew on the subject of a London visit. At a moment when Joe Kennedy was feeling miserable at his post, alienated from the Churchill administration on one side and from the Roosevelt administration on the other, he wrote of his great sadness at being separated from his wife and children through all this: "The big difficulty, of course, is being lonesome," he told Rose, "but I have to keep my mind off that or I'd throw up the job and go home."

Kick wasted no time writing back to propose that she might be just the person to assuage Joe Kennedy's loneliness: "I wish I could come to

England to keep you company," she declared on the sixth. "Is there any chance of it? I should so love it." Given the concerns that had motivated the ambassador to repeatedly reject previous appeals, was it reasonable or realistic to think that he would let her come over at a moment when the defense of the island—perhaps even the fighting in the fields and streets evoked by Churchill—threatened to begin at any time? Probably not, but when it came to Billy, Kick was not then in a condition of mind that might adequately be described as reasonable. The young man she loved was facing another monumental fight for his life, and she wanted to be there with him.

So Kick sent off her request, though by that point her father was plainly as desperate to escape London as she was to get there. His ambassadorial heyday had coincided with the premiership of Neville Chamberlain; there was simply no comfortable place for the defeatist, anti-interventionist Joe Kennedy in Winston Churchill's Britain. Enraged that in its dealings with Churchill and the British, his own government had transformed him into, in his bitter phrase, no more than "a $75 a week errand boy," Kennedy longed to quit.

If he remained on the job, it was because he wanted to avoid being charged with cowardice for abandoning his post and his president at a time of grave danger. As he suggested to Rose Kennedy and others, he wished to do nothing to jeopardize his family's reputation and thereby harm the two eldest boys' futures. The White House, though it had ceased altogether to trust Joe Kennedy's judgment or recommendations, was content to leave him in place for now. It seemed the lesser evil to keep Kennedy in London than to bring him home during the run-up to the 1940 presidential election, when any critical public comments by a disaffected former U.S. Ambassador to the Court of St James's could prove highly damaging to Franklin Roosevelt.

In early September, Hitler, having failed in his efforts to outmatch the Royal Air Force in combat, shifted tactics. Over the course of nine months, German planes attacked London in an effort to terrorize and demoralize the British people and leave them begging for peace. Night after sleepless night, the face of the city was transfigured by relentless bombing. Thousands of German aircraft filled the skies like swarms of buzzing bees. Craters opened in the streets. Buildings burned. Residential and shop windows blew out. Walls shook, cracked, and collapsed. Billows of acrid smoke befouled the air. Emergency crews scrambled to rescue survivors trapped in the mountains of rubble. The death toll climbed to more than twenty thousand.

Fragments of the city that Kick had come to know so well in 1938 and 1939 began to vanish. A Nazi bomb pulverized the balcony in Grosvenor Square where she had sat late one night listening to Tony Loughborough hold forth on the future of Europe. Another bomb gutted the Cavendish family house where the duchess had made the audacious gesture of seating Kick to Billy's right, in the position of honor, at his twenty-first birthday party. Still another bomb destroyed the Earl of Airlie's residence, where Kick had often lunched with Jean Ogilvy, Debo Mitford, Gina Wernher, and other debs.

At length, both Jean and Debo were shipped off to live with Nancy Astor. Debo worked in the hospital for Canadian soldiers that had been set up at Cliveden, while Jean traveled daily into London, where she was employed at the Women's Voluntary Service caring for victims of the Blitz. Formerly the most sheltered of the debutantes in Kick's group, Jean would walk from Cliveden to the main road, a distance of about a mile, where she would hitchhike into town, usually in a truck, before reversing the process at the end of the workday. Some two and a half years after "the two Joes," as Kick and Jean had dubbed their fathers, agreed about the wisdom of avoiding a second world war, Joe Airlie had become an ardent and active supporter of the fight against Nazi Germany. Back in the uniform he had worn in the First World War, he was stationed near the Tower of London, where, as a member of the Home Guard, he watched for fires and participated in rescue missions.

The Germans had calculated that Britons would react to the mass bombing by ejecting the Churchill government. But, as the American broadcast journalist Edward R. Murrow told his listeners on September 10, 1940, "It's more probable they'll rise up and murder a few German pilots who come down by parachute." On not a single occasion, Murrow continued, "have I heard man, woman, or child say that Britain should throw in her hand."

On the very day that Edward R. Murrow spoke those words to his CBS radio audience, Joe Kennedy was writing home with a rather different picture. Kennedy reported that while Britons kept saying that their chins were up and that they would not be beaten, "I can see evidence of some people beginning to break down." As far as his own response to the bombardment of London was concerned, he insisted: "Haven't the slightest touch of nervousness." That, however, was far from how the British people perceived his behavior. Kennedy's nightly search for safety in a house in the country caused contemptuous Londoners to refer to him as "Jittery Joe." Foreign Office documents characterized him as "thoroughly frightened" and as having "lost his nerve" and "gone to pieces" as a consequence of the Blitz. Whether because of fear of the German bombers, a sense of his inefficaciousness in London, resentment about how the White House had been treating him, or some mixture of those factors, Kennedy finally decided that he had had enough. Given that Roosevelt was intent on keeping him in London until after the election, Kennedy sent word, via U.S. Under-Secretary of State Sumner Welles, that if he were not allowed to come home at once he would publish an indictment of the administration in the American press a few days before the presidential contest.

Oddly, the U.S. ambassador made similar claims at the time to British foreign secretary Lord Halifax, boasting of the impact his printed comments promised to have on the outcome of the election. Roosevelt, threatened in this manner by one of his top diplomats, reluctantly consented to summon Joe Kennedy to Washington, though with the stipulation that Kennedy make no statement to the press until he and the President had had a chance to agree upon what ought to be said.

Roosevelt instructed Kennedy to come directly to the White House on his arrival in the U.S. Soon, official word went out that Ambassador Kennedy was being brought back to America for consultations.

Newspaper accounts in the U.S. described Joe Kennedy as coming back for a brief vacation, for a prolonged stay, or for good. There was meanwhile much concern in high British quarters about the role Kennedy might play in the American election when he went home. The Churchill government emphatically preferred Franklin Roosevelt to his Republican challenger, Wendell Willkie, and there was anxiety that, once he was safely back in the U.S., Kennedy would announce his support for the latter. Halifax, unlike a good many of his colleagues, predicted that Kennedy would agree to support the very candidate he had been threatening to attack.

At LaGuardia Airport in New York, Kick and her sisters Eunice, Pat, and Jean rushed forward like so many well-synchronized ballerinas when Joe Kennedy finally came into view amidst the numerous reporters who were clamoring to ask about the circumstances of his departure from London. Had Kennedy come home for good? Did he intend to resign? What were his plans otherwise? How did he feel about the reelection of Franklin Roosevelt? And what about Wendell Willkie? The ambassador's return had been postponed for two days due to severe storms over the Atlantic, and the delay seemed only to have intensified public curiosity about the purpose of his trip. Kennedy had refused to answer press questions when he changed planes in Portugal, and he proved to be similarly uncooperative now.

The inrushing Kennedy girls crowded round the old man in such a way as to temporarily block the correspondents' access. Their father proceeded directly to the White House, where he signed on to campaign for Roosevelt in the expectation that at length the President would accept his resignation and find a new official post for him in Washington. Kennedy delivered a highly effective radio address on Roosevelt's behalf that was broadcast on more than a hundred stations nationwide, and he appeared beside the President at a rally in Boston, which some commentators later saw as having been key to Roosevelt's successful reelection bid.

That same month, Kennedy went on to damage himself immeasurably by a rabid interview with *The Boston Globe* and a similarly ill-considered address to film industry figures in Los Angeles. In both venues, he reiterated his predictions of social and economic apocalypse should the U.S. allow itself to be drawn into the war. And this time he seemed to go even further. "Democracy is finished in England. It may be here," Kennedy informed the Boston newspaper in what he later insisted had been off-the-record remarks. The ambassador predicted that even if the Germans were to win the war, the U.S. would continue to trade with Nazi-dominated Europe. The speech in Los Angeles that followed struck attendees as being shot through with anti-Semitism, when Kennedy warned Jewish producers and film studio executives to stop making anti-Nazi motion pictures lest Hollywood and the Jews later be blamed for the horrors and hardships that would ensue should the U.S. join the fight against Hitler.

Referring to the *Globe* interview, the *New York Herald Tribune* accused the ambassador of telling the Germans quite what they wanted to hear and to believe. Old Joe, full of self-pity, privately lamented that while the bombers might be tough in London, "ill-disposed newspapers" were even tougher in the U.S. Taken together, his Boston and Los Angeles performances constituted a spectacular act of self-destruction. By the time Roosevelt finally accepted and announced Kennedy's resignation, in December 1940, it was not just old Joe's ambassadorship that had come to an end; it was his public life as well.

During the past year and a half, Kick's arguments for being allowed to return to London had all been predicated on her father's ongoing presence there. After his resignation had been accepted, she could no longer talk of living with him again at Prince's Gate or of playing a role in mitigating his loneliness. If Joe Kennedy had refused her pleas in the past, he was not likely to assent now. Less tenacious souls might have lost hope at this point, but Kick was nothing if not resolute. Her attach-

ment to Billy and Britain had become intrinsic to her sense of herself as
a soloist rather than as a mere member of the Kennedy girls' corps de
ballet.

She cabled Billy at Christmastime 1940 to communicate that she had
not abandoned her goal: "Hope the New Year brings us together again."
Was she worried that her beloved would be discouraged by the ambassador's departure from the London scene? Did she fear that, in the matter
of love, blue-blooded Billy would prove less stalwart than she? Soon,
Nancy Astor was signaling that Kick might indeed have reason to be
concerned. Ostensibly, her February 22, 1941, letter to Kick was about
the impending marriage of Debo Mitford, aged twenty, to Andrew Cavendish, who had just turned twenty-one and seemed exceedingly young
to Lady Astor. Having imparted the news of the one brother's wedding
plans, she went on to pointedly say about the other: "Your Billie [sic] is
still heart-free." This was surely a hint that, devoted to Kick though Billy
still was, he might not remain hers for long in the present climate. Read
in the context of other of Lady Astor's letters (both to Kick and other
correspondents), it seems clear that she was not alluding to any potential lessening of Billy's ardor. She was speaking of the changed reality
that faced all the young people there, and of how that new reality might
affect Billy's thinking with regard to waiting for Kick.

Death had become a factor in the young people's lives in a way it simply hadn't been before. Constantly, inescapably, one was reminded of
one's mortality. Tony Loughborough—now Tony Rosslyn, the 6th Earl
of Rosslyn—wrote to Jack Kennedy of how unsettling it was to realize
that friends with whom one had attended Eton, boys with whom one
had once played games, suddenly no longer existed: "Every few days one
reads of another shot down in the air or killed at sea." Jean Ogilvy nar-
rowly escaped being killed when she and a Women's Voluntary Service
coworker with whom she had dined in London changed plans at the last
minute, staying the night at her family's surviving mews cottage
rather than at the friend's residence, which a bomb proceeded to destroy
that very evening. And of course there was the prevailing sense that if

the Germans ever did manage to occupy Britain, it would be, in Tony Rosslyn's words, "over the dead bodies of all our 44,000,000 that are old enough to bear arms." Under the circumstances, Debo and Andrew were far from the only couples who found themselves rushing into marriages they might otherwise have put off for years, or perhaps never have entered into at all. As Nancy Astor was to declare in another context, it was difficult, if not impossible, for anyone who was not then in Britain to comprehend quite what it was like there as a consequence of the war: "Nobody could—it has all changed so."

Two weeks after Nancy Astor sent off her warning to Kick, there occurred in Billy's life precisely the sort of event that had been causing a good many young people of late to drastically rethink their personal timetables. Billy had an evening off in London, where the nightclubs were regularly packed with merrymakers determined to live life to the fullest, not so much in spite of the bombs as in defiance of them. He and the other young grandees tended to travel in packs, and since Kick's return to the U.S. he had regularly squired various young women whom he'd known for much of his life and whom he regarded as "pals," such as Rene Haig and Sally Norton.

On this particular Saturday evening, March 8, 1941, he and Sally Norton arrived by taxi at Coventry Street in Soho, shortly after a pair of 50-kilogram high-explosive bombs had hit the Café de Paris, killing thirty-four customers, club staff, and band members, and gravely injuring dozens of other people. Bodies were being removed as the taxi pulled up, and Billy rushed into the club to assist.

Illuminated by torches and cigarette lighters, the scene that greeted Billy on the plush dance floor, some twenty feet belowground, was horrific—headless, limbless bodies; blood and death everywhere. Having encountered similar piles of mutilated corpses of the innocent in France, he found that he was strangely numbed to the nightclub carnage. The establishment's subterranean location had been generally assumed to provide a modicum of safety against the aerial pounding. Tonight, however, the bombs had roared down a ventilation shaft from the roof, exploding in the midst of the crowded dance floor. Billy, when he told the story afterward to his brother, emphasized that had he and his companion arrived but ten minutes earlier one or both of them might have been killed.

On April 19, 1941, Billy served as best man at his brother's wedding ceremony in London's oldest surviving church. Andrew and Debo had been attracted to St. Bartholomew the Great, which had been in continuous use since the twelfth century, for its reassuring aura of permanence and stability in a world that seemed to have been turned "upside-down" by war.

As it happened, the setting for the reception that followed, the ballroom of Lord Redesdale's house in Rutland Gate, bore the marks of the random violence and sudden, shocking upheaval that the young people had been hoping to escape for at least a few hours on their wedding day. Shortly beforehand, bombs had blown out all of the windows, shredding curtains and littering floors with broken glass. By the time the guests arrived, Debo's mother had had the debris removed and the windows covered over with faux curtains, in the form of gray and gold wallpaper strips that left the house precariously exposed to the elements. Fortunately, the weather proved to be mild that day.

For the members of the set, there was something upside-down as well about Andrew's being the first of the brothers to marry. Even he had been heard to exclaim, on the eve of his nuptials, that he was much too young to be doing this. The second son had long striven to catch up to Billy. And indeed the previous November, much to Billy's annoyance, Andrew had been commissioned as an officer in the same battalion of the Coldstream Guards, the Fifth, in which Billy was already serving. Billy and Andrew soon often found themselves to be near neighbors when training, and the arrangement appeared to work out no better than when, as boys, they were forced to share a room. Now, Andrew had taken the lead over his brother by becoming a husband—and more.

The newlyweds honeymooned at Compton Place, where German bombers nightly roared overhead, en route to London. Not long after the honeymoon, Debo announced that she was "in pig," as she referred to being pregnant. She and Andrew were wonderfully happy together during this period, living in the various improvised quarters of a soldier's marriage while he trained in various parts of the country.

There would come a day in the not too distant future when Billy would write to Kick: "It was a very long time before I gave up all hope of marrying you." It is impossible to pinpoint exactly when that abandonment of hope occurred. But surely the process began in the wake of Ambassador Kennedy's resignation, when Billy had had to absorb that Kick was not likely to return before the end of the war. He might have been able to bear that knowledge with equanimity had he still been the person whom Kick had last seen in September 1939. As it was, what he had confided to Jean Ogilvy in June of 1940 remained powerfully true many months later. To his cousin's perception, at moments Billy appeared almost to be living more in Belgium and France than in London. Far from having abated, his need to go back and finish the fight seemed to have grown the more urgent and intense. He saw himself as having come home to England but "temporarily." He regarded it as unquestionable that he must return to battle before very long; and he would tolerate no suggestion, however well meant, to the contrary. If he were to become a husband and a father, if he were to produce an heir, if he were to enjoy at least some portion of the private happiness that most men desire, he sensed that he must accomplish all of these things before he left.

By degrees, the people around Billy began to detect a shift in his relations with Sally Norton. Rene Haig, to her manifest disappointment, ceased to be an alternate companion when Billy was on leave. Now, it was left solely to Sally Norton to accompany him to fashionable London restaurants and nightclubs on her days off from war work. She held a top-secret position at Bletchley Park, where she applied the language skills that she had honed at a German finishing school before the war. On official orders to give no hint of her role in the breaking of Nazi codes, she steadfastly described herself to family and friends, including Billy, as a Foreign Office clerk. Less discreet about her new role in the

life of the duke's heir, Sally made a point of routinely, and to not a few
ears gratingly, referring to him in company as "my Billy." The duchess
certainly noted the altered dynamic; so did Debo, Andrew, Jean, Fiona,
and others. Within that circle, it was said disparagingly of Sally Norton
that she was "after Billy." Billy would later reflect that during this
period he attempted to make up his mind that under the circumstances
he "should have to make do with second best."

Kick had told Billy that she hoped 1941 would bring them together
again, and in the late spring a dramatic change in Germany's war strategy seemed to make that objective somewhat less impracticable. On May
9, 1941, the last and worst of the bombing raids on London took place,
leaving a record fourteen hundred people dead and reducing to rubble
the Chamber of the House of Commons. In the weeks that followed,
though sporadic bombing persisted, it soon became apparent that the war
was moving in a different direction. On the twenty-second of June, the
Germans unleashed their military might against the Soviet Union. The
invasion of Russia meant that for a time at least, the threat of a Nazi invasion of the British mainland seemed to be in abeyance. London was
no longer the impossibly dangerous place it had been during the Blitz.
As Kick would soon argue to her father, though bombs continued to fall
on London, she was as likely to be hit by one there as she was to be struck
by an automobile at home in the U.S.

Ironically, it was Joe Kennedy who inadvertently provided Kick with
the opportunity she had long been seeking. When she earned her junior
college diploma that spring, her father suggested that she consider a
career in journalism. He had encouraged his two eldest sons to make
their mark by writing about world events and the European scene, and
now he had it in mind for Kick to find employment at a newspaper in
Washington, D.C. Working there would put her in what he portrayed
as "the thick of things" in the world's most important capital at a critical time in history. Though her father clearly never planned for her to
use the job to catapult herself back to London, that, she would later acknowledge, had been her intention from the first when old Joe's friend

Arthur Krock arranged for her to be hired as a secretary to Frank Waldrop, executive editor of the ultraconservative, isolationist newspaper
the *Washington Times Herald*.

In the *Times Herald*'s culture, assisting Waldrop was regarded as a
stepping-stone toward other more important assignments. Waldrop liked
to try out new girls, often wealthy former debutantes like Kick (and in
later years Jacqueline Bouvier, the future Mrs. John F. Kennedy), to determine whether they were serious about journalism or merely intended
to "hang around" until they made a suitable marriage. Meanwhile, being rich, they provided the newspaper with a cheap form of labor. If at
length Waldrop judged a girl to be sincere, he liked to take his time de-
ciding exactly where she belonged in the organization.

Hardly had Kick moved to Washington and reported to work in September of 1941 that it seemed as if she were about to demonstrate to
Waldrop that a career in news was far from her priority. Obviously it
was going to take a while before she advanced to the reportorial position she saw as her ticket to London. So, for all of her grand talk to her
parents about wanting to be a journalist, she was very happy indeed when
another friend of her father's, Carmel Offie, told her that he could arrange to get her over to London immediately. By this point, Kick had
heard nothing from Billy for, in her phrase, "simply ages," so the short-
cut suggested by Offie could scarcely have been more opportune.

Offie, the former assistant to U.S. ambassador to France William
Bullitt, had the reputation of a "fixer"; his methods were frequently illegitimate or in the neighborhood thereof. In the present instance, he
promised to use his personal influence with his new boss, the recently
designated U.S. ambassador minister to the exile governments in London, Anthony Drexel Biddle, to provide Kick with the coveted visa. Offie
assured her that Biddle would "do anything" for him. On October 3,
1941, Kick wrote to tell Joe Kennedy of Offie's involvement, and to let
her father know that the one thing she still needed was his consent. She
underscored that she had a good many friends whom she would really
like to see, "and even if the British feel a little embittered about your

opinion in the present struggle I don't think any real friends such as I have would let that bother them. And even if it does as Offie says 'the hell with them.' "

On October 20, 1941, Kick had yet to hear back from Joe Kennedy when she had lunch in Washington with Dinah Brand. Nancy Astor's niece had just arrived in Washington to live with her widowed father, Bob Brand, who was then the director of the British food relief program. She brought with her urgent messages, both written and spoken, for Kick. Dinah handed Kick a letter in which Debo and Andrew implored her to come at once and "save" Billy from Sally Norton, who had him "in the bag." Other friends had asked Dinah to personally convey similar pleas. Even after Dinah had left Britain en route to the U.S., during a stopover in Portugal she had encountered Fiona Gore, who'd added her own forthright voice to the chorus. Andrew, for his part, wrote at the urging of his mother. Sally Norton was not what the duchess wanted for her son; nor, she believed, was Sally quite what Billy himself wanted and needed. The duchess remained determined that he marry the girl of his heart, not the girl he had lately chosen as a matter of wartime expediency. Indeed, that it was Kick whom Billy still really loved was the underlying assumption of all the people who reached out to her through Dinah Brand. He and Sally Norton were set to publicly announce their engagement in January of 1942. Andrew, Debo, and the others were certain that Kick needed only to come back to prevent that from taking place.

After lunch, Kick returned to the office, where she poured out the news in a frenzied letter to her father. Two weeks before, Kick had been careful to maintain the long-established pretense that she wished merely to see old friends in London. In this follow-up message, she made no effort to conceal why she was really so anxious to travel to the war-ravaged city even though she had just begun a new job. This time, there was no subterfuge, no artifice; there was, after all, not a moment to be lost. She spoke openly of the urgent messages about Billy that had just been transmitted to her, and of the engagement announcement that

she yet hoped to prevent. And she was honest about the chaos of her emotions: "I am nearly going mad," Kick disclosed to her father. ". . . I am so
anxious to go back that I can hardly sit still."

This was her condition of mind when, on the evening of the twenty-
first, she received the letter in which Billy spoke of having waited a very
long time before he'd given up hope of marrying her. He said he had
never been engaged before, thanks to Kick. He fondly reflected that what
sense of humor he possessed he owed to her. He related the news that
(unbeknownst to him) she had already heard from Debo, Andrew, and
the rest; and more than a little oddly, he asked her to keep writing in
spite of his engagement to Sally Norton.

For two years, Kick's sense of her own emergent identity had been
tied up with her feelings for Billy. For two years, she had regarded herself as merely marking time until she managed to be reunited with him.
For two years, she had used every stratagem and argument that she could
devise to persuade her father to allow her to go back to London. Quite
often, her efforts had had a quixotic air. Now, just when she finally had
what looked to be a viable plan in place, Billy had decided that he could
no longer wait for her.

Prior to receiving his letter, she had been wild to reach London. That
ceased to be the case after she heard directly from Billy. By the time Kick
reported Billy's change of heart to her father on the twenty-second, she
had had a full night to process all that had just occurred. If Billy's letter
had provoked tears, she had given herself ample time to wipe them away.
If she had experienced hurt and humiliation, she had since endeavored
to armor herself against such feelings. If Billy had proven himself to be
weak, she would not allow the same to be said of her. "Rather sad, don't
you think?" Kick commented contemptuously on Billy's performance.

As if the defection of her first great love meant little to her, she went
on to blithely enlighten her father about her busy social schedule in
Washington, and about her weekend plans to attend the races and a dance
in Middleburg, Virginia—with another of her young men.

Six

Six days after Kick received the terrible news from Billy, Jack Kennedy, aged twenty-four, joined her in Washington, D.C., where he was set to begin active duty in the Foreign Intelligence Branch of the Division of Naval Intelligence. Not surprisingly, Jack had failed his draft physical, but at length his father had arranged for him to pass a specious new exam, in which the second son's lengthy history of grave medical difficulties was made to disappear, if only on paper, via a notation in his official records that he had suffered nothing in excess of the "usual childhood illnesses." Jack thereupon received his commission as an ensign in the United States Naval Reserve, with an eye toward being reassigned to sea duty.

For Kick, Jack's arrival was fortuitous, coming as it did in the wake of Billy's defection. Now that that relationship was at an end, Kick discovered that she was very grateful indeed to be able to cling to her collective Kennedy identity by again forming a duo with Jack. No sooner did her brother come to town than she and he were constantly dashing in and out of each other's apartments, dining and entertaining together, attending cocktail and dinner parties, filmgoing, and in other ways diverting themselves in a city she had until only recently intended to use as a mere springboard. From this point on, America's capital, not England's, would have to be where her real life and real friends were.

Immediately, she began sending out autographed copies of Jack's critically well-received, bestselling book *Why England Slept* to all the leading Washington hostesses, in an effort to secure invitations to their tables. The Kennedy Kids, as they came to be affectionately known, soon emerged as popular dinner guests. It was not just their youth, physical attractiveness, high spirits, and intriguing twinlike behavior that made them so appealing to prominent Washingtonians. At a moment when there was much dinner table debate about Winston Churchill, Franklin Roosevelt, the war, and whether American interests would be best served by joining the fight against Nazi Germany or by steering clear, Jack's and Kick's firsthand experiences of Britain on the eve of the declaration of war had huge appeal. As Joe Kennedy's children, they also possessed a certain curiosity value; as Kick later recalled, hardly a night would pass that someone did not inquire or make remarks about the old man's controversial statements and opinions.

Kick, of course, rarely if ever hesitated to speak up, at table or elsewhere. But on these occasions it was Jack in particular who was known to hold forth, more often than not about subjects he had written about in his book, such as Stanley Baldwin's politically motivated pursuit of a tepid policy of rearmament, and Neville Chamberlain's dilemma when he encountered Hitler at Munich.

Interestingly, on the matter of potential U.S. intervention in the war, Jack, who had previously sided with their father, had begun to come round to Kick's way of thinking. At least he affected in public to have done so. Jack now maintained to fellow dinner guests that if a "quick victory" were possible he would be inclined to support an American decision to go in. At evening's end, when Jack delivered Kick to her one-bedroom apartment on Twenty-first Street, she would change into a bathrobe and sit up late with him, dissecting the various eminences they had met that night, as well as plotting their own next moves on the chessboard of Washington society.

As it happened, there was a third Kennedy sibling residing in Washington at the time, though few people in town were aware of her existence. Rosemary Kennedy, who had been rendered intellectually disabled by a lack of oxygen at the time of her birth, was now twenty-three and confined to a residential facility. Prone to bouts of depression and violent tantrums, she resented being forcibly cut off from her siblings and from the world they inhabited. Many nights, while Jack and Kick were establishing themselves socially in the capital, Rosemary went missing from her room at St. Gertrude's School and spent hours wandering the dark city streets until the nuns who maintained the facility found her and brought her back. Rosemary's parents feared that in the course of these perambulations she might be sexually assaulted or otherwise harmed. Late in the fall of 1941, Joe Kennedy permitted doctors at George Washington University Hospital to perform a lobotomy on Rosemary.

The outcome of the procedure was disastrous. Rosemary emerged from the operation unable to walk or talk. Deemed permanently incapacitated, she was removed at once on her father's orders to Craig House, a psychiatric hospital in Beacon, New York, where she lived in secrecy and seclusion for years to come. In the wake of his having moved Rosemary to Craig House, Joe Kennedy sent occasional reports on her to Kick and other of the siblings; but he alone visited the eldest Kennedy daughter there.

Kick, meanwhile, was by no means spending every evening in Washington in her brother's voluble company. Prior to Jack's arrival, she had begun to form a friendship with a wild-eyed, tattooed, always sloppily dressed, Harvard-educated feature reporter at the *Washington Times Herald* named John White, who was nine years her senior. Apart from being one of the best and most prolific writers at the paper, he was also the best talker, a freethinker and left-winger who loved few things more than to debate and disagree.

Attracted as Kick tended to be to whatever was most amusing and exciting, she had warmed from the first to the colorful and contrary White. Fellow interventionists in a nest of isolationists, he and she seemed to disagree about almost everything else. Though his fierce combativeness, which bordered at times on obnoxiousness, was rather too pronounced for many people's tastes, Kick at this stage enjoyed and excelled at the cut and thrust of her encounters with him. And he marveled at what he judged to be her prodigious powers of retort. Quite often in conversation, he took what he described as "the devil's position," arguing for argument's sake, not because he actually believed what he was saying. And she, in turn, frequently struck him as not necessarily speaking her own mind about issues. Rather, it was as if Kathleen—as he insisted on calling her, mainly because everyone else addressed her as "Kick"—was testing her parents' values and views by laying them out for her iconoclastic colleague to demolish.

For the moment anyway, though White spoke openly about wanting a good deal more from the relationship, passionate argument about such freighted topics as the Pope, birth control, and premarital sex was about as far as matters had progressed. In the early autumn of 1941, Kick believed herself to be on the verge of obtaining a visa, and of being reunited with Billy. As she conspired with Carmel Offie; as she awaited Joe Kennedy's consent; as she lunched with Dinah Brand; as she reflected on Debo and Andrew's urgent message; as she desperately appealed to her father anew; and even as she found herself reeling from the letter in which Billy spoke of his engagement to Sally Norton—all the while John White had been preoccupied with what was for her but a minor subplot. As he had done with other of Frank Waldrop's young, pretty secretaries, White, a self-styled lady-killer, had been intent on adding Kick to his list of sexual conquests.

It was not until the month after Kick received Billy's game-changing letter that John White was finally able to record a first small but hopeful sign of progress in his at times comical pursuit of her. Given what had been Kick's resistance to all sexual overtures, he seems to have regarded even the most minimal physical contact as a potential turning point in their sweet and sour relationship. "Tonight for the first time I held the hand of KK," White exulted in his diary on November 30, 1941, ". . . and do now wonder what will become of us."

Kick, when she finally allowed John White to take her hand in his, was of course facing a drastically different future from the glittering one of castles and coronets that had appeared to beckon to her but a few weeks before. Now the struggle to become, in her phrase, a person in her own right shifted to new ground. Like Billy before him, John White offered an alternative to her family's view of the universe. White was quite simply of greater mental vitality than the Zeke Colemans and George Meads of this world.

To be sure, White was seeking to break down her sexual defenses by patter, debate, and perhaps not a little sophistry. At the same time, by repeatedly and explicitly challenging the religious and moral principles of her Kennedy upbringing, he emerged as a central actor in Kick's ongoing drama of identity.

White was hardly the first man on earth to flatter himself that, far from trying to seduce a sexually inexperienced young woman, he was really seeking to enlighten and awaken her. Not so much in spite of his efforts to land her in bed as because of them, he viewed himself as a beneficent presence in her life. With typical pomposity, he compared her to a chick that has yet to break out of its shell, and he described it as his role to helpfully nudge the process forward. With characteristic grandeur, he spoke of loosening the bonds that constrained her.

As a socialist, White professed to despise all aristocrats as a matter of principle. He had an especially low opinion of Billy, in part no doubt because Kick herself had been so contemptuous of Billy when she was still dealing with all of the hurt and heartbreak attendant on the end of their relationship. White's abiding view of Billy as pitifully weak reflected how Kick regarded him, or at least how she affected to regard him, when, in the late fall and winter of 1941, she believed that he was forever lost to her. Further, White viewed with disdain the younger man's failure to initiate and educate her sexually, as White himself now magnanimously proposed to do.

White was no less critical of Kick's father, though of course for very different reasons. He was horrified by the degree of control that old Joe exerted over Kick and her siblings. As early as White's second or third outing with her, she seemed to know all sorts of details about his background as the son of an Episcopal minister in Tarboro, North Carolina, that he was certain he had never mentioned to her. Pressed as to how she suddenly knew so much about him, she disclosed that her father routinely had all of his children's would-be girlfriends and boyfriends investigated by detectives. What, White demanded to know, had been the finding with regard to him? "Frivolous, but harmless," she flung back.

As if he were intent on proving the contrary to be the case, White more and more cast himself as the antagonist of Joe Kennedy. Years afterward, he liked to tell the story of finding himself with Kick in a hotel suite, whose outer door she insisted must be left open because her father's operatives were almost certainly watching. In the narrative that the newspaperman constructed of her life, he saw it as his role to help bring her to the point where she was finally ready to shut that door, with all that might suggest about the diminution of old Joe's power.

White never actually met Billy; and it would be many months before he finally beheld the other object of his derision, Joe Kennedy. Of the important male figures in Kick's life, the one with whom White's relations were most fraught and complex was Jack, whom he had little choice but to meet on a regular basis. From the moment Kick's favorite brother materialized in Washington, White perceived him to be, in his phrase, "in the way," and he sensed that Jack felt a similar antipathy to him.

Thus began a strange and uncomfortable relationship that would persist long after Kick was dead, when both John White and Jack Kennedy were, each in his own manner, orbiting the young Jacqueline Bouvier in postwar Washington. The two men would have seemed to have much in common. Both had prodigious sexual appetites (and indeed would

later pursue and succeed with many of the same women). Both were vo-
racious readers, with highly refined literary tastes.

But whereas John White took pride in being a free spirit who dis-
dained the personal ambition that drove many, if not most, other men,
the Jack Kennedy who arrived in Washington in 1941 was unabashedly
ambitious. Jack of course had not always been that way. There had been
a time when the second son had had to conceal his desire to displace his
older brother as the family front-runner. Now, the critical and commer-
cial success of *Why England Slept* had profoundly altered Jack's position in the Kennedy hierarchy. In the wake of Jack's bestsellerdom, Joe
Kennedy Sr. had begun to proudly refer to him in public statements,
where once he might have referred to Joe Junior; and the patriarch had
allowed himself to rely as never before on Jack's strategic counsel and
even on his efforts as a speechwriter and a ghostwriter. Jack's publishing triumph was supposed to have been young Joe's, but the firstborn's
tortured literary efforts had come to naught, only one of his many articles and essays (a piece about his travels in Spain) having finally made
it to print.

To make matters worse for young Joe, Jack soon turned his attention to outdistancing him in another, even more critical area. Jack began
to speak, however lightheartedly, to his sister and their circle of close
friends in Washington of the possibility that he might seek the presidency
one day. At times, these antic discussions resembled a party game that
Betty Coxe affectionately dubbed "Jack's Future." Among the Kennedys, it was young Joe, not the second son, who had long been assumed
to be destined for political preeminence. For Kick, who from the time
she was a child had championed Jack in the face of formidable opposition and seemingly impossible odds, his ascendency both in the family
and in the world was as gratifying as it was thrilling.

Kick also seemed pleased—at least initially—when a female colleague of hers at the paper, Inga Arvad, quickly came to share the elec-
tric intensity of her excitement about Jack. A statuesque blond Danish

beauty then living apart from her second husband, Arvad was a highly valued contributor to the *Times Herald*. She wrote a popular interview column known as "Did You Happen to See . . . ?" that spotlighted new-comers to the Washington scene. Early in her career, she had been a European beauty queen, a film actress, and a reporter for a major news-paper in Copenhagen. She had traveled to prewar Germany, where she interviewed Hitler, who, pronouncing her a perfect specimen of Nordic beauty, invited her to join him in his private box at the 1936 Olympics in Berlin.

Subsequently, she had attended the Columbia University School of Journalism in New York City, where Arthur Krock offered to find her a job in Washington. As he would later do to help launch Kick, he sent Inga to Cissy Patterson, publisher of the *Times Herald*. On the basis of Inga's experience in Europe, Mrs. Patterson immediately signed her on as a staff writer.

Inga became fast friends with Kick when the latter arrived at the paper. On the eve of Jack's move to Washington, Kick touted him to Inga, who soon had a chance to judge that her coworker had not been exaggerating: "He had the charm that makes the birds come out of their trees," Inga later wrote of her first meeting with Kick's brother. "He looked like her twin, the same mop of hair, the same blue eyes, natural, engaging, ambitious, warm and when he walked into a room you knew he was there, not pushing, not domineering, but exuding animal mag-netism." Or, as Inga confided at the time to her other chum at the *Times Herald*, John White, "I have gooey eyes for him."

With a nod to the European tradition of the older female who under-takes to educate a young lover, Inga declared that Jack, four years her junior, still had a lot to learn and that she was pleased to be the one to teach him. The pedagogical dimension of her relationship with Jack was not limited to matters of sex, however. Inga also discussed politics and history with him, read and critiqued his writings, and in a tone that Betty Coxe described as "motherly" advised him shrewdly with regard to his virtues and limitations were he indeed to pursue a career in politics. Half in earnest half in jest, Jack told Inga that if he ever did seek high office he would want her to be his campaign manager. Meanwhile, in her column on November 27, 1941, she enthusiastically introduced Jack Kennedy to *Times Herald* readers as "a boy with a future." Inga wrote that at twenty-four years of age Jack had already produced a "much praised book" and that "elder men like to hear his views which are sound and astonishingly objective for so young a man."

By the time those words appeared in print, Inga and Jack had enlisted Kick and John White to help them carry on what was after all an extramarital affair on Inga's part. Her Hungarian-born husband, Paul Fejos, then living in New York, was known to be explosively jealous. By design, Kick and John would conspicuously appear with Inga and Jack at the start of an evening, as though they planned to make a sprightly quartet. Before long, however, Kick and her companion would discreetly leave the lovers alone for a time, then rejoin them at evening's end for all the world to observe. The arrangement naturally put a good deal of additional pressure on Kick, who was by no means as eager to take instruction from her self-appointed sex tutor as Jack was from his. When she and John White peeled off from the lovers, he sometimes brought her to "the cave," as he called the grungy, book-filled basement apartment he occupied in the house on Dumbarton Avenue in Georgetown owned by his sister Patsy Field. He would read to Kick from his pantheon of authors, argue with her peremptorily, act as if he knew what was best for her better than she did herself, and otherwise vainly endeavor to maneuver her into bed.

In three months' time, Kick's relationship with this eccentric, at once exasperating and endearing older man who had fallen infernally in love with her had developed its own distinctive rhythms and routines. Notable among them was a fast-paced, combative style of conversation that self-consciously echoed the Hollywood screwball film comedies that she and John, playing hooky from the paper, often slipped off to see together of a workday afternoon.

For all of the insults ("big bag of wind," "ignorant, thick headed

Mick," and many others) that they were forever hurling at each other, their friendship at this point was filled with, quite simply, fun and enjoyment. However much being called upon to serve as beards for Jack's affair with a married woman complicated their own relationship, Kick and John also found it to be a great game that was exceedingly amusing. And however persistently Kick countered John's arguments for a greater degree of physical intimacy, even she seemed to enjoy at least playacting at being a couple in the fullest sense of the word when they double-dated with her brother and Inga.

But the hilarity of Washington life as Kick had come to savor it in the waning months of 1941 was about to draw to a rather abrupt end.

On Sunday, December 7, Kick joined John White and Patsy Field for lunch at a local restaurant. In the course of the meal, a radio blasted the news of Japan's surprise attack on Pearl Harbor. White later acknowledged that as a newspaperman he really ought to have rushed to the office immediately. Kick as well would have been expected to go in to assist her boss, who was already at his desk frantically phoning a football stadium where he knew many of his circulation men to be spending the afternoon. Frank Waldrop requested that an announcement be made on the arena's public address system directing all *Times Herald* employees to report to work immediately. But there was no such announcement in the restaurant, where Waldrop's secretary on the one hand and his premier feature writer on the other kept up the bantering tone of the conversation that had preceded word of the attack.

They had been discussing what John intended to do were there to be a war. John had declared, as she had often heard him do, that he did not believe a man should fight. In truth, this was far from what he thought. The claim that he was a pacifist was merely his way of returning the ball over the net, of initiating a debate by affecting a bohemian attitude with which Kick was certain to disagree. Now, revisiting the theme in light of Pearl Harbor, Kick again asked about his plans. Again, he suggested for argument's sake that he would refuse to serve. Though Patsy was eager to talk in a more serious vein, John and Kick persisted in laughing and disputing as they took their time finishing lunch.

No thanks to John and Kick, the *Times Herald* was the first paper in town, possibly in the nation, to hit the streets with comprehensive news of the attack. Waldrop's triumph did nothing to improve the publication's reputation, which plummeted in the aftermath of Pearl Harbor. Roosevelt asked Congress to declare war on Japan; and three days after that Japan's ally, Germany, declared war on the U.S. In such a climate, the *Times Herald*'s long-held fervent opposition to American intervention, coupled with a controversial editorial decision, three days before Pearl Harbor, to publish secret U.S. war plans, caused not a few Washingtonians to regard the paper very suspiciously indeed.

Given the leaked war plans, some figures in the Roosevelt administration viewed the people at the *Times Herald* as traitors who bore personal responsibility for Pearl Harbor. The paper's publisher, in turn, privately voiced suspicion that Roosevelt might actually have "arranged" for the attack to take place in an effort to force the country into war. At length, Cissy Patterson came to believe that the President had at least known in advance about the Japanese assault. Frank Waldrop would long take a similar view.

Amidst all the fear and finger-pointing, a rumor suddenly circulated at the *Times Herald* that there might even be a Nazi spy planted among them. The evidence was a news photograph in the paper's morgue showing Inga Arvad with Hitler in his box at the 1936 Olympics in Berlin. On December 12, Kick informed Inga of what was being said about her. Inga complained about the rumor that she was a spy to Cissy Patterson, who found herself in a most difficult position.

Inga insisted that she had been at Hitler's side in her capacity as a freelance journalist; and her employers at the *Times Herald* were inclined to believe her. Still, Mrs. Patterson understood that at a moment when her paper was regarded in some Washington quarters as virtually a fascist organ, the Nazi rumors about one of its staff members were not likely to be helpful. The publisher urged Inga to tell her story in full to the Federal Bureau of Investigation, in the interests both of clearing herself and of removing this additional taint from the paper.

Inga did as suggested, but the result of her long interview with an FBI agent proved to be far from what she or her employer had been hoping for. Instead of exonerating her, Inga's testimony prompted the bureau to launch an intensive monitoring operation focused on the espionage suspect's daily existence. Federal agents watched the front door of her residence and tapped her phone. Initially, the agents remained clueless about the identity of the tousle-haired young man known, in the words of one official report, "only as Jack," who was Inga's regular bedmate. When at length Jack's full name and status did emerge, his superiors in Naval Intelligence and his father were soon united in their consternation.

Soon, Kick informed John White that their regular foursomes with Jack and Inga might have to be discontinued. She explained that her father, who had initially approved of the idea of an older, worldly instructress for Jack, was no longer prepared to accept Inga's presence in his son's life. Old Joe, Kick reported ominously, was "getting ready to drag up the big guns." And so he seemed to do following the January 12, 1942, publication in Walter Winchell's syndicated column of a reference to Jack's affair: "One of ex-Ambassador Kennedy's eligible sons is the target of a Washington gal columnist's affections." Reporting that the woman had already spoken to a lawyer about a divorce from her husband, Winchell concluded: "Pa Kennedy no like." The next day, Jack received word that he was to be transferred immediately to the Charleston Navy Yard in South Carolina—or, as he bitterly referred to his new assignment many miles from Inga, "Siberia." Prior to leaving town, he bequeathed to Kick his much nicer apartment, at Dorchester House on Sixteenth Street, which she arranged to share with Betty Coxe, who was then enrolled in a foreign service course at Washington's Walker School.

Hardly had Kick and Betty moved in than visitors were greeted by a prominent display of Kick's personal photographs, which were arrayed on a large table in the living room—framed pictures of Billy and other of the aristocrats who had courted and feted her in Britain just before the war. The display reflected the fact that Jack's departure from Washington was not the only critical event to have taken place in Kick's life just then. Some two and a half months had passed since Jack arrived in town shortly after Kick had learned of Billy's engagement. Now, suddenly, she had had unexpected news from Cliveden.

Nancy Astor wrote to report that Billy had broken off with Sally Norton. Though Lady Astor provided few details, according to Billy's sister Anne their mother had been a prime mover in the breakup. Also, in the aftermath of Debo and Andrew's message imploring Kick to come back and "save" Billy, Debo had given birth two and a half months prematurely to a son who had lived for but a few hours. The couple's ineffable sadness over the loss, and the manner in which Andrew had striven to comfort the woman he loved, seemed to affect Billy profoundly, reminding him as it did that it was Kick he truly cared for, and wanted to be with when life's worst misfortunes struck. At Christmastime 1941, he decided that he could not go forward with his present marital plans.

Nancy Astor, of course, was eager that Kick come at once. For a moment, it almost seemed as if in her great haste to reunite Kick and Billy, she had overlooked the inconvenient matter of America's recent entry into the war. Kick, by this time, was better acquainted with the obstacles. "I long to come over," she told Lady Astor, "but it looks quite impossible." She added that if Dinah Brand went over in the spring she would "definitely" (Kick packed a good deal of personality into that adverb) accompany her. Quite how she would manage to bring off the trip remained as yet unclear. But for the moment, one thing was evident: Whatever Kick's hurt and anger had been the previous October, all was instantly forgiven with regard to Billy.

Soon, he as well wrote to her of the sundered engagement. Confident that Britain, having stood alone since 1939, had amply disproven the opinions so often expressed by Jack and old Joe, Billy prompted Kick to ask her brother whether he still believed that the British were "decadent." Kick fired off this playful challenge in a February 13, 1942, letter to Charleston; and before long the old jousting dynamic that the trio had been known to exhibit before the war—between her beloved on the one side and her brother on the other, with Kick in between—had been pleasantly reestablished.

Where did this altered dynamic leave John White? Not in an optimal position, to be sure. Though no doubt all-consuming to him, his earnest efforts to advance his relationship with Kick had become again but a minor subplot to what was for her once more the thrilling main action. Since hearing from Nancy Astor, Kick had again been living essentially ad interim, focused on returning to Billy by the spring of that year. She believed she might have found a way when, in early February 1942, as her twenty-second birthday drew near, she was finally promoted to the staff writing post that she had regarded as her ticket to London when she first went to work at the *Times Herald*. By Kick's calculations, her new job as the paper's film critic made her eligible for the journalistic credentials she needed to go over.

The extent to which Kick's sights had altogether shifted from caves to castles is suggested by Jack's March 10, 1942, response to Billy's question about whether he still believed that the British were "decadent." Addressing her, as he liked to do, in a fanciful strain, Jack cast his reply specifically in terms of Kick's recently revived travel plans. "I would advise strongly against any voyage to England to marry an Englishman," he wrote at once archly and unrepentantly to his sister. "For I have come to the reluctant conclusion that it has come time to write the obituary of the British Empire." Jack painted "the English way of life" that he and she had witnessed on the eve of the war as very much a "dying" phenomenon. Far from impressed by Britain's ability to stand alone, as Billy had expected him to be, Jack pointed to Churchill's reliance on the Americans to defeat Hitler as a sure sign that the Britain of old could not possibly survive the war. Though of course, in a very different tone, Joe Kennedy had been saying as much for years.

John White, rather than acknowledge that at this point Billy and the life he offered had become an insurmountable obstacle to his intentions, much preferred to look upon Kick's father as his principal nemesis. When White lamented that he was sick of fighting with her about their relationship; when he countered her claims about what the Roman Catholic Church prohibited her from doing with indignant demands that she seek a dispensation; when he vowed to renounce her, only to resume hysterically chasing and quarreling with her shortly thereafter; when he spoke in a desultory manner of hoping that they might marry one day; when he finally gave up begging and badgering her for sex, insisting that he would happily settle for kissing and cuddling instead—he seems to have had no clear comprehension that whatever window of opportunity he may have enjoyed between late October 1941 and early January 1942 had shut swiftly and forever as soon as she'd learned that Billy was free. She did not wish to hurt John, but she could not give him what he wanted, either—certainly not now. When Lem Billings visited Kick and Betty Coxe soon after they inherited Jack's apartment, he observed with amusement that among the young men's photographs displayed on the living room table, there was not a single image of Kick's current suitor, John White.

Inga, too, regarded old Joe as her particular enemy, but in her case this was not a misperception. When he learned that she and his son had been rendezvousing in Charleston and, worse, that Jack was contemplating marriage, he went into overdrive to end the affair. He knew about it partly from Kick, who now admitted to being jealous about the depth of Inga's intimacy with her brother, and partly from the detailed reports that the FBI regularly sent on to him. The agency bugged the Charleston hotel room where the lovers' pillow talk included, among other matters, Jack's belief that "the British Empire is through," his annoyance with Churchill "for getting this country into the war," his bitterness about his father's political downfall, and his sense that old Joe had finally quit speaking out against intervention because he feared that were he to persist he "might hurt his sons in politics."

This last concern, or so the old man claimed, was what motivated him now to do all that he could to compel Jack to give up Inga. She was a married woman, after all, and even were she to divorce her husband and marry Jack, she threatened to prove a significant liability should he run for office as a Catholic candidate who hoped to appeal to the Catholic vote. Jack initially sought to resist his father. He brought Inga to meet the old man, who, by Inga's account, made a pass at her when his son was out of the room.

After Jack learned about the FBI surveillance of his trysts with Inga, he reluctantly agreed to see her no more. Inga seems to have accepted the end of the affair with an air of stoicism. She told Jack that were she "but 18 summers" she would "fight like a tigress for her young, in order to get you and keep you." As it was, she considered herself too old, and Jack's bond to his father and to his family too strong. Not long after the breakup, Inga left the paper, where Kick inherited her column.

In the end, Jack had capitulated with regard to the woman he had hoped to marry. Kick, though no less attached to her father and family, was unwilling to lose Billy in the same manner. Presently, she told her parents of a letter that Nancy Astor had sent to the Brands, calling on Kick to stop the foolishness and come back to marry Billy without delay. Was Kick's mention of Lady Astor's remarks her way of preparing her parents for the inevitable? Certainly, she made no effort to hide the fact that the possibility she might marry the heir to the Duke of Devonshire was still very much in play.

Intent on going over in the capacity of a journalist, Kick made the rounds of various U.S. State Department offices in Washington in quest of the special permissions that would be necessary for a trip that, she told Inga over lunch one day, she was prepared to undertake at her personal expense. In the beginning, she was confident that her status as Joseph P. Kennedy's daughter would open all doors. However, that proved to have been a miscalculation. Kick complained of the futility of her efforts to Jack, noting that the U.S. government had an agreement with London about the number of correspondents they could send over. She, unfortunately, had failed to make the cut. Also, one's visa had to be approved by the British Embassy, which, she noted sardonically, she did not believe the British would be "too happy to do" in her case.

After he had lost Inga, Jack, despite his privately stated antipathy to the war, began an officers' training course in Chicago in eager anticipation of finally being reassigned to sea duty in the Pacific theater. John White, powerless against the magnetic pull that Billy and Britain seemed to exert on Kick, joined the Marines. By this point, White had abandoned his efforts to persuade her to sleep with him, or even merely to cuddle and kiss. He reasoned that her convictions with regard to premarital sex were so deeply ingrained that to seduce her would be truly to violate her, and that he loved her too much to knowingly do that. Instead, he asked for no more than to be allowed to spend chaste but affectionate evenings with her at Dorchester House. At bedtime, Kick would rush into the bathroom to change into a flannel nightgown. Then she would position herself in bed in anticipation of permitting John to tenderly massage her back until she fell asleep, or at least until she pretended to sleep in the interest of hastening his departure.

Finally, John White left Washington for boot camp in South Carolina and later a stint at the Brooklyn Navy Yard in New York. Prior to his being shipped out to Northern Ireland, Kick invited him to spend the Labor Day weekend with her family at Hyannis Port. There he would have an opportunity to encounter for the first time the Kennedy patriarch who had loomed so powerfully and ominously in the younger man's imagination.

The meeting between old Joe and his self-appointed nemesis proved anticlimactic, to say the least. It took place outside the main house, where John White, who had missed his bus to the Cape, was making a tardy and somewhat awkward arrival. Joe Kennedy, walking past the hired car that had delivered his daughter's houseguest, uttered but two clipped words of welcome: "You're late!" The shabby newspaperman, clutching his little overnight bag, was left to scurry up to the main house on his own.

Directly, he found himself drawn into the vortex of game playing and

frenetic activity that epitomized life among the younger Kennedys. He
could not possibly have known it, but as he saw Kick match, if not ex-
ceed, the savage ferocity and competitiveness of her siblings on the tennis court, he was witnessing the identical phenomenon that had riveted
the attention of a very different group of young people one long-ago prewar day at Hatfield House. At last, it was not really old Joe, or even
Billy, who had thwarted John White. He had been defeated by Kick's
high-mettled spirit, the inner demon that drove her to keep pounding
for what she wanted when less obstinate souls might have long since
given up.

When, in November of 1942, she heard from Billy that he might soon
stand for the Devonshire seat in Parliament, she conspired with the former Hearst correspondent in London, William Hillman, to get her over
to England so that she could put her journalistic experience to work in
helping to advise Billy, and to assist him with his speeches. When Hillman's efforts came to naught, she approached the publisher of the
Woman's Home Companion monthly about signing on as its London correspondent.

Finally, after three years of failed attempts that had invariably been
followed by hopeful new efforts, Kick found the path back to London
that she had been seeking. Early in 1943, Betty Coxe proposed that they
travel together to England as part of a Red Cross program that was then
recruiting young women to assist in aiding American military person-
nel overseas. When Kick quit the *Times Herald* to enroll in the Red Cross
training school, she could not be certain that she would be assigned to
London, of all conceivable destinations. Nonetheless, she expressed
confidence that her father could be cajoled into calling in the necessary
favors, opposed to Billy though he remained.

When, in the waning phase of Kick's relationship with John White,
she had spoken to him of Billy, she depicted Billy as still pining for her,
and she painted his great need for her as but one factor among many in
her calculations about England. Almost certainly that had been her way
of bringing poor, dear, mad John White back down to earth as softly

and gently as possible. By contrast, in the course of many conversations with an important new friend whom she acquired during this period, Lord Halifax's son Richard Wood, she made it clear that she was nothing less than, in her word, "desperate" to be with Billy again.

Richard Wood had never met or seen Kick before when, in 1943, she came to the British Embassy in Washington, where his father had been appointed ambassador on the death of Lord Lothian. But the twenty-two-year-old Richard had certainly heard and read and thought a great deal about her in years past. As he would recall more than half a century later, Kick's legend had utterly captivated him in 1938 and 1939, when there was so much talk, at his school and elsewhere, of the "fabulous Kennedys," and especially of Kick's triumphs among the aristocratic cousinhood. In those days, Richard, handsome and athletic, a superb cricketer, had been a student at Eton, where he was a classmate of Andrew Cavendish.

Kick, when Richard first learned of her existence, had seemed somehow achingly out of reach, a girl far more likely to be interested in Oxford and Cambridge fellows, who were all slightly older than he. One of Richard's own elder brothers, Peter Wood, was friendly with most of the young grandees who admitted to being besotted by her. Peter had been with David Ormsby-Gore, Jakie Astor, and Hugh Fraser in the car crash of 1937 that figured prominently in the myth of their group. Now, he regaled young Richard with stories of Kick. Andrew Cavendish supplied other tantalizing details. At a time when Joseph P. Kennedy was at the pinnacle of his popularity in London, Kennedy came to Eton to address the school's Political Society on the theme of "America." The ambassador was accompanied by Joe Junior and Jack, both of whose dashing good looks and air of glamour had the effect of stoking young Richard's dreams about their fabled sister.

Richard longed to meet or even simply to glimpse Kick in person. To his immense frustration, however, by the time Kick returned to the U.S. with her mother and siblings, any such encounter had yet to take place.

Meanwhile, the British declaration of war had led to a major change in Richard's plans for life after Eton. Instead of going up to Oxford as previously intended, he worked briefly at the British Embassy in Rome, prior to enlisting at nineteen years of age in the King's Own Yorkshire Light Infantry. Later, as a member of the King's Royal Rifle Corps, he fought with the 8th Army in North Africa. In the course of a raid in the Libyan desert in December 1942, Richard was pinned beneath a bomb that had been dropped by a Nazi Stuka bomber. The bomb failed to explode, but both of Richard's legs were crushed, and had to be amputated under primitive conditions. At length, brought to Washington to possibly be "fitted up" for a pair of artificial limbs, he resided at the British Embassy, where Lord and Lady Halifax encouraged him to have groups of young people in to dine.

For all the world, Richard strove to appear to cheerfully accept what had happened to him on the sands of Libya. He liked to jest that he had survived only because he had been hit by a bomb that anti-Nazi Czech munitions workers had deliberately misassembled. The remark was lent pathos by the fact that Richard's brother Peter had been much less fortunate, losing his life in the Battle of El Alamein, two months before Richard's ordeal. But what sort of life could Richard expect to have?

Despite Richard's carefully maintained outward air of acceptance and good humor, he was, by his own subsequent account, privately in crisis. Could he really ever enjoy anything approximating a normal existence? He insisted to others that he could and would, but he experienced many agonizing moments of doubt. It was in this tumultuous condition of mind that Richard finally found himself face-to-face with the very girl whom he had once ached to meet. But so much had changed for him since that earlier time. Could he possibly relax and enjoy himself now, as though he were any twenty-two-year-old in the company of a highly desirable young woman?

Many years afterward, he would reflect that it was Kick who first taught him to answer that question in the affirmative.

She began to restore his sense that he was a man like any other. By Richard's lights, in the days and weeks that followed their initial encounter, Kick plunged him back into vibrant life. She reintroduced him to a world of young people partaking of ordinary pleasures. Early on, she escorted him to his first baseball game, an experience that he would long treasure, not because of any great passion on his part for the American sport, but rather because it was such simple, everyday fun, light-years away from all he had endured in the war zone.

Also coincident with Kick's Red Cross training program, she and Richard enjoyed many spirited conversations. They spoke about their life-changing experiences, his in the Libyan desert and hers in fashionable London society; about Anglicanism and Roman Catholicism; and about their nations' cultural and political differences. In these discussions, there was nothing of the combativeness associated with the talks that she had had over the course of many months with John White. John had been hectoring and argumentative; Richard's nature was genial and contemplative. John had been a freethinker; Richard was deeply religious. John had a permissive attitude toward sex; Richard was a man of exacting morals.

Unlike John, Richard had no illusions about the intensity of Kick's feelings for Billy. He understood that his conversations with Kick were a prelude to her return to Britain and the man she loved. Richard had finally met Kick, after all, at a time when every element was at last in place for the transatlantic journey that, she made clear, she had long been struggling to arrange. To his perception, she regarded their talks as a means of working out certain of the issues of religion and national identity that were about to confront her in England. So, as generous as she had been with Richard, their friendship proved a boon to her as well. The trouble, from Richard's perspective, was that she saw him wholly as a friend, nothing more. In view of Kick's impending departure, Richard resigned himself to the necessity of concealing that he, too, had fallen hopelessly in love with her.

On the evening of June 23, 1943, Kick, habited in a tin helmet and raincoat, with a canteen and first-aid kit fastened to her waist, sailed for the port of Glasgow, Scotland, whence she was due to proceed by train to London. Nearly four years had passed since she'd returned to the U.S. from England at the start of the European war. At the time of that earlier voyage, she had not yet been twenty years of age. In the autumn of 1939, whether she would be able to retain her new sense of herself as a person in her own right had yet to be tested. Whether in the face of much familial opposition and many new obstacles and distractions she would persist in her determination to be with Billy again was still to be seen.

First love is often meteoric. One minute it dazzles and dominates the thoughts and senses, and then, in a twinkling, it is no more. But in 1943, Kick's very presence on the liner *Queen Mary*, along with a contingent of Red Cross girls, seven of whom she shared a cabin with, and some eighteen thousand U.S. troops attested to the fact that her feelings for Billy had endured, after all. Indeed, she didn't even have Betty Coxe by her side, her friend having been dispatched to North Africa instead.

Kick, when Betty first spoke to her of the Red Cross, had viewed the job as an expedient, like all the expedients that had come before, including her work as a journalist. And now it is not too much to suppose that she saw herself less in a tin helmet than in a tiara, the former being the necessary prelude to the latter.

Meanwhile, in a round-robin letter to her family from the *Queen Mary*, she complained about the crowded conditions in her cabin; about the annoyance of her "giggling" female cabinmates, who liked to sit up until about half past one every night; about the "pathetic" living conditions of the American soldiers who seemed to be "packed in all over the ship"; about the "crude circumstances" in which she and other worshippers had been forced to have Mass; and about the limited deck space available for her daily mile-long walk. "Mother," Kick declared, "you wouldn't recognize this boat as the same one you made that comfortable luxury cruise on in 1936." Life on a military troop transport, she went on, "seems so unreal and far removed from anything I've ever known that I can't believe I'm part of it."

She insisted that she recognized that much in England had altered in her absence.

Still, after so much carping, the very fact that Kick felt compelled to portray herself as "quite prepared for the changes" suggests that she had perhaps begun to fear that she was not.

Seven

On June 28, 1943, Kick arrived in London on a crowded troop train from Glasgow, where the *Queen Mary* had docked earlier in the day. Though Kick was technically part of the same military buildup as the soldiers, she and they were operating in terms of two decidedly different narratives. For Kick, London was the end of the journey, the destination she had been fighting to get back to, where she would finally be reunited with Billy and resume the life she had been forced to leave behind in 1939. For the soldiers, the war-scarred city, large sections of which had been destroyed in the Blitz, was to be but a stopping-off point.

One month before, in Washington, Winston Churchill and Franklin Roosevelt had agreed to a plan for an expedition across the English Channel, with the aim of invading France. Prior to that, there had been much contention between the British and American sides about how best to attack the Germans. Churchill had preferred to go in through what he called the "soft underbelly"—that is, via Italy and up through Southern Germany. Among other reasons, the British prime minister maintained that this approach would have important political ramifications in the postwar world. Also, mindful of the tremendous loss of life sustained by the British in the First World War, Churchill believed that his plan would result in fewer Allied casualties than would the strategy favored by the White House, which had argued for crossing the English Channel and going in through France.

Finally, in May of 1943 a compromise had been reached whereby the main thrust would be an assault through France, to be preceded by a subsidiary attack via the soft underbelly.

The eighteen thousand soldiers who had just come over on the *Queen Mary* were the latest installment of a gigantic massing of American troops that had begun one year before. The objective at this point was to have an estimated one and a half million U.S. soldiers in place by the time of the cross-Channel invasion, to be undertaken in conjunction with divisions of British and Canadian troops, as well as more modest contingents from other countries. Every fiber of the troops' collective being was concentrated on this make-or-break operation, in anticipation of which the new arrivals would shortly join their many American predecessors in a program of intensive military training.

Kick had not told Billy in advance that she would be coming over on this particular ocean crossing. He knew about the Red Cross scheme that she had hatched in collaboration with Betty Coxe, but she had given him no specific date on which to expect her.

So now Kick sent word through the Ormsby-Gores that she had managed to return at last. David, who was in training near Hatfield with the Territorial Army, knew how to get word to Billy without delay, precisely as Kick had expected. She further assumed that when Billy learned that she was in London he would come to her instantly.

Instead, it would be nearly two weeks before he could obtain leave. He could not simply break off from his training maneuvers and rush to Kick in London whenever it pleased him to do so. Whether Kick liked it or not—and, as would become increasingly clear, she most certainly did not like it—that was the stark new reality that confronted her upon her return to England.

Meanwhile, she also had much to be dissatisfied with in her new Red Cross posting. A good many strings had indeed been pulled to win her a choice assignment at the Hans Crescent Club for soldiers, located behind Harrods department store in Knightsbridge. Through a contact at U.S. Army Headquarters in London, old Joe had managed to prevent Kick from being sent off, like most other new girls, to military encampments far from the nation's capital for a six-month preparatory program. Though Kick was pleased to be able to remain in London, she was unhappy about the requirement that she live at the club, where her responsibilities would consist of talking to homesick soldiers, helping them to write letters, playing cards and Ping-Pong with them, and otherwise ministering to their spirits.

Eager to see old friends in and about London, she was dismayed by the mere one and a half days per week that she had off from her duties. In turn, her coworkers and superiors were not entirely delighted with her. There was resentment that another Red Cross girl had had to be transferred out of London so that Ambassador Kennedy's daughter might take her place; and there was annoyance that Kick received too many personal phone calls at the club and had too many visitors.

Hardly had Kick's old friends heard of her return than there was a great rush to see her, take her up, invite her out, and otherwise incorporate her back into the aristocratic cousinhood. There were evenings out at the 400 Club, where Tony Rosslyn, William Douglas-Home, and other of her former devotees again paid court to her, though as Tony lamented in a letter to Jack Kennedy: "As far as I can see, she is not particularly interested in any of them."

Advised by the Hans Crescent Club management to scale back her social life, Kick wrote home that both the club director and the program director were driving her "nuts." She mocked the former as "a very second rate kind of person" and the latter as a "Jewess" who was "very jealous" of her. Kick left no doubt that she would have preferred a job in Red Cross public relations, but for fear of losing her London perch she'd decided to put up with "a tough situation," at least for now. All of which led to further complaints from colleagues that she treated her duties at the soldiers' club as though they were an imposition, that she had come to London in pursuit of the duke's heir, and that for a Red Cross worker she seemed oddly oblivious of the war.

These charges were by no means without foundation. German bombs had transfigured the face of the city, where more than a million buildings, including ones that Kick knew well, had been reduced to rubble. Yet in a letter to her brother she wrote, rather oddly, that London appeared "quite unchanged" since last they had seen it and that the blitzed areas were "not obvious." In 1939, when Kick had returned to the U.S. after eighteen months abroad, she had anticipated that much at home would have changed in her absence, as she perceived herself to have changed. So, when life in Bronxville had struck her as "just the same," that plaintive phrase, in a letter to her father, was freighted with her longing for all that she had just been forced to give up.

By contrast, in 1943, as she had remained constant to them during her prolonged absence, she seemed to want the world and the people she had left behind in 1939 to be quite as she remembered them. Most of Kick's anxiety in this regard was naturally concentrated on Billy.

Certainly, he did not look entirely the same when, on Saturday evening, July 10, 1943, he arrived at the Hans Crescent Club to collect Kick for a night out in London. There had been a time, when Kick first met him in 1938, that Billy had appeared as one who had not yet quite grown into his large body. Five years later, his six-foot frame was covered with lean muscle, the consequence of what his brother liked to call the Army's "toughening up" program. This consisted of training maneuvers that were often as arduous as and at times even more punishing than anything one might encounter on an actual battlefield, exercises in the course of which men were known to die. One moment the troops were scaling cliffs and clearing minefields, and the next they were being sprayed with blood from a slaughterhouse and being forced to eat almost-raw liver.

At twenty-five years of age, Billy was, in his sister-in-law Debo's phrase, "film star handsome." In the wake of his return from France, Jean Ogilvy had begun to notice that wherever she went with Billy in London, heads turned to stare at him because he was "suddenly so attractive." Though Billy was not literally taller than he had been before the war, he was unquestionably more physically imposing; and when he and Kick were reunited now, he appeared to loom over her even more than he had in 1938 and 1939.

But it was not anything to do with his physicality that caused people to, in Kick's phrase, "put their heads together" when he and she appeared in public together that first night. As reported to her family, there was already "heavy betting" in London on when she and Billy planned to announce their engagement. Many people seemed to believe that she was prepared to give in on the religious issue, but she firmly denied to her family that she had any such intention. By evening's end, however, one thing had become evident. As Kick would much later tell her mother, that night she and he discovered that they still loved each other as before.

Though at this early stage Kick was loath to disclose this to her parents, Billy had no such compunction about speaking frankly to his mother. At his request, the duchess invited Kick to Compton Place for the first weekend that he could manage to obtain leave. In London, he and Kick had had but a few hours together. At Compton Place, where they had first become an established couple, they had the consummate luxury of an entire day to themselves.

"For twenty-four hours I forgot all about the war," Kick later wrote to her brother Jack of her idyll with Billy at Eastbourne. "Billy is just the same, a bit older, a bit more ducal but we get on as well as ever." In other words, aside from the newly imposing physical presence that she registered as ducal, Billy struck her as being quite the fellow he had been before the war. Or at least he behaved that way when he was with her.

Billy looked upon the delightful hours he spent with Kick as, in his brother's carefully considered phrase, "a return to innocence." He welcomed the opportunity she gave him to become again, if only for a short while, the person he had been of old, before his entire world had been upended in the war zone. The strange, almost obdurate blindness that had annoyed and angered Kick's coworkers at the Hans Crescent Club was, by contrast, immensely appealing to Billy. She saw him as he longed to be, undefiled by the experiences that had in fact changed him forever.

Strange to say, before Kick's letter had had a chance to reach her brother, Jack had had a traumatic confrontation of his own with killing and death, when a PT boat he was captaining in the Pacific theater was split asunder by a Japanese destroyer, killing two of Jack's men and leaving him and the surviving crew members stranded in dark waters. Seamen on other PT boats in the area spotted the flames, but gave Jack and his men up for dead. Meanwhile, Jack rescued a badly burned member of his crew from a patch of flaming gasoline. Then he swam out once more from the wreckage of the PT boat and saved two additional crew members. Finally, perceiving that the wreckage was about to sink, he ordered the survivors to make for a small island some four miles distant. As the burned man was unable to swim, Jack placed the straps of the man's life jacket between his teeth and towed him to safety, a journey that took five hours to complete.

Kick called the news of her brother's heroism "the most exciting thing" she had ever heard. "There wasn't a very big piece in the English newspapers," she wrote home to Hyannis Port, "but quite big enough for me to gather that he did really big stuff. Loads of people here saw it and they were all thrilled."

Then and later, Jack was much applauded for his bravery, but the praise and publicity meant little to him. He obsessed about the crew members he had lost. He tearfully dwelled on the possibility that if the other PT boats had come to assist early on, he might yet have been able to avert the two men's deaths. He blamed himself for not having put one of the men off the PT boat earlier, after the fellow had been deeply affected by the killing of a crew member who had happened to be standing next to him when death came. Jack, far from taking pride in the lives he had managed to save, focused on what he perceived as his personal failures in the course of the ordeal, and on all that he might have done differently.

Meanwhile, after that first weekend at Compton Place, Billy was determined to see Kick as much as possible. As far as he was concerned, quiet meetings at his family's homes, Compton Place and Churchdale Hall, were best. So he was displeased when she accepted invitations to Cliveden and to another house where she was to become increasingly in demand—Sledmere, the residence of Joe Junior's onetime girlfriend, the former Virginia Gilliat. Virginia was now Lady Sykes, the wife of Sir Richard Sykes, who was more than a decade her senior. The tumult of life at Cliveden had long been repugnant to Billy. He objected to weekends at Sledmere, because the Sykeses and the set they gathered around them in their Georgian country house in Yorkshire were too "racy" to suit his austere tastes. To his consternation, Kick rather liked the gatherings at Sledmere House and the opportunity that weekends there afforded her to encounter interesting new people. As Billy's cousin Jean would point out years afterward, Kick "liked to experiment"; Billy decidedly did not.

If he absolutely had to see Kick among people other than his parents and sisters, Billy much preferred that the setting be Pimlico House, the residence of Fiona and Arthur "Boofy" Gore, where the company tended to be familiar to him and where he could usually count on having Kick more or less to himself. Fiona was then working in the Women's Royal Naval Service, Boofy in the Ministry of Information. The Gores, who had bought the Hemel Hempstead property in 1936, had yet to fully occupy the main house, so at that point most of their living and entertaining took place in a diminutive, redbrick gardener's cottage.

There was not much furniture, so Billy would pass the night in a sleeping bag on the floor of the cottage's tiny dining room, which was barely able to accommodate a man of his height. Kick, by contrast, was herself so petite that she slept quite contentedly in an upstairs bathtub, which she insisted was "more like a bed." During the day, the couple tended to spend a good deal of time together, merrily teasing one another in a manner that their hostess regarded as "childlike" and otherwise talking the hours away.

Despite such happy interludes, as the autumn of 1943 progressed Kick and Billy seemed to be operating on drastically different timetables. She had spent the past four years plotting and planning to get back to him. Now that she had succeeded, she appeared utterly relaxed and in no particular hurry about anything. She was not driving forward anymore, and for the moment she seemed to want only to be with Billy and to have fun.

His situation was a good deal more complicated. Though when he was with her he contentedly playacted at being very much the boy he had been before the war, at other times the unfinished business of 1940 continued to obsess him. When he was in the latter state of mind, it was as if he were living entirely for the fast-approaching day when he would return to battle. Much as he sought to keep Kick uncontaminated by all that, before long he began to perceive a connection between his desire to spend his life with her on the one hand and his need to finish the fight on the other. Given that his orders might come at any time, Billy became convinced that if he and Kick were to be married, the great step must be taken without delay.

Yet, despite his sense of urgency, he hesitated to explicitly broach the subject of marriage. It was not that he feared that Kick would refuse him. It was that he knew that in proposing marriage, he must also ask her to capitulate in the matter of religion. Whatever Kick may have thought or hoped at the time, and whatever she may have suggested to her family, a compromise on Billy's part was never a possibility. In view of the traditional role and responsibilities that would one day fall to him, he knew that he could never agree to raise his children in any but the Anglican faith. That being the case, before he formally approached Kick he wanted to be sure that she could really be happy were she to make the great sacrifice he was about to demand. As Billy later explained his reasoning to her mother, if in fact he believed that he was condemning Kick to live the rest of her life with a sense of guilt, he would not be justified in asking her to be his wife.

During all this time, Billy at least had the comfort of being able to speak of his concerns in confidence to his cousin Jean, who now lived in Yorkshire, not far from where he was stationed. Though Jean had long been in love with Nancy Astor's son Michael, in 1942 she had married David Lloyd, the 2nd Baron Lloyd of Dolobran. The parents of a baby girl, Jean and her husband had rented a small house some three miles outside of Scarborough, where David was serving in the Welsh Guards. The cramped, comfortless, unheated dwelling lacked a telephone, so Billy would often arrive unannounced to talk to Jean for a few hours, and, whenever he could, to stay the night with her and her husband.

One afternoon early in November of 1943 Jean, responding to an unexpected knock at the front door, discovered Billy in something very much like the state of frenzy that she had witnessed three years previously upon his return from the fighting in France.

On the present occasion, the cause of Billy's outburst of emotion was Andrew's having received his orders to leave immediately to fight in Italy. Though by this time it had been agreed between the Americans and the British that the invasion of France had priority, Churchill had insisted that Rome must yet be taken. Some of the most seasoned troops were coming home from the Italian campaign in anticipation of the invasion of France, and reinforcements like Andrew were being sent over to replace them.

Again, Billy was almost in tears. Again, his words poured out in a torrent. He insisted that it should not be Andrew, who had an eight-month-old daughter and a pregnant wife, who was called up to fight. "It should be me," Billy repeated over and over.

Jean's initial reaction was that Billy was being protective of his younger brother. She assumed at first that he was merely making the point that, as a bachelor, he ought to be the one at risk. But the more he talked, the more another possibility began to present itself to her. Somehow Billy seemed terrified that Andrew's having been sent off to fight might prove an obstacle to the older brother's receiving his long-awaited orders as well. The Cavendish brothers were not just any soldiers, after all. Whether Billy knew it or not, their paternal grandmother, Duchess Evie, had already attempted to ensure that the two brothers would not be at the front at the same time. Though the dowager duchess had been unsuccessful, her efforts in this regard reflected the family's abiding concern that were both brothers to die in battle, there would not at present be a direct heir to the dukedom. So, Billy was far from wrong to think that Andrew's presence in Italy might subsequently pose a problem for him.

Billy seemed absolutely frantic at the prospect of being held back. In the middle of talking about how unfair it was that the second son should go instead of him, Billy, who almost never raised his voice in any circumstance, suddenly began to shout about all the ghastly things he had seen in France. "Things you can't imagine." Then he repeated the lines Jean remembered from their fraught encounter at her home in London three years before. "We ran away! We ran and we ran!"

By the time Kick had lunch in London with Debo and Moucher on the eleventh of November, Andrew had indeed already embarked with the 3rd Battalion, to which he had been transferred. Debo had come in from the country to spend her young husband's last few days of leave with him. And now, both she and her mother-in-law conveyed to Kick their immense sadness at his having gone. Andrew's departure would cast a shadow over a large party that Kick was about to give, in partnership with Fiona Gore, in London on the thirteenth.

Kick billed the event at the Mayfair home of Mrs. Violet Cripps as London's first young people's party in two years. Particularly pleasing to Kick was that at least a dozen of the girls on her guest list had not been to a party of any sort since the beginning of the war. A number of the debs she had been friendly with in 1938 and 1939 were present, notably Fiona, Jean, Debo, and Sissie, all of whom were now wives and mothers themselves, living lives considerably less comfortable and felicitous than anything they had been accustomed to before the war.

For the most part, the dances, parties, balls, and country house weekends were but a memory. So were the more than a million servants who had been employed in 1939, some having entered the military and others having been moved to work that was deemed essential to the war effort. Even the nightclubbing and other revels associated with the early phase of the war were at best a rarity now. Girls who had been brought up in great luxury had had to learn to live with coupons, queues, and other forms of discipline. They had endured the bombing of London, and they all knew people who had been killed. By the late autumn of 1943, a general air of war weariness and exhaustion had palpably begun to set in, not just among the aristocrats, but among the whole population of Britain.

Kick, by her very obliviousness, seemed to offer an antidote to all that. Unlike her colleagues and critics at the Red Cross, her old friends found it refreshing that she had returned to London seemingly determined to pick up just where she had left off in 1939, as though nothing had altered in the intervening years.

Tonight she had hired a six-piece band; she had arrayed the tables with fragrant flowers; and she had issued a last-minute invitation to the composer Irving Berlin to perform at the piano for her guests. There was much drunkenness and not a little rowdiness. The evening's guest of honor, Kick's brother Joe Junior, recently arrived in England, entered the party in a visible state of inebriation; so did the members of his naval squadron who accompanied him.

But it was the excessive drinking of one of the young English soldiers, Ned Fitzmaurice, Charlie Lansdowne's brother, that nearly led to disaster, when the Guardsman accidentally set a match to the new evening dress worn by Billy Hartington's seventeen-year-old sister, Elizabeth Cavendish. Given the ill feeling many of the English soldiers harbored for the Yanks, whom they resented for, among other offenses, paying excessive attention to British women, Kick was pleased that on the present occasion it was one of the American boys who deftly extinguished the flames.

In the end, Lady Elizabeth seemed less upset than exhilarated by the incident. She had never been to a party before. Lest anyone fear that the episode might have scared her away from attending other such parties in future, she gaily declared to her mother, who had accompanied her daughter to Kick's soiree, "Before I was set on fire the boys didn't pay much attention to me, but afterwards I was very popular."

All in all, Kick's English friends delighted in her efforts to re-create, if only for a few blissful hours, the frivolity and freedom from care that they associated with the lost prewar world. Still, the very darkness that Kick had endeavored to banish from that large, crowded, noisy room on South Audley Street asserted itself forcefully and unavoidably in the form of two prominent guests who had already been horribly injured in the war.

Robert Cecil, the glamorous bad boy of prewar days, was at this point still recovering from a friendly-fire incident in 1942, in which twenty-three soldiers had been machine-gunned to death. Robert had been hit in both his lung and his right hand, the latter wound making it impossible for him to hold a cigarette. Despite his wounds, he was determined to participate in the invasion of France. Richard Wood, a double amputee who was still waiting to acquire his artificial legs, had lately returned from Washington with his mother, Lady Halifax. Through no intention of their own, Robert and Richard together served as a stubborn reminder to the revelers of what the war had already cost.

Taken on top of the inveterate partygoer Andrew Cavendish's widely remarked upon absence from the festivities on the evening of the thirteenth, the sight of numerous young men in military uniform, both American and British, hinted at the bloodletting yet to come.

Indeed, even as Kick had been making last-minute preparations for the party the day before, Churchill had left for Cairo to confer with Roosevelt, after which the British and American leaders were due to meet Stalin in Tehran, Iran, where final arrangements for Operation

Overlord, the code name for the invasion of Normandy, would be completed.

Reminiscing about Kick's famous party after more than half a century had elapsed, a number of attendees grimly remarked on how many of the boys who laughed and drank and sang that night were soon to die. Before the Germans were defeated, Mark Howard, Charlie Lansdowne, Ned Fitzmaurice, and Dicky Cecil (Robert's brother) would all be dead. So would Kick's brother Joe Junior.

So would Billy Hartington.

Not long after the party, Duke Eddy had a talk with Billy that, in unexpected ways, was to impact profoundly on Kick's future. The duke reported that his brother-in-law, Henry Hunloke, who had taken his seat in the House of Commons when Eddy moved on to the House of Lords in 1938, had decided to divorce the duke's sister Anne. In conjunction with his severance from the Cavendish family, Hunloke also intended to resign as MP for West Derbyshire, a seat that the duke looked upon as something of a family heirloom. With the exception of two painful interludes when the Liberals won the seat, in 1918 and 1922, it had long been a stronghold of Cavendish power. In conversation with Billy, Eddy proposed to arrange for him to obtain leave from the Coldstream Guards, so that Billy might stand as the candidate of both his party and his family in the by-election, a special election conducted to fill a seat that has become available between general elections. Eager to complete all of the delicate arrangements before anyone else could suggest an alternate Conservative candidate, and before any potential opposition had had a chance to mobilize, the duke was especially—and as it would turn out, disastrously—keen at this point to prevent any word of the impending vacancy from being made public.

Eddy anticipated settling the matter with his son right away. But in this, as in many other things just then, the duke miscalculated. His scheme confronted Billy with a formidable dilemma. Already frantic about the potential impact upon himself of Andrew's participation in the

Italian campaign, Billy worried that the duke's manipulations might throw yet another obstacle in his path back to battle. Did the duke intend for his son and heir to sit comfortably in Parliament while other men fought? That, Billy made clear, would be unacceptable to him. In the end, Billy consented to do as his father wished, but only on the strict condition that win or lose he be allowed to return to his regiment following the by-election. The duke had no choice but to agree.

When the Cavendishes forgathered at Churchdale Hall at Christmas of 1943, the duke was consumed with laying out the choreography whereby the West Derbyshire seat would be safely kept in the family. He strategized with the Conservative Party whip, James Stuart, who was his sister Rachel's husband, and with another of his sisters, Dorothy Macmillan, who had the well-earned reputation of being an astute political hand.

Exhibiting what Kick, in a different context, would later describe as "the certainty of a Duke," Eddy Devonshire seemed serenely confident about Billy's candidature. Quite apart from the Cavendishes' long association with the seat, Billy would also presumably benefit from the truce among the Conservative, Labor, and Liberal parties, which had pledged not to oppose one another in by-elections for the duration of the war. The whole point of Churchill's wartime coalition government had been for all parties to act as one in winning the war, to which end it had seemed prudent to refrain from engaging in politics as usual.

Not every Cavendish family member shared the duke's optimism about the by-election. Lady Dorothy's husband, Harold Macmillan, minister resident in the Mediterranean, wrote to point out that the wartime truce had in fact begun to wear "rather thin." In a sign of the changing times and of an increasingly radicalized electorate, an amalgam of independent socialists known as the Common Wealth Party was now poised to present a significant challenge to Conservative candidates. Macmillan predicted that there would be trouble from Alderman Charles White, whose father, a local cobbler, had twice vanquished the duke himself, in the key contests of 1918 and 1922. Macmillan warned that Sir Richard Acland, one of the founders of the Common Wealth Party, could be counted on to back Alderman White's efforts to secure the seat.

Nonetheless, until it was too late the duke appeared to persist in the belief that the 1944 West Derbyshire by-election would be, in his phrase, a "walk-over." But was he really so blind to the growing class resentment throughout Britain that threatened to transfigure the post-war political landscape? Had Eddy Devonshire been entirely free from concern about his ability to hold on to the seat, would he have been as obsessed with keeping Henry Hunloke's imminent departure from Parliament a secret until Billy was officially designated the Conservative candidate, and a writ for the by-election moved?

Meanwhile, as always when Billy came home on military leave, his mother had arranged that every element be in place to minister to his happiness. Among other preparations, the letters of Georgiana, Duchess of Devonshire, that Billy loved so well, along with some of the family's collection of Old Master drawings, were carted over from Chatsworth for his delectation. The jazz recordings he liked to endlessly play as he lay upon a sofa reading and rereading the letters, and examining the drawings, were carefully stacked and ready. Billy's rambunctious black standard poodle, Lupin, was bathed and clipped in anticipation of his beloved master's arrival.

And this year, for the first time, the duchess invited Kick to be part of the holiday celebrations. She did this with her son's, but also with the Cavendish family's, future in mind. By such efforts to enfold Kick into the Cavendish family, she was thinking politically and strategically every bit as much as, if not rather more creatively and effectively than, the duke, for all of his frantic electoral calculations. Not so long ago, Ambassador Joseph P. Kennedy had been much reviled for predicting that the Britain of old could not possibly survive the war. Yet that was precisely the dizzying new reality that was about to confront the Cavendish family in particular and the patrician elite in general over the course of the landmark 1944 West Derbyshire by-election. While her husband clung futilely to the past, the duchess had had the wit to embrace none other than Joseph P. Kennedy's daughter, in the hope that Kick might one day help Billy, his family, and all that the Cavendishes represented in British life to weather the changes that would unavoidably face their class in the new world that was bound to emerge following the war.

Kick's presence at Churchdale Hall at Christmastime 1943 had a powerful emotional impact on Billy. Together he and she sat on a sofa, where they read aloud from Georgiana's correspondence and looked over Old Master drawings. They rode pony carts to Chatsworth, which had been leased to a girls' boarding school, and which, like other great houses during the war, had been allowed to fall into decrepitude and dilapidation.

Billy spoke to her of the upcoming West Derbyshire by-election and of his dream that, whether or not he managed to secure the seat this time, he might have a useful political career after the war. He spoke of the principle so dear to his father, and to the dukes who had come before, that the great landowner looked out for his tenants, who, in turn, were expected to yield to his political leadership. He spoke not only of Georgiana, but also of other duchesses of Devonshire, of the power and influence the duchesses had wielded, and of the role these women had played in the history of Britain.

To be sure, Billy had talked to Kick of such matters before. But, as the hour drew near when he must return to combat, their conversations in this regard took on a new heat and urgency. It was as if he were portraying for Kick the life she would have, if only certain critical obstacles could be made to vanish. Andrew's presence in Italy; Debo's pregnancy; the duke's political maneuvers; the imminent invasion of France—all of these factors contributed to Billy's sense that the moment had arrived when he must force the issue with Kick.

In Washington, there had come a point in her relations with John White when the newspaperman had reflected that Kick's beliefs were so deeply ingrained, so intrinsic to who she was, that to keep pressing her to abandon them would be to harm her. John White professed to love

Kick too much to risk doing anything like that. Now, Billy took quite the opposite approach. Billy reasoned that, precisely because he loved Kick as he did, he could not risk losing her. He maintained that the great love they shared, a love that had been tested by years of separation, left him no choice but to act before it was too late.

After much reflection, Billy concluded that Kick was, in his phrase, "so holy and good" that God would continue to help her after her capitulation, and that as a consequence she could indeed be happy. So, after Christmas, he did what he had long been putting off. He asked Kick to marry him, with the proviso that, given his future ducal responsibilities and given the fact that sooner or later his son and heir would be called on to preside in his place, Kick must be the one to compromise. She must agree that any children they might have would be brought up Anglican.

On this vital matter, Billy, who in their prior relations had always been so kind, gentle, and even malleable, made it clear that he intended to be absolutely firm. He cast the great concession that he demanded of Kick entirely in terms of religion, not realizing that for her it was going to prove a good deal more complicated than that.

Eight

Heretofore, Kick had insisted to her family that in spite of what anyone in England might think, hope, or anticipate, she had no intention of giving in on religion. She had affected an air of great amusement at the anxiety that her reunion with Billy had provoked in some British quarters. She had jested that certain of Billy's Cavendish and Cecil ancestors must be nearly ready to "jump out of their graves" for fear of the threat she posed to their "ancient traditions." She had left her parents with the impression that it would be up to Billy to make the great compromise, if he wanted her badly enough—which of course she had no doubt that he did.

Now, the unambiguous terms in which Billy had cast his marriage proposal left it entirely up to her whether he and she would ever become husband and wife. Kick could no longer pretend to others, or to herself, that it would be simply a matter of waiting for Billy to cave.

Thus began what David Ormsby-Gore, who had previously agreed that his own children would be brought up in his wife Sissie's Roman

Catholic faith, was to sadly characterize as "a strange episode" in Kick's life—strange in the sense that had it not been wartime, indeed had it been but two years later, David believed that Billy would hardly have been "so insistent" about the matter. As it was, David judged that by making the particular demands that he did, Billy "was putting unnecessary pressure on Kick." Persuaded as he was that Billy's requirement could only "hurt" Kick and her family, David would have talked to his cousin "in detail" with the objective of changing Billy's views. But as David later lamented, the war deprived him of that opportunity. The rush of events before Billy followed his brother into battle ruled out the kind of passionate and lengthy discussion the cousins had so often enjoyed and benefited from in years past. To David's lasting regret, there was to be no "nose-to-nose" with Billy on this monumental matter.

Meanwhile, the pressure on Kick was intensified many times over by the tendency—or, more accurately perhaps, the strategy—of Billy's mother to treat it almost as a fait accompli that the marriage would soon take place, the religious obstacle having been overcome by some grand compromise on Kick's part. In this regard, the festivities surrounding Elizabeth Cavendish's January 8, 1944, coming-out party did double duty as a means of presenting Kick, in her new role as Billy's future bride, to the rest of the family. Seated next to the duchess's erudite and endlessly amusing brother, David Cecil, whose quicksilver conversation at once thrilled her and left her with the impression that she still had much to learn, Kick was indeed subjected to the "good going over" by Billy's relatives that she had nervously anticipated having to endure at Elizabeth's party. No one, apparently, mentioned Billy's marriage proposal; but everyone seemed to know about it and to be waiting to see what Kick's next move would be.

In all of this, the duchess's aim was less to secure the Cecil and Cavendish relatives' approval of Billy's beloved than, quite simply, to make Kick feel as if she were already an established member of the family. Perhaps that is also why, at a time when Eddy Devonshire was intent that his political plans remain secret until his son and heir could be smoothly and safely installed as the Conservative candidate in West Derbyshire, Kick nonetheless knew all about those plans—and freely, some might say indiscreetly, wrote of Billy's candidature, as well as of the military leave that had been granted to him for the duration of the electioneering, in a January 20, 1944, letter to her family. Not long afterward, Kick was invited to join the duchess, Elizabeth, and other members of Billy's family for the final three days of the campaign prior to the February 17, 1944, by-election. The contest in West Derbyshire would prove to be a critical event in British political history—and in Kick's life.

Five days before, on February 12, she went to spend a few quiet days with Richard Wood at his sister Anne Feversham's house in Yorkshire. By now, Richard had acquired a pair of wooden legs, but it was an immense effort for him to walk on them and it would clearly be some time before he would be able to cover any real distance. Whenever Richard and Kick saw each other during this period, they easily fell back into the unique rhythms of the relationship, rhythms they'd established in Washington.

At his sister's house, once again Richard was cast in the role of helping Kick to work out certain of the agonizing questions that faced her with regard to any future she might or might not have with Billy. Once again, Richard's unspoken feelings lent a considerable amount of tension to their colloquies. When he was not staying with his sister, he lived alone at Garrowby Hall, the estate where the earls of Halifax had long dwelled. His mother having returned to the U.S., Kick worried that Richard spent too much time at Garrowby by himself. Mindful as always of her feelings for Billy, Richard refrained from disclosing to her that he would then have given almost anything to share his life there with her.

On the present occasion, Richard was encountering Kick at a moment when her Christmastime discussions with Billy were still fresh in her ears. She talked a good deal to Richard of Georgiana, and of other past duchesses of Devonshire. She talked of her sense that, were she to accept Billy's marriage proposal and the particular terms attached to it, she might one day become, in her pointed phrase, "a woman of influence."

As he listened to Kick, it struck Richard that she was both "very ambitious" and, as never quite before, "very clear on what she wanted." Her whole conception of herself and of all that she could be had suddenly come into much sharper focus. There had been a time when it had meant everything to Kick to be a person in her own right apart from her identity as a Kennedy daughter. Five years later, what she wanted was at once much larger and much more specific than anything she had spoken of in 1939. And again, it was her experience of England and of English life that had allowed her to conceptualize herself in this new way.

As Richard perceived it, Kick saw herself in the future as playing the part of "a great political hostess," in the manner of previous Devonshire duchesses. Kick made it clear by her remarks to Richard that she was keenly interested in the beneficent "power and authority" that would eventually be hers and Billy's to exercise over the tenants who lived and worked on Cavendish-owned land, and had traditionally submitted to ducal leadership in political affairs. She made a great point of the dynamic between landowner and tenant in Britain being so much more satisfactory, in her view, than that between the classes in the U.S., where, as she saw it, the upper classes took no comparable personal responsibility for the people in their employ.

Ironically, it was precisely the long-held assumption in British politics that broad acres conferred upon their owners the right to wield political power that had already come under spectacular assault during the run-up to the 1944 West Derbyshire by-election. The left targeted the anachronistic old duke, who had never doubted that the seat in Parliament was his to do with as he wished, as well as the politically callow son and heir with whom he had had the effrontery to seek to fill it. The Common Wealth Party's Sir Richard Acland, who, in line with Harold Macmillan's prediction was enthusiastically supporting Alderman Charles White, framed the debate early on by his insistence that the duke regarded the constituency as his preserve. Commenting on Eddy

Devonshire's efforts to rush the election, Acland scathingly accused him of treating the forty-eight thousand people in the constituency as though they were "the goods and chattel" of the Cavendish family.

The by-election quickly emerged as far more than merely a local affair. The rowdy contest became a first significant referendum on what Britons wanted the nation to look like in the postwar era. Curiously, the Marquess of Hartington, aged twenty-six, represented the old order, the upper-class dictatorship in British political life that many electors nationwide apparently wished to forever relegate to the past, while Alderman White, aged sixty-three, who symbolically launched his campaign in the shilling-a-week cottage of his birth, represented the new order that hoped to prevail after the war.

The duchess later called the 1944 West Derbyshire by-election "the worst and dirtiest fight" in all of the elections she had fought. Billy, when he addressed political meetings in village halls throughout the rural constituency, was consistently booed, heckled, and drowned out by loud hissing and foot stamping. As Billy had privately stipulated beforehand that win or lose he intended to return to his regiment after the poll, it stung all the more when White accused him of having accepted the nomination in hopes of evading service.

Billy and his family knew the latter charge to be utterly untrue. White managed to get closer to the bone when he pandered to the wide national antiaristocratic sentiment that had swelled with the controversial recent release from prison of the British fascist leader Sir Oswald Mosley and his wife, by pointedly reminding electors that Diana Mosley was Debo's sister. The Mosleys had been let out in November on account of Sir Oswald's ill health. Churchill sought to justify the decision by arguing that people could not simply be kept in jail indefinitely because they held opinions that were abhorrent to others. That, he argued, was among the very principles that Britain and the U.S. were then fighting for. But the prime minister's case was undermined by the fact that others who had been jailed during the war for similar reasons remained imprisoned even as the Mosleys went free. The case provoked a national uproar, and many critics charged that the couple had been accorded preferential treatment because they were aristocrats.

Billy responded to White's efforts to link him to the Mosleys by pointing out that his brother was then fighting in Italy and by emphasizing that both Andrew and Debo were "violently anti-Fascist." Billy went on, "So am I. In any case, am I my brother's keeper?" But of course, matters were a good deal more complicated than that, not so much because of ideology as because of Debo's painfully divided loyalties.

Through all the storms that swirled around the Mosleys, then and in later years, Debo, portraying herself as apolitical, persisted in her devotion to her unashamedly Hitler-worshipping sister Diana. Quite simply, Debo loved Diana. She visited Diana in prison, took an interest in her children, railed against "Cousin Winston" as he allowed Diana to languish in jail, and rejoiced when she was freed. During Diana's incarceration, her young sons visited Churchdale Hall, where Max Mosley, as outspoken at age three as he would be in later years, instructed Eddy Devonshire not to smoke at the table. Later, Billy was drafted to entertain the Mosley boys, while they were staying with their pregnant aunt Debo at the Rookery. None of which meant that Debo, or Billy for that matter, in any way sympathized with Diana's reprehensible views. But because of Debo's intense ongoing relationship with her, Diana would long burden the Cavendishes with no small amount of unwanted moral and political baggage.

Meanwhile, in a measure of all that was perceived to be at stake in the by-election, cabinet ministers came down from London to speak on Billy's behalf; and even Winston Churchill was heard from, in a public letter addressed to the Conservative candidate: "My dear Hartington," the prime minister began, "I see that they are attacking you because your family has been identified for about three hundred years with the Parliamentary representation of West Derbyshire. It ought, on the contrary, to be a matter of pride to the constituency to have such long traditions of constancy and fidelity through so many changing scenes and circumstances. Moreover, it is a historical fact that your family and the people of West Derbyshire have acted together on every great occasion in this long period of history on the side of the people's rights and progress." But how could Churchill possibly help Billy, when the wartime leader was himself about to fall victim to the very same forces of change that were at work in the West Derbyshire by-election? Indeed, Debo would later describe Billy's unsuccessful candidature as "the straw in the wind" that foretold Churchill's electoral defeat in 1945.

Sure enough, the prime minister's attempt to intervene in the by-election backfired. The people of West Derbyshire—a great many of them anyway—decried Churchill's public letter as an example of the very paternalism they were seeking to eradicate. Conservative efforts to sell Billy as "the patriotic candidate," a vote for whom represented a vote of confidence in the wartime coalition government, proved similarly counterproductive. Though Hitler had yet to be defeated, many Britons, weary of wartime stringencies, were already eagerly looking beyond the war to better, more prosperous and egalitarian times.

When Kick joined Billy and his family on the fifteenth, her presence had to be downplayed as much as possible, the duke's political agents having ruled that a connection to the Kennedy family would do Lord Hartington's candidature no more good than a connection to the Mitford family. Remaining for the most part in the background, Kick thrilled to Billy's ability to maintain his poise and good humor despite all the harassment. She marveled at the duchess's oratorical skills, when on numerous occasions Moucher Devonshire spoke eloquently and forthrightly on her son's behalf. And she delighted in the family's marathon nightly strategy sessions.

The adrenaline rush of politics was by no means unfamiliar to Kick. Nor could any Kennedy offspring have failed to be elated by the sight of the many press people, American as well as British, who descended upon the villages and hamlets of the dale to cover this historic and emblematic election. Elizabeth Cavendish's chestnut pony, Poppet, started back in fright when American journalists leapt out of their automobiles and began snapping pictures and asking questions of anyone they could find. The press invasion proved similarly disconcerting to not a few lo-cal residents. By contrast, for Kick, who had finally been permitted to canvass for votes with Billy's sister in a gig decorated with gaudy campaign posters, the clicking cameras were as a drug.

As Kick later told Richard Wood, the whole experience of the by-election—the press, the crowds, the noise, Billy's bravery and beauty on the speaker's platform, the intensity of the feelings on both sides, and the magnitude of all that was at stake—had "the most overwhelming impact" on her.

Had the duchess staged it all, had she constructed sets and hired crowds of extras, with an eye toward beguiling Kick, the older woman could hardly have proven more efficacious.

Strange to say, Kick fell in love with a world and a set of traditions at the very moment when both were in the process of being radically transformed. It was as if she had found exactly what she was searching for, the ideal outlet for her ambitions, only to see it instantly snatched away by history. When, at last, Billy received but 41.5 percent of the vote to Alderman Charles White's 57.7 percent, Kick could scarcely conceal that she was "hysterically upset"—both for her young man's sake and for herself.

The duke shared Kick's sense of desolation. "I don't know what the people want," Eddy Devonshire bitterly lamented.

To which his son cheerfully flung back: "I do. They just don't want the Cavendishes."

The Common Wealth Party, meanwhile, pointed to Billy's loss as proof that "Britain will not be content to return to the old 1939 world when we have defeated the enemy."

Finally, Billy made a short speech to about one thousand local Con-servative supporters, who by turns cheered and wept at what he had to say. "It has been a hard fight, and that is the way it goes," he declared. "I am going now to fight for you at the front. After all, unless we win the war, there can be no home front. Better luck next time."

Debo, standing in the crowd, heard one old woman beside her remark regarding Billy's imminent return to the front, "It's a shame to let him go, a great tall man like he is, he's such a target."

At any rate, unlike his father, Billy had emerged from the cut and thrust of the campaign curiously invigorated. That so many of Billy's long-held assumptions about life had been upended in the Battle of Flanders may have helped him now to accept what Eddy Devonshire still could not bring himself to acknowledge. Billy saw that the centuries-old traditions that he and his father cherished and earnestly believed had always served England best could not possibly survive the war. At the same time, as a West Derbyshire neighbor would later write of Billy, he was "no less determined to play his part in directing the current and not merely to be swept away by it." Billy's parting words to supporters, "Better luck next time," signaled his intention to return to politics after the war.

By the time Billy uttered those words, there was no longer any doubt on Kick's side that, when he did return to the political fray, she intended to be there with him.

Billy's father signaled that the time was fast approaching to make the gesture that his son had demanded of her, when, three days after the election, on the occasion of her twenty-fourth birthday, the duke presented Kick with a beautiful old leather volume of the Book of Common Prayer, the book of prayers and services used in the Anglican Church. Kick laughed and thanked him, but the duke's message to her was clear. Initially, she pinned her hopes on old Joe Kennedy's being able to obtain a dispensation on her behalf through his contacts in the Roman Catholic hierarchy. In league with Francis Spellman, the Archbishop of New York, old Joe attempted to pull strings at the Vatican.

But in the end, the ambassador and the archbishop were unable to secure the special arrangement that would permit Kick to marry Billy and bring up their children as Protestants while she herself remained in the good graces of the Catholic Church. "Frankly I do not seem to think Dad can do anything," Rose reported to her daughter. "He feels terribly sympathetic and so do I and I only wish we could offer some suggestions.

When both people have been handed something all their lives, how ironic it is that they can not have what they want most."

Characteristically, given the choices that Rose had made in her own life, she counseled her daughter to find solace for her disappointed hopes in a renewed commitment to her duty. "It is Lent now," Rose went on, "and I am praying morning, noon and night, so do not be exhausting yourself and running your little legs off going to Church, as your first duty is towards your job. The little verse—'Do your duty, that is best; leave unto the Lord the rest' may be Protestant or Catholic, but it really teaches us that our first responsibility is towards our immediate job."

Rose seemed confident that in the absence of a dispensation, Kick would not dare go forward. The case, as far as the Kennedy matriarch was concerned, was closed.

Kick, however, continued to struggle. She spent two days at Churchdale Hall, where the duchess had arranged for her to confer with her great friend, the Reverend Edward Keble Talbot, who was King George VI's chaplain. The clergyman reviewed what the Cavendish family stood for in the English Church and reiterated "the impossibilities" of any son of Billy's being brought up as a Roman Catholic.

He spoke in detail about the significant differences between the Anglican and Roman churches, and expressed the hope that Kick might be able to find "a substitute" in Anglicanism for the faith in which she had been raised. As she later reported to her parents, Kick countered "that something one had been brought up to believe in and which was largely responsible for the character and personality of an individual is a very hard thing for which to find a substitute." She further told the clergyman that it struck her as "rather cheap and weak" to capitulate in the first real crisis that had presented itself to her in life.

At the same time, as Richard Wood perceived, she had never been more lucid about what she wanted and what she must do to obtain it. At once complicating and clarifying her situation was the fact that Billy's father had suddenly gone so far as to tell him that were he to give in to Kick on the religious question, the family would not cut him off. On the face of it, this was a huge development. Duke Eddy's altered position would have seemed to obliterate the obstacles before her. But it quickly became apparent that that was far from the case.

Henceforth, it was Billy alone who saw it as a matter of his own bounden duty to insist that Kick be the one to capitulate. She was not battling the duke anymore; she was battling the man she loved.

Yet for all the anguish Billy's inflexibility caused her, she also found much to admire in the stance he had taken. "Poor Billy is very, very sad but he sees his duty must come first," Kick wrote to her parents. "He is a fanatic on this subject and I suppose just such a spirit is what has made England great despite the fact that Englishmen are considered so weak-looking, etc." Did she intend the latter sentence as a riposte to her father and older brothers, who had often been heard to portray the British as weak?

During this period, Kick grew fonder than ever of Billy's mother, who showered her with empathy and understanding. "The duchess is so wonderful and kind," Kick reported to Joe and Rose. "She wants me to consider wherever they are as home and really couldn't be kinder. She is writing to Mother." Moucher Devonshire conveyed to Kick her understanding of how difficult it must be to be alone in England without her parents at a moment when she was going through so much. "I know how lonely you must feel and how forsaken," the duchess wrote to Kick after the unproductive meeting with the clergyman, "but we must trust in God that things will come out for the best. I do hope you know how much we love you and if there is even the smallest thing we can do to help you have only to say—and always please come and see me at any time if you feel like it and come and stay. There is always a bed for you—you have only to telephone."

Kick sought the counsel of, among others, Bishop James Matthew, the auxiliary bishop of Westminster. This prominent Roman Catholic endeavored to assuage at least one of Kick's fears about what might happen were she to marry without the sanction of her church. "No one can say you are committing a sin," he assured her, "because a sin is done from a selfish motive. What you are doing is done from an entirely non-selfish motive."

Kick was much comforted by this interpretation. Far less satisfying was Bishop Matthew's suggestion that, given what would almost certainly be the Vatican's reluctance to move quickly and publicly in such an exceptionally high-profile case, it might perhaps be best if she and Billy were to marry first and then hope for a dispensation to be granted at some much later date. Kick judged that were she and Billy indeed to wait for Rome to act, the process might take years—time that, under the circumstances, she and he simply did not have.

The scarcity of time was further driven home to her when, in early April, Billy called to say that he did not believe that there was any hope of securing additional leave to visit her in London. The lovers still had so much to settle, yet from this point on the only way to see one another was for Kick to come to Billy. Fortunately, they both had access to Jean and David Lloyd's cottage in Yorkshire, not far from where Billy was stationed.

So it was that on Wednesday, April 19, 1944, Kick, having obtained a brief leave of her own from the Red Cross, took a train up from London to spend three days as Jean's houseguest. The plan was for Billy to join her when he was off duty in the evening, or when he otherwise managed to grab a few stray hours.

Kick associated Jean with the splendor of her upbringing at Cortachy Castle. Yet when Kick entered the Lloyds' exceedingly modest cottage that first day, she found her hostess down on the floor, awkwardly sweeping the surface as best she could, given the heavy plaster cast that encased her left leg. Jean had broken the leg several days before as she dashed upstairs to make the bed for Billy, who had arrived unexpectedly to spend the night in the claustrophobic space that the Lloyds referred to with a dash of irony as "David's dressing room."

Visibly aghast at the picture that greeted her, Kick broke out, "What are you doing?"

Jean, usually the kindest and gentlest of souls, replied sharply, even angrily, "You can see what I'm doing!"

At that moment, all of the war weariness, all of the exhaustion and frustration, that had been pent up in Jean for so long erupted in her expression of displeasure with Kick. Since Kick's return nine months previously, the aristocratic cousinhood had been charmed by her ability to remind them of what life had been like before the war. But on this particular spring night in 1944, Jean found herself bristling at Kick's abiding, almost willful blindness to how much in British life had changed, a good deal of it perhaps forever.

Jean's upset quickly dissolved, so pleased was she to see her old friend, with whom she was soon laughing, gossiping, and gaily talking about better times. Jean felt more than a little guilty about her outburst, so she was glad that she had already planned something of a feast to cook for her guest's breakfast.

David Lloyd had to be off by seven A.M., so the next morning Jean was up at dawn stoking the fire for hot water and preparing a meal that almost certainly would have been beyond them in London. Kick, Jean, and David were sitting in the kitchen feasting on eggs and bacon when the front door opened and in came Billy, a sack of oranges in one hand.

Tossing the precious bag to Kick—in wartime, citrus fruit was a rarity—he looked at her with immense pleasure and declared, "We're off!" As Billy uttered those words he rubbed the palms of his hands together. Jean, to whom he had often spoken of his abiding, at times all-consuming need to go back, knew at once that the long-awaited invasion was finally at hand.

Billy contentedly chatted with Kick and the Lloyds for a bit, but he had to leave almost as abruptly as he had appeared. He promised to return sometime that evening. Clearly, the moment for Kick to reply one way or another to his marriage proposal had also finally arrived.

Over the course of the day, Kick trailed Jean about as her hostess performed household chores. Kick later wrote to tell her family about how "fantastic" it was to think of the way Jean had lived before the war and "how easily" she had now adapted to her new role in Scarborough. Kick reported Jean's opinion, which had been seconded by her husband, that there would be no returning to the kind of life they had once enjoyed. Though Kick made a point of assuring her family that, in her capacity as the Lloyds' houseguest, she had been "most efficient around the house," Jean would laughingly recall years afterward that beyond making a huge display of assisting her, Kick had actually been of little help. Jean felt it was not that Kick did not really want to help; it was that she simply did not know how.

That evening and the next, Billy appeared with a bounty of lobsters and champagne. Both nights, there was much table talk about the deprivations and depredations wrought by the war. Billy acknowledged that he did not expect to inhabit Chatsworth—ever. Kick could scarcely conceal from her hostess the feeling that such an idea was very difficult for her to accept. She had long been building castles in the air; now, she had to face the possibility that, though she might make the great sacrifice, the castle, and the opportunity to restore it to its previous glory, might never be hers after all.

Meanwhile, on both nights, when the Lloyds went up to bed, Kick and Billy remained behind in the sitting room. At daybreak, when Jean appeared downstairs to prepare hot water, she found the couple still conversing in an animated fashion—but not, she emphasized many years later, in the teasing, bantering style they had often exhibited in the past. Crucial decisions remained to be made, and though Jean did not hear what they had said in the course of the night, their talks on these occasions had an unaccustomed air of gravity about them that was not entirely dissipated by the hostess's entrance.

There was no news that first morning, but at breakfast on Saturday Kick excitedly informed Jean and David that she had at last accepted Billy's marriage proposal. Both she and Billy struck the Lloyds as wondrously happy. It was an occasion that called out to be recorded—and so it would be.

As Billy was about to return to his regiment, he and Kick wandered out into the garden. They were followed there by Jean, who had her old Brownie box camera in hand, the same apparatus that she had used to record a great many signal occasions in the prewar lives of their group of young people. In those days, many of the debs, as well as their mothers, had kept their Brownie box cameras constantly at the ready to register the various landmarks on the road to marriage and adulthood—house parties, dances, race meetings, picnics, and the like, images that the girls would later lovingly affix to the heavy pages of their scrapbooks. In 1944 Jean still possessed not only her Brownie, but also all of the reflexes that, now as then, drew her irresistibly to any moment that looked to be a beginning.

On the sunny April morning that Jean photographed the couple, Kick was at last truly about to become Lady Hartington. It had taken her six years to reach this point. She had had to overcome the numerous obstacles that warring nations, not to mention both the Kennedy and Cavendish families, had put in her path. Then, when the duke had finally conceded to his son that, even if Kick were to insist upon their children being brought up as Roman Catholics, the marriage would have his and the duchess's blessing, it had been Billy himself who had presented Kick with one last, really formidable hurdle that she would have to surmount alone. In effect, he had asked her to abandon certain of the principles with which she had been inculcated from an early age. Without actually saying so, he had demanded that she give up the comfort of what she herself would later longingly refer to as "the protecting walls of the convent."

In place of Catholicism, Billy had offered her an alternate way of making sense of the world and of creating order out of chaos. In the end, Kick had managed to find that new and necessary sense of meaning not in Anglicanism, but rather in the traditional societal structure that she had had an opportunity to observe firsthand in West Derbyshire.

As for Billy, he too had been hurtling toward this point for six years, though his trajectory had contained rather more detours than Kick's, the most notable of which had been a much-regretted engagement to someone other than the girl of his heart. But it was also the case that, even now, Billy was traveling along a separate, but no less propulsive course, whose final destination he was achingly on the verge of reaching. As Jean understood, the picture she took of him with Kick on the morning of April 22, 1944, captured a moment of what was for Billy perfect satisfaction, as both his marriage to Kick and his return to the war zone were finally assured.

Back in London, Kick faced the ordeal of disclosing her decision to her family. Putting off the inevitable cataclysm for at least a few seconds, she began her April 24, 1944, letter to her parents and siblings by speaking not of the freighted subject of her impending marriage, but rather of a topic that was always a supremely happy one between her and her mother. She wrote of a package of clothes that had arrived from home two weeks previously, commenting that they were all "awfully nice" with the exception of an evening dress of her mother's. Kick felt that the evening dress was "really too old for me," and promised to bequeath it to "some deserving British soul."

Stalling before she had to commit the dreaded words to paper, Kick went on to write in detail of the fate of a mirror that Rose Kennedy had recently sent over as a gift to the Queen. As no message of gratitude had been received chez Kennedy, Kick had recently made an inquiry of Tommy Lascelles, the King's secretary, whose note of response she now had in hand and quoted to her parents and siblings in full: "The mirror certainly reached the Queen safely; and equally certainly a letter was sent to your mother within a few days of its arrival. But the letter seems to have gone astray—maybe through enemy action—and a copy of it is being sent at once to Mrs. Kennedy. Mind you, let me know if this too fails to turn up!" Kick proceeded to write at length of her visit with Jean and David Lloyd in Yorkshire, and of Billy's nightly visits to the household. All of which led her to confess at last.

"I have definitely decided to marry him."

She assured her parents that she would let them know the date in advance, once it had been set. "You understand that the ceremony would have to be performed in a registry office which is rather sordid but the only thing to do as I wouldn't have an Anglican service."

Rose, when she learned of Kick's intentions, recorded in her diary that she was at once "horrified" and "heartbroken." Tellingly, foremost among her considerations at the moment was the extent to which Kick's marriage to a Protestant would constitute "a blow to the family prestige." Once Kick had done it, Rose reflected, would not other young girls ask, "If K Kennedy can—why can't I?" Rose insisted that prior to this, "everyone pointed to our family with pride as well behaved— level headed & deeply religious."

As Rose expressed this sentiment in the privacy of a diary, it is worth asking to what extent she actually believed that the world perceived her family to be well behaved and religious. Had she refused to acknowledge the crude reality of her life for so many years that she had begun to confuse a personally and politically useful image with the truth? Had she been complicit in old Joe's mythmaking for so long as to have become blind to the fact that his and his eldest sons' behavior was often rather squalid? Far from being the problem, Kick was in fact truer to the idealized image than either of her older brothers. Yet now, as far as Rose was concerned, it was Kick whose actions threatened to heap shame upon them all.

Rose urged old Joe to fly to London immediately, but to her chagrin he seemed to think that such a trip would be impossible. Tortured by the thought that her husband really ought to have gone over a month or two previously, she barraged Kick with frantic telegrams, as well as with pleas and warnings transmitted through various envoys whom she tasked with extricating her before it was too late.

The dilemma that confronted Kick had to do with a good deal more than simply religion or rebellion per se. It had to do with her conception of herself as a kind, caring person. It had to do with her part in the fragile familial ecosystem that, since virtually the time of Kick's birth, had helped to sustain Rose. Kick—who had long been Rose's staunchest supporter in the family; who had refused to join her older brothers in mocking and disparaging their mother; and who had declined to countenance the humiliations to which old Joe by his relentless womanizing had callously and often publicly subjected his wife—suddenly found herself cast in a new and unwanted role. To her horror, Kick became the family member who was conceivably about to do greater harm to her mother than any of the others had ever even approached doing.

Bishop James Matthew had previously explained to Kick that were she to marry Billy, she would not be committing a sin. No one, however, could offer her comparable assurances that by going forward in the absence of a dispensation, she would not be wreaking havoc upon the mother whom she called "the dearest person in the world." Given the poignancy of Rose's life, Kick saw it as her duty to be always supremely caring and protective of her. Kick scoffed at Rose's threats, which came aplenty that first week of May 1944, that if she went ahead with the wedding she would no doubt be damned and go to hell. According to Billy's sister Anne, by this point Kick was at peace with her decision to marry and with the accommodations she had finally decided to make.

What Kick was by no means at peace with, however, was the prospect of hurting Rose, who, by all indications, was about to take her daughter's actions very hard indeed.

An ambassador designated by Archbishop Francis Spellman to speak to Kick on behalf of her parents soon perceived that at this point there existed only one individual who might yet succeed in stopping the wedding, which was now scheduled to take place at the Chelsea Register Office on May 6. After conferring with Kick on the third of May, Archbishop William Godfrey, the apostolic delegate to Britain, sent word to the U.S. that his efforts had been in vain. Though Kick remained absolutely firm about her decision to marry Billy outside of the Roman Catholic Church, she was still, however, clearly very upset about her mother's reaction. Accordingly, the archbishop suggested that the Kennedy family's one last remaining chance to halt the ceremony was for Rose herself to "try again with all her power."

Kick with her oldest siblings. Joe Jr., Jack, Rosemary, Kick, and Eunice. COURTESY JOHN F. KENNEDY LIBRARY

Teddy, Jean, Bobby, Pat, Eunice, Kick, Rosemary, Jack, Rose, and Joe Sr. Kick was her favorite brother Jack's beloved mascot. © BETTMANN/CORBIS

Joseph P. Kennedy and his wife, Rose. Kick was her father's favorite child and he was the great fixer in her life. Kick was her mother Rose's self-appointed protector. COURTESY JOHN F. KENNEDY LIBRARY

In 1938, Joe Kennedy went to London as America's very unexpected Ambassador to the Court of St James's. COURTESY JOHN F. KENNEDY LIBRARY

In England not long after their arrival in 1938. Kick almost immediately began the process of becoming a person in her own right. © BETTMANN/CORBIS

Andrew Cavendish, Jean Ogilvy, and Billy Hartington. These three were to become the key figures in Kick's next chapter. COURTESY JEAN LLOYD

Gina Wernher, Debo Mitford, and Billy Hartington. COURTESY JEAN LLOYD

Debo Mitford,
Sally Norton, and
Tony Loughborough.
COURTESY JEAN LLOYD

Jean Ogilvy, Robert
Cecil, Sissie Lloyd
Thomas, and David
Ormsby-Gore.
COURTESY JEAN LLOYD

Charlie Lansdowne and Andrew Cavendish. COURTESY JEAN LLOYD

Kick Kennedy and Billy Hartington at
Goodwood in 1938. © GEORGE W. HALES/
HULTON ARCHIVE/GETTY IMAGES

Kick Kennedy and Billy Hartington.
COURTESY JOHN F. KENNEDY LIBRARY

The Cortachy house party at Airlie Castle with the Dowager Countess of Airlie. Debo, Jean, Kick, Granny, Robert, Ivar, Billy, and David. COURTESY JEAN LLOYD

Lord Airlie. At Cortachy the imminent danger of war had Jean's father constantly on edge with the young boys. COURTESY JEAN LLOYD

At Cortachy. Ivar Colquhoun, David, Debo, and Billy. COURTESY JEAN LLOYD

The Kennedys at the coronation of Pope Pius XII in March 1939. While they were in Rome, Hitler moved again and suddenly war now seemed unavoidable to all of Kick's friends.
COURTESY JOHN F. KENNEDY LIBRARY

The boys in Kick's set lived now even more wildly knowing the coming war was imminent. There was a series of dangerous car crashes. Here are David Ormsby-Gore and Jakie Astor. David had already lost his teeth in one crash and Jakie had been left with a scar on his face. COURTESY JEAN LLOYD

Kick and Billy in 1939 as the coming war intensified the pressure on their romance. © BETTMANN/CORBIS

Billy Hartington's Coming of Age in August 1939. The Duke and Duchess of Devonshire and the twenty-one-year-old Marquess of Hartington greeted some 2,500 of their guests at the celebration. Kick was distraught that her parents refused to allow her to attend.
COURTESY JEAN LLOYD

Hugh Fraser.
COURTESY JEAN LLOYD

Billy and David Ormsby-Gore as Billy works on his Coming of Age speech.
COURTESY JEAN LLOYD

Derek Parker Bowles, Sybil Cavendish, David Ormsby-Gore, and Andrew Cavendish.
COURTESY JEAN LLOYD

Chatsworth illuminated for Billy's Coming of Age. © HERITAGE IMAGES/
HULTON ARCHIVE/GETTY IMAGES

Maurice Macmillan, Andrew Cavendish, and Charles Granby. Granby would serve as best man
at Billy and Kick's wedding. COURTESY JEAN LLOYD

Billy's Cecil grandmother and his Cavendish uncle at his Coming of Age. Lord Richard Cavendish told Lady Alice Salisbury: "These Catholic girls are a menace!" COURTESY JEAN LLOYD

September 3, 1939— Joe Jr., Kick, and Jack Kennedy rushing to the House of Commons, where Prime Minister Chamberlain was about to declare war. Kick was sent home to the U.S.—much against her wishes—when war was declared. She and Billy, in spite of their parents' objections, considered themselves unofficially engaged. Billy was now a soldier in the Coldstream Guards. COURTESY JOHN F. KENNEDY LIBRARY

Kick returned to England in 1943 as a Red Cross worker. © KEYSTONE/ HULTON ARCHIVE/
GETTY IMAGES

Billy and Kick in London in 1943 shortly after her return. © RANDY FARIS/CORBIS

Kick in a photo taken at Jean's house the day she finally accepted Billy's marriage proposal. COURTESY JEAN LLOYD

May 6, 1944, Kick's wedding day. The Duchess of Devonshire, Billy Hartington, Kick, Joe Kennedy Jr., and the Duke of Devonshire. © BETTMANN/CORBIS

At the Bakewell Fair, August 1944. Debo Cavendish, the Dowager Duchess of Devonshire, and Kick. This was the day Kick finally proved herself to the Duke of Devonshire. COURTESY JOHN F. KENNEDY LIBRARY

Kick's favorite photograph of Billy, with his dog Lupin. On September 9, 1944, just four months after their marriage, Billy was killed by a German sniper's bullet in Belgium. COURTESY JEAN LLOYD

Kick just a few weeks before her death in 1948. She was then Kathleen, Marchioness of Hartington. COURTESY JEAN LLOYD

After Billy's death, Kick became romantically involved with the married nobleman Earl Fitzwilliam. Here Peter Fitzwilliam is pictured with his wife, Obby. © KEYSTONE/ HULTON ROYALS COLLECTION /GETTY IMAGES

Even as Rose was bombarding her daughter with pleas and threats, all of England was physically and psychologically in upheaval, as soldiers began to move en masse from bases throughout the nation. Their clockwork procession to southern England during the first week of May constituted the greatest mass movement of soldiers in British and American military annals. Restricted to designated marshaling locations, the troops would shortly be briefed about the Normandy invasion, which was now scheduled to take place at the beginning of June.

To his vast disappointment, Billy was not to be among these troops. He had expected to cross over the Channel with the first mighty wave of soldiers. Instead he was assigned to remain behind with his unit, which was set to be brought in as reinforcements at some point after the initial assault. Billy's orders cast a blight on his happiness in anticipation of the wedding. But then, had his departure not been put off, the marriage ceremony could never have taken place when it did. Nor, obviously, could he have obtained leave for a honeymoon, confined as he would have been to one of the marshaling areas in southern England. As it was, the newlyweds were to have six nights together at Compton Place before Billy would be required to return to duty.

Meanwhile, the one Kennedy sibling who supported Kick unequivocally in her decision to marry outside the Roman Catholic Church was Joe Junior. Kick conferred with him by telephone each time a new angry or despairing message from their mother arrived. He saw Bishop Matthew on her behalf to determine if there was any way a dispensation might yet be acquired, and later he met with the Duke of Devonshire's lawyers to read over her marriage settlement. He wrote to offer personal assurances to his parents that Billy was clearly "crazy about Kick" and that it was evident to all who saw them that they were "very much in love." On the day of the wedding, young Joe would be the family's sole representative at both the ceremony and the reception afterward.

Some observers at the time believed that the romantic relationship Joe had recently embarked on with Pat Wilson, the wife of an English soldier who was then fighting in Italy, a relationship Joe's parents clearly would not approve of were they to have learned of it, made him more open to what Kick was about to do. Others connected it to his state of free fall within the Kennedy family hierarchy. Frantic that the second son, who was now not only a successful author but also a war hero, had displaced him in their father's eyes, Joe seemed eager to at least take Jack's place as the intimate of Kick, the patriarch's favorite. He supported Kick within the family as she had once supported Jack.

In the current controversy, Jack proved rather less supportive of his sister than their past history might have led one to expect. When Jack weighed in on the subject of Kick's wedding plans, it was only to say that he believed it was time for Billy to make a concession of some sort. That of course was scarcely what she would have wished to hear. Other siblings as well seemed to take their mother's view of the matter. Twenty-two-year-old Eunice was indignant over what she regarded as her sister's apostasy, and eighteen-year-old Bobby was, as he recalled to David Ormsby-Gore in later years, "very shaken and shocked." There had been a time when Kick longed to find an identity apart from her family—but now, so much disapproval from her siblings was almost too much for her to bear.

Even more distressing was a newspaper report that her mother was extremely ill and had had to be hospitalized as a consequence of her upset over the impending nuptials. To make matters worse, Kick's father seemed suddenly to have abandoned his long-established policy of backing her even when her views did not coincide with his own.

As far as Kick's relationship with Billy was concerned, several times in recent months old Joe had conveyed to her that she ought to marry whomever she thought best. "I'll gamble with your judgment," he had told her on one occasion. "The best is none too good for you, but if you decide to marry a Chinaman, it's okay with me. That's how much I think of you." He seemed to view matters differently, however, as soon as the actual wedding date was announced. At that point, the patriarch went disturbingly silent. Nor, despite Kick's anguish, was there any reassuring word from old Joe as to her mother's condition. "The power of silence is great," Joe Junior would at length angrily telegram his father. And so, on the bittersweet occasion of Kick and Billy's wedding day, it proved to be.

On Saturday morning, Lieutenant Joseph Kennedy, in naval attire, delivered Kick to the Chelsea Register Office. They arrived there some twenty minutes late, Joe Junior's vehicle having taken a few wrong turns en route. Billy, in the uniform of a captain in the Coldstream Guards, met them there, as did his sisters, parents, and grandmothers, the Dowager Duchess of Devonshire and the Marchioness of Salisbury. In the absence of Billy's brother, who was in Italy, the young Duke of Rutland, also an officer in the Coldstream Guards, served as Billy's best man. Debo, who had lately given birth to her and Andrew's first son, Peregrine, was still recovering at Churchdale Hall and therefore unable to attend.

Other guests at the wedding ceremony included Nancy Astor and Marie Bruce. The latter was a London friend of Mrs. Kennedy's, who, highly sympathetic and loyal to Kick, had done everything she could to act in loco parentis. Mrs. Bruce's services to the young bride ranged from providing Kick's simple, street-length, pale pink crepe wedding dress, to seeking to comfort her the night before in the face of her mother's abiding disapproval.

Following the ceremony, which took but seven minutes to complete, the newlyweds were feted at a reception for some two hundred family members and friends, including some of the same Red Cross coworkers who had previously been so critical of Kick, at the home of Lady Hambleden. After the last champagne toast had been raised, Kick disappeared upstairs to change into a going-away costume that consisted of a black and white flowered crepe dress, a simple black coat, and a black and white halo hat. Before she and Billy left Lady Hambleden's, they telephoned Jean Lloyd, who was in the hospital with a bout of jaundice and had therefore been unable to come to the reception. Kick and Billy took turns regaling his Ogilvy cousin with all of the day's details.

At last, pelted by rose petals, the young marquess and marchioness departed for Victoria Station, where they boarded an unoccupied first-class compartment of a train headed for Eastbourne. In the course of the day, Kick had striven to smile and laugh whenever members of the press, British and American alike, pointed cameras and shouted pointed questions at her. Otherwise, such had been her agitation about her parents, especially her mother, that, after the festivities ended, Joe Junior, Lady Astor, and Mrs. Bruce all contacted the Kennedys, urging them to break their silence by wishing their daughter well.

By the time the newlyweds reached Eastbourne and began the half-mile walk between the train station and the family mansion at Compton Place, it had been an exceedingly long and worrisome day. At this point, Kick still had no idea how her mother was, or how to account for her father's eloquent silence. Billy, who had previously avowed that, above all, he wished to do nothing to make Kick unhappy or guilt-ridden, could scarcely be sure that he had not done precisely that by forcing her to marry outside of the Roman Catholic Church and thereby alienating her from her family.

In her Washington days, Kick had made it clear to John White, when he attempted to lure her into bed, that she intended to remain a virgin until her wedding night. When at last she and Billy entered the bedroom at Compton Place that had been specially prepared for them, she was astonished and horrified by something that he did. In the room, two beds had been pushed together to form one large bed. Whether on account of fatigue, fear, a reluctance to deprive her of the innocence he prized, or some other reason or combination of reasons, Billy immediately pushed the two beds apart.

Kick wasted no time assertively pushing the beds back together. The gesture was the culmination of two narrative lines in Kick's life. The first emanated from all of the arguments that she and John White had had about sex. She was a married woman now. It was time. This was the occasion she had long been deferring. But, to whatever degree Kick knew or sensed it to be the case, she was also at that moment enacting a scenario that had much more at stake than merely her own personal fulfillment. Joseph P. Kennedy's daughter had been brought in, as other nonaristocrats had in centuries past, to improve the breed. The pressure on Kick was great, as the future head of the house of Cavendish was but weeks away from returning to the battlefield. If an heir to the dukedom was to be produced, there was very little time left to begin the process. But by Kick's own account to both Fiona Gore and Jean Lloyd, the wedding night proved to be a disaster and a disappointment, mainly, she insisted, because of Billy's inexperience.

The tumult of her emotions can scarcely have helped matters. When at last Kick received word from her father, she responded to say how much hearing from him meant to her, and how worried she remained about her mother. After old Joe sought to assuage her concerns, Kick wrote to her mother at once and at length, on Tuesday, the ninth. "A telegram arrived from Daddy this morning with the news that you are well. I was very worried about a newspaper report here that you were very ill. They made out that it was because of my marriage."

Kick went on to assure her mother that the marriage in no way called into question the raison d'être that Rose had fashioned for herself around the time of her second daughter's birth. "You did your duty as a Roman Catholic mother. You have not failed. There was nothing lacking in my religious education. Not by any means am I giving up my religious faith—it is most precious to me. Billy wants it to remain as such."

Having addressed these spiritual matters, Kick moved along to the sort of material details that would no doubt interest her mother. Kick described the wedding and the reception, her pink crepe wedding dress, and the jewels and precious gifts that had been lavished upon her. She wrote of her engagement ring, a square-cut sapphire with diamonds on each side; of the diamond bracelet Billy's father had given her; and of the gold-diamond-and-pearl pin she'd received from Fiona and Boofy Gore. She begged Rose not to be sad—about anything. "I'm very, very happy," she emphasized, "and quite certain about what I've done."

The resumption of contact with Joe and Rose began to lift the veil of anxiety that had clung to Kick since her arrival in Eastbourne. Still, matters were far from settled with her family. And three days after the wedding, Compton Place continued to be deluged with letters from what Kick described as "irate Catholics" who charged her with having sold her soul for a title. Unwilling to hear his bride disparaged, Billy took it upon himself to personally reply in writing to every one of Kick's critics.

Despite all of this turbulence, however, the honeymoon, while far from idyllic, did prove to be a happy one. The weather was perfect. The newlyweds sunbathed in gardens lush with flowers. And, as Kick later confided to both Fiona and Jean, Billy finally, in her phrase, "figured out how to do it."

Billy reported to his military camp on Friday. But he rejoined Kick in London on Tuesday the sixteenth of May in anticipation of their spending the night at Hatfield House as the guests of his Cecil grandparents. Since the days when Kick had famously shown her mettle there, the family seat had been converted into a military hospital for the duration of the war. Billy's maternal grandfather and grandmother lived on the ground floor in one corner of the massive Jacobean edifice.

Neither grandparent had a history of welcoming Catholics into the family. Lord Salisbury was the family leader who before the war had objected to his grandson Robert Cecil's relationship with Veronica Fraser on the grounds that a union between them would amount to the renunciation of the Cecils' traditional role as leaders of the Anglican community. And it had been Lady Alice Salisbury who, at the time of Kick's first momentous visit to Hatfield, in 1938, had instigated some of the rough treatment to which the Catholic newcomer had been subjected.

Now, six years later, Kick was returning as more than just a new member of the family. Like other brides before her who had come to Hatfield from diverse ranks of society, she represented the hardier stock on which the future of the line was thought by some to depend. When, as Kick reported afterward to the Kennedys, the various old Cecil relatives and their servants gave her "the eye," it was probably as much with curiosity about whether she might already be pregnant as with the disdain and dismay that she herself seemed to perceive.

Following their visit to Hatfield, Kick and Billy moved to a small hotel on the main street in Alton, near to where Billy was stationed. The newlyweds were given the premier suite at the Swan Hotel, an English inn dating to 1554, where the staff were obviously delighted to have a marquess and marchioness in residence. The Irish bellboy happened also to be named Kennedy, and he insisted that he and Kick might be related. It amused and pleased Kick greatly that each time she or Billy so much as peeked out into the hotel corridor, there was the bellboy waiting to march in front of them. "This way, Marquess," little Kennedy would loudly declare as he threw open some door for the noble guests, who were the future Duke and Duchess of Devonshire, after all.

Billy daily traveled by motorbike between the hotel and the military camp. It had fallen to him to supervise and keep up the spirits of some two hundred men, not a few of whom seemed as disappointed as he at having been relegated to the status of reinforcements. He and his men were scheduled to receive their orders at some as yet unspecified date after the initial cross-Channel invasion had been undertaken. Kick, meanwhile, had a bike of her own so that she could get about in the market town while Billy was off during the day.

Their time together at the Swan proved to be an immensely happy one. "I am feeling better now than I have since I left America," Kick reported to her family. "This is the first really good rest I have had for a year. Have put on some weight and am getting plenty of sleep. MARRIED LIFE AGREES WITH ME!" Billy, for his part, would later speak of his month with Kick as the most perfect of his life.

Still, these days of joy were lived against the vivid and unavoidable background of the long-anticipated invasion of Normandy. Some 156,000 Allied soldiers landed in Normandy on D-day, June 6, 1944. That first day alone saw about 10,000 Allied casualties, with more than 4,000 troops known to be dead. And that was only the start of the massive bloodletting.

As Kick and Billy savored Sunday picnics, laughed fondly over certain of their wedding pictures, and made postwar plans that included a trip to the U.S. so that he could meet all of the Kennedy and Fitzgerald relatives—a prospect he was far from certain that he looked forward to—Allied soldiers were trying to battle their way across the Normandy countryside, where they encountered fierce resistance from German forces.

The newlyweds were aware that these could well be their final days together, but when Captain the Marquess of Hartington received his orders at last on June 13, 1944, he attempted to treat their parting as no different, really, from the other forced separations that they had had to endure. "This love seems to cause nothing but goodbyes," Billy wrote to her before he left for the military camp, where he would be confined until the eighteenth of June, when he embarked for France with the 5th Coldstream Battalion under the command of Lieutenant Colonel the Lord Stratheden. By these tender words Billy seemed to suggest that, as he and Kick had been reunited before, so they would be again.

Nine

Four weeks after Billy waded ashore in the rain from his landing craft on June 23, 1944, he could no longer pretend with Kick that their latest parting would surely be like all the others. Too much had happened in the violent and bloody month since he and Kick had said good-bye.

The 5th Coldstream Battalion had arrived in Normandy three days before General Sir Bernard Montgomery, the commander of Allied ground forces in Normandy, opened a major offensive, Operation Epsom, with the objective of taking the German-occupied city of Caen. The Guardsmen were assigned to hold defensive positions at St. Manvieu and Marcelet, to the west of Caen. Just before dawn on a rain-drenched July 2, Billy and other members of the No. 4 Company, of which he was second in command, went out to patrol a patch of scrubby country-side where the air was thick with the nauseating stench of dead cattle. The men had to withdraw when they came under heavy fire from the Germans, but so far they'd suffered only two minor casualties.

As the day wore on the rain persisted, but the frequent shelling that the English soldiers had already learned to anticipate as a daily fact of life seemed somehow less intense at the moment. At about two P.M., however, the men had a sharp lesson in the randomness and unpredictability of war, when a splinter from an airburst shell struck the company commander, Mark Howard, in the neck.

Major Howard, aged twenty-six, died almost instantly. He was buried near the spot where he fell. A week after Billy arrived in Normandy he stepped in to replace his lifelong friend and former Trinity College, Cambridge University, classmate as company commander.

In retrospect, Debo would cite the news about her great friend Mark Howard as the beginning of the grievous period that she dubbed "the summer of death"—when, one after another, the young men of their group were killed. Good-looking, vital, and high-spirited, Mark Howard of Castle Howard had been a much-loved and much-admired member of the set. Like Billy, he had been intent on launching a political career after the war. He had been one of the fellows in military uniform who had cavorted at the famous London party the previous November, at which Kick and Fiona had attempted to recapture, if only for an evening, some of the frivolity and freedom from care they associated with the aristocratic cousinhood's halcyon prewar world.

Word that Mark Howard had fallen and been immediately replaced by Billy Hartington caused shock waves among the members of their group who remained behind in England. Many years afterward, Billy's sister Anne remembered thinking that had the shell splinter's trajectory been but slightly different, it might have been her brother who died that day.

Indeed, the fact that death had come so close to Billy so soon after he arrived in France heightened anxieties at Compton Place, where Kick had elected to remain with his parents, for the time being at least. She had originally intended to return to the Hans Crescent Club in London in a volunteer capacity as soon as her husband embarked for France. But the Germans' V-1 buzz bombs, or doodlebugs, each carrying a ton of explosives, which began to pummel London on the very day Billy received his orders, helped persuade her to alter her plans. Part of the psychological effect of the doodlebugs, which were launched from various sites on the French coast, was the eerie twelve-seconds-long interval between the abrupt shutting off of the engine and the deadly roar of the explosion. Kick, who had not been in London at the time of the Blitz, found the V-1s terrifying.

Soon, these precursors of the cruise missile were raining death and destruction on the English coast as well. Nonetheless, Kick still felt safer in Eastbourne, where her presence did double duty by offering comfort to the Duke and Duchess of Devonshire. Before he left, Billy had written his mother to say that his marriage had brought him complete happiness. Kick's presence among the older couple now served as a cherished reminder of their son's joy in having won her at last. Besides, the tacit assumption, not only of Billy's parents but also of the tribe in general, was that Kick might be in the early stages of pregnancy. So at this point it seemed wisest and best to keep her as close to the family as possible.

Meanwhile, the 5th Coldstream Battalion went on to participate in its first battle, Operation Goodwood, named like its predecessor Operation Epsom for a British racecourse. On the eve of the fight, the men jested that the battle was likely to be "a day at the races." Soon, however, quite the opposite proved to be the case. Among a host of other problems, the British tanks that had been confidently expected to smash through the German defenses faltered when they came up against the formidable earthen walls laced with tree and brush roots that were a prominent feature of the terrain. Nor did the tanks of the Guards Armored Division maneuver easily in the soupy marshland that was to present yet another major obstacle in the course of the Normandy campaign.

Billy's battalion was shelled in Démouville. British casualties were heavy, culminating on the last day of Operation Goodwood with the wounding of Lieutenant Colonel the Lord Stratheden. When this immensely popular and inspiring battalion commander, who had been personally responsible for raising and training the men, had to be temporarily replaced by Major Michael Adeane, morale plummeted. The 5th Coldstream presently withdrew to Giberville, near Caen. There, subjected to intermittent artillery fire and bombing, the British forces attempted to reorganize and regroup in anticipation of the next battle.

It was during this interlude that Billy, who had now been fighting in France for a month, wrote to confront Kick with the possibility that this time they might not be reunited after all. His letter to her from Giberville was one that she would at length have much occasion to reread and reflect upon. "I have been spending a lovely hour on the ground and thinking in a nice vague sleepy way about you & what a lot I've got to look forward to if I come through this all right," Billy wrote on July 26, 1944. "I feel I may talk about it for the moment as I'm not in danger so I'll just say that if anything should happen to me I shall be wanting you to try to isolate our life together, to face its finish, and to start a new one as soon as you feel you can. I hope that you will marry again, quite soon—someone good & nice."

So there it was. He had said the unsayable.

In the year since Kick and Billy were reunited in 1943, there had been much of innocence and denial in their relations. For reasons of his own, he had prized her obdurate blindness to the ravages that the war had wrought. But now, having come so close to death in recent weeks, he at least had to prepare her for the possibility that, like Mark Howard and the rest, he could fall at any moment. As his brother Andrew—who was nearly killed in Italy the day after Billy wrote of death to Kick—later reflected, Billy knew by this time that survival was going to be "all about luck" and that luck was unpredictable. The chances were that, as an infantryman, he would eventually be hit. If he was lucky, he would merely be wounded. If he was unlucky, he would be killed.

Kick had already read Billy's letter when, on August 8, 1944, she made her first public appearance in Derbyshire as Lady Hartington, the wife of the future Duke of Devonshire. As she later recalled, the fear that her young husband might die was to gnaw at her throughout the summer. Six months previously, she had had to be kept very much in the background in the course of the by-election. Today, by contrast, Kick, attired in her summer-weight Red Cross uniform, was front and center as she attended the Bakewell Fair in the company of Duchess Evie, also in the garb of the Red Cross, the Derbyshire branch of which Billy's paternal grandmother was both founder and president. Debo attended the fair as well; but as the wife of the second son, she wore civilian dress, a simple cotton skirt and blouse, that emphatically distinguished her from the dowager and the marchioness.

Not that Debo minded that the spotlight was suddenly on her new sister-in-law; on the contrary, she was delighted, both for Kick and for herself. The previous June, Debo, who was still living at the Rookery near Chatsworth, had been called upon to stand in for her mother-in-law, the Duchess of Devonshire, speaking at various fairs and fetes in Derbyshire, an experience that, in correspondence with her sister Nancy, she had professed to loathe from the outset.

Nor, it seems, was she otherwise envious of Kick. Debo liked Kick personally very much, and does not appear to have coveted, even to the most minimal extent, what looked to be Kick's future life as a duchess. At this point, Debo was exceedingly happy with Andrew and pleased with married life. By now, the couple had had two healthy children, Emma and Peregrine, the latter of whom had recently been christened. What had mattered to Debo at the time of Peregrine's birth was not that he had been a son, but rather, given the fate of her firstborn, that the baby had survived. It was Kick who, as the heir's wife, had to be concerned with producing a male offspring.

As contented as Debo had been with Andrew before he left for the front, she looked forward to even better things after the war. Given his refined literary tastes and his abilities, Andrew hoped to become a publisher in the manner of his uncle Harold Macmillan. Andrew also intended to have a political career. But first, of course, he had to come back safely from Italy, where he had been fighting for almost nine months. Mark Howard had been Debo's closest male friend, and the news of his death in the Normandy campaign had exacerbated her fears about Andrew.

So both young Cavendish sisters-in-law had reason to be desperately worried about their husbands, a circumstance that Duchess Evie had striven unsuccessfully to avoid when she tried to ensure that both of Eddy's sons would not simultaneously find themselves in jeopardy at the front. It was not, however, Kick's and Debo's serenity of mind that the dowager had been concerned about; it was the dukedom, and her desire to guarantee a smooth succession. At any rate, on the day of the Bakewell Fair, Duchess Evie kept a sharp eye on her new grand-daughter-in-law, as Kick met and addressed many of the very same electors who by their votes had removed the traditional Cavendish seat in Parliament from the family's hands. There had been a time when Kick had been the recipient of the dowager's "dirty looks." Today, the looks that Duchess Evie cast her way were strictly those of approba-tion. Billy's paternal grandmother was mightily impressed by Kick's as-sured presentation at the fair. Notably, the old woman was not alone in her assessment. The duke's longtime political agent, also in attendance that day, was pleased to observe that the fairgoers seemed to abso-lutely adore Billy's American bride.

Though at the time of her marriage Kick had acquiesced totally to the duke in his wishes about the religious training of his future grand-children, she was aware that he persisted in seeing her as, in her phrase, "a sort of evil influence" who had somehow insinuated herself into his family. Indeed, shortly before the Bakewell Fair he had been heard to expound on what one listener, the diarist James Lees-Milne, described as his "ferociously anti-Catholic" views at a dinner party at the Dorches-ter, presided over by Emerald Cunard: "I am a black Protestant and I am proud of it. . . . Papists owe a divided allegiance. They put God before their country." In the course of the dinner party, Duke Eddy had spoken of an ancestor of his who had been cut off by his family because he had so much as stayed at Hatfield House, a Tory High Church household whose religious practices were, in the view of the

Cavendishes, dangerously akin to those of Catholicism. And he had spoken of how, for similar reasons, his own father, Duke Victor, had "looked askance" at Eddy's marriage to Moucher.

Kick, faced with Eddy Devonshire's abiding horror of anything to do with Catholics and Catholicism, had vowed early on to try to prove herself to him "over a period of years." As it turned out, she accomplished that objective a good deal more swiftly. At the Bakewell Fair, Lady Hartington won people over with her charm and vivacity, not to mention the hint of glamour provided by the silk stockings that she had had sent over from the U.S. and that, owing to their great rarity in wartime, riveted the eyes of her audience.

The political agent reported her effect on the crowd to the duke, who wasted no time crowing about Kick's triumph to her father. In a letter to old Joe Kennedy, Eddy Devonshire delightedly predicted that if Billy proved unable to win back the family seat in Parliament himself, Kick no doubt would "win it for him." She had previously made clear how much she wished for a public role in England and for the power that would come with that role. Her success at the Bakewell Fair certainly suggested that she might be about to get exactly what she wanted.

But ironically, this first triumph, which seemed to bode so well, had come at a moment when Billy's letter from Giberville had asked her to consider a starkly different outcome.

Indeed, since he wrote to her of death, the 5th Coldstream had been engaged in days on end of the "bitter and confused fighting" known as Operation Bluecoat, in the course of which Billy—now Major the Marquess of Hartington—had twice been called upon to replace a fallen commanding officer. On August 1, Colonel Adeane, who had only recently replaced Sandy Stratheden, was himself wounded in battle. Billy thereupon assumed temporary command of the entire battalion until Major B. E. "Buster" Luard took charge. The new commander remained in place for a mere twenty-seven hours, however—on August 2, Luard himself was wounded during heavy shelling by the Germans.

Yet again Major the Marquess of Hartington was left in command.

The following day, Billy's men encountered unexpectedly heavy fire. The Guardsmen, perched atop tanks driven by their Irish comrades, bounced up and down "like ships in a heavy sea" as they rode over the hedgerows. Throughout, "Billy was magnificent," one of the soldiers, Lady Astor's son-in-law James Willoughby, later recalled; "he never lost his head or his good spirits in spite of the hard time his Battalion was having, no sleep, no food and continual casualties. . . . On the last day we were counter attacked continuously from 6 o'clock in the morning until 10 o'clock at night and Billy's Battalion had to stand the brunt of the attack."

Finally, on the fifth of August, Major the Marquess of Hartington was relieved by Colonel Roddy Hill, aspects of whose technique Billy would subsequently have occasion to emulate. Billy and his weary, ragged men looked on in amazement and admiration as the impeccably attired, almost eerily serene new commanding officer communicated by his appearance and demeanor a sense that, in spite of all that the men of the 5th Coldstream had just endured, and in spite of all that they yet faced, everything was going to be "quite all right." One of his men later recalled: "There was about him an air of unhurried disregard for the immediate alarums of the moment that was wonderful to see. We felt we'd never seen such imperturbability, and the effect on everyone was miraculous." On the day Kick and Debo toured the stalls at the Bakewell Fair in the company of the dowager, Billy, under Colonel Roddy Hill's command, was fighting near Estry, amidst the putrefying cattle, burnt-out tanks, and freshly dug graves that pocked the terrain.

Three days after Kick's triumph at Bakewell, the mood of euphoria at Compton Place turned to horror when Duchess Evie's twenty-two-year-old nephew, Ned Fitzmaurice, the soldier who had tipsily set fire to Elizabeth Cavendish's dress at Kick and Fiona's party nine months earlier, died in a burst of machine gun fire during his first battle. And the day after that, another relative who had been at the party, Dicky Cecil, an RAF pilot, died in a motorcycle accident in England. At the dowager's behest, Duke Eddy immediately began efforts to arrange for

Ned Fitzmaurice's older brother, Charlie Lansdowne, to be brought back from the fighting in Italy, lest their father, Evie's brother, be left without an heir. It was in the midst of this desperate undertaking on the duke's part that further appalling news reached the household on the same day that Dicky Cecil died.

On Sunday, August 13, 1944, Kick had a call informing her of the presumed death of her brother Joe Junior, whose naval aircraft had exploded over the Channel the evening before. He had completed his antisubmarine missions and had been scheduled to return to the U.S. But he had volunteered to remain in Britain in hopes that by securing the European campaign medal, he might yet match the glory that had been won by his brother Jack. When Kick attended his birthday celebration dinner on the twenty-fifth of July at the home of Pat Wilson, he had said that he was going to be doing something secret for the next three weeks. It turned out that the mission on which he had pinned his great hopes aimed to destroy a V-1 launch site near Calais. The plan was for Joe and a copilot to parachute out of their explosives-laden aircraft, which from that point on would be guided to its target by a remote-control device. Instead, the aircraft had exploded before either volunteer had had an opportunity to parachute to safety. For his feat of bravery, Lieutenant Kennedy would be posthumously awarded the Navy Cross, the Navy's highest decoration.

Kick was with Billy's family when she learned of young Joe's death. In a letter to Joe Kennedy Sr. written the next day, the duke expressed gratitude that at least she had not been alone at the time. "I am afraid she will feel the loss of her brother terribly," wrote Eddy Devonshire on the fourteenth of August, "and that it will add to the burden of her husband's absence in France, but we will do the best we can to find a home life for her." When the duke sent off this message he assumed that Kick meant to remain with her husband's family. Eddy's letter was intended both to offer condolences for the loss of young Joe and to assure the ambassador that Kick was being loved and taken care of at this terrible time.

Presently, however, Kick stunned the duke and duchess by express-
ing a wish to return to the U.S. as soon as possible. There was some feeling among her husband's family and friends that her decision to leave
England just then was a betrayal. It was not so much that anyone in
England questioned the sincerity of Kick's concern for her parents or
her desire to comfort them in person. But there was a sense, which was
by no means without foundation, that she was also fleeing the war, the
mounting toll of young men, the terror of the V-1 attacks, and a household
environment that was then dominated by the duke's frantic, fruitless efforts to bring Charlie Lansdowne home from the war zone. And there
was sentiment that at such a time, her duty as Lady Hartington was to
remain with Billy's parents and sisters—and not fly to the Kennedys.

Even after more than half a century had passed, Debo, Jean, and
Billy's sister Anne all expressed perplexity and disappointment about
Kick's decision to go "home" that long-ago August of 1944, while her
husband remained in peril in France. When she agreed to marry Billy,
had she not tacitly promised that from then on she would regard Britain
as her home?

Whether or not Kick sensed the distress she was causing in the Cavendish family circle, once again she asked her father to use his connections, and before long Joseph P. Kennedy had arranged for her to travel
to New York on a troop transport aircraft.

Kick, attired in the same summer-weight Red Cross uniform that she
had worn on the day of her triumph at the Bakewell Fair a little over a
week before, stepped off her plane at LaGuardia Airport in New York
on August 16. She thereupon boarded a flight for Logan Airport in Boston, where her brother Jack was waiting to collect her. If indeed, as
Billy's people sensed, she had hoped to escape their "summer of death"
to whatever degree possible, Jack's war-ravaged appearance when
she beheld him for the first time since his ordeal in the Solomon Is-
lands plunged her back into the very sort of horror from which she
had just fled.

Until this moment, Jack's heroism in the Pacific had been little more than an abstraction to her. She had rejoiced in the glory and the publicity that he had managed to win. Since childhood, she had frequently observed him in the throes of one grave illness or another, but nothing in her brother's sickly past could have prepared Kick for the sight that confronted her now. His face and body were cadaverous. His skin had a yellowish tint, owing to a bout of malaria. He was in constant, wrenching pain, the consequence of a botched operation he had had that spring for a herniated disc. He was physically and psychologically traumatized—burdened, despite a Navy and Marine Corps medal and other honors and accolades that had been heaped upon him—with a sense of guilt about the crew members he had been unable to save. Kick embraced her brother. Then she dropped her head onto Jack's shoulder and wept.

Though old Joe encouraged his children to get on with their lives despite the family's great loss, he himself grieved deeply and passionately for his son, and often shut himself away in his room in despair. Kick's father could not seem to get over his feeling that young Joe had died in spite of all of the patriarch's efforts to avert this war, which, no less than it had in years past, still struck the elder Kennedy as pointless and misguided. Time and again he had implored London and Washington to find a way to come to terms with Hitler. But his efforts had been in vain, and he seemed to blame his eldest son's death on his own failures in the diplomatic arena. Rose, meanwhile, threw herself ever more deeply into her religious devotions, intent, as always, on numbing the pain.

Kick viewed herself as having come home to comfort her parents at a terrible time. Still, to Jack's eye, even in this mournful atmosphere Kick could not entirely suppress her "great happiness" as a newlywed. As Jack would later recall, Kick's immense pleasure in having recently married Billy "even shone through her sadness" about her brother's death. Kick's delight in her marriage and in all that the future held for her as Billy's wife "was so manifest and so infectious," Jack wrote, "that it did much to ease the grief of our mother and father."

Still, there could be no denying that Kick felt more strongly bonded to her new young husband than to the brother she had just lost. For, as she would later write in a different context, whereas Joe and Rose Kennedy had lost a part of themselves when young Joe died in the war, it was Billy—not her late brother—with whom Kick had felt as one.

In England, Kick had opened a breach between herself and the Cavendish family by her controversial decision to go back to the U.S. while her husband was still in jeopardy in France. In America, the intensity of her emotional connection with Billy inevitably distanced her from her parents, focused as they were on the death of young Joe.

Kick had carried with her to the U.S. Billy's July 26 letter from Giberville, in which he had bid her to face the possibility that he might not survive the war. For all of her outward air of happiness, there were times now, as her father told Eddy Devonshire, that she seemed "distraught," craving as she did some news of "Billy's hazards." Unfortunately, hardly had Kick gone back to America than the duke and duchess suddenly stopped receiving letters from their son. His silence greatly alarmed the duchess because, as she later said, "he was always so wonderful about writing and saving as much anxiety as he could." Presently, word of the August 20 death of Charlie Lansdowne, whose return from Italy Eddy Devonshire had been desperately trying to secure, caused immense sadness and further heightened concerns at Compton Place.

The Allies entered Paris four days later, sparking hopes that the war might soon be at an end. The news confronted Kick with a new decision about where her duty properly resided. If, as she suspected, the liberation of Paris meant that her husband was about to return home, she wanted to be at Compton Place to welcome him back. But she was also eager to stay in the U.S. as long as possible in hopes of repairing her relationship with her mother.

In the end, Kick chose to risk not being in England when Billy came home. Lest he appear in her absence, she'd asked Marie Bruce to explain her decision both to him and to his parents.

For all of Kick's efforts, however, her mother seemed never to recover fully from the shock and disappointment of her marriage. Early on, Billy's mother had written tenderly and understandingly to Rose, and had thereby perhaps embarrassed her into making at least a polite show of acceptance and approval. Now, however, Kick persisted in feeling, and at times rather resenting, what she took to be an element of censure in some of her mother's pointed looks and remarks. Particularly hurtful was the hint of regret in Rose's tone whenever she proposed that they attend Mass together. To Kick's perception, it was as if her mother were tacitly commenting on the fact that, though Kick was still allowed to go to Mass, she was no longer permitted to take Communion.

Kick spent the Labor Day weekend with Jack and a group of his naval buddies, whom he had invited up to the Cape. As far as he was concerned, these men—who would in effect constitute his new claque—seemed to understand him as no one in the civilian world appeared capable of doing. To Jack, they alone comprehended the ordeal that even now he persisted in endlessly replaying in memory in a futile effort to determine if there was anything he might have done differently. Jack's obsession with the two PT-109 crew members whom he had failed to save had driven him to further damage his own health when, in the wake of the episode, he had insisted on serving four months more in the Pacific in the belief that he might somehow avenge them, though in view of his condition he ought to have been sent to the U.S. immediately for medical treatment.

At Hyannis Port that September of 1944, there was much laughter and merriment when Jack and his naval buddies got together—sailing, golfing, tossing a football about. But there was also a palpable sense that, for Jack, a great deal remained excruciatingly unresolved.

At the very same time, quite the opposite was proving to be the case for Billy. The advance toward Brussels, one of the great advances of the Second World War, began at the end of August. The Guards Armored Division, after passing various landmarks familiar to British soldiers who had been there in 1940, made its triumphant entry into the Belgian capital on the third of September. Singing, cheering Belgians greeted the British with champagne and flowers, kisses and embraces, and words of gratitude that they chalked on the liberators' tanks. For the British in general, the taking of Brussels was a glorious moment, a reversal of past humiliations and a resumption of the noble project that had had to be set aside temporarily at the time of the Dunkirk evacuation.

But for those, like Billy, who had participated in the ill-fated Battle of Flanders, the entry into Belgium represented something at once larger and more personal. When Billy had returned to London four years before, he had confided his anguish to his cousin Jean. In bitter tones, he had spoken of his sense of guilt at having survived when so many others—not just fellow soldiers, but also innocent men, women, and children—had perished. Billy had often in the intervening years found himself living much more vividly and intensely in the war zone than in Britain, where he was in body, but not always in mind. At times during those years it had been as if he were living simply for the moment when he would go back and finish the fight and avenge all of those lives he had been powerless to save in 1940. That moment had come at last.

On September 4, the day after the liberation of Brussels, Billy wrote a long, lovely letter to Kick, who was then celebrating Labor Day with Jack and his naval buddies. She would not receive the letter until sometime later. Speaking of the euphoria of the past several days, Billy reversed—no doubt unconsciously—his despairing, long-ago statement to his cousin Jean on that terrible day after the fall of France, in 1940: "We ran and we ran!" Now, manifestly at peace in a way that he simply had not been in years, Billy wrote to Kick of the triumphs of the past six days: "We have advanced and advanced and advanced . . ."

He wrote of his sense of what a wretched time the Belgians had had under Nazi rule, and of their great loathing for their now vanquished German oppressors. He wrote of the tears of happiness and of the embraces with which he and the other British liberators had been greeted. He spoke of his never having suspected that the human race could be capable of such an outpouring of emotion, and of his sense of being somehow unworthy of all that gratitude, "living as I have in reasonable safety and comfort during these years while they have been suffering such terrible hardships under the Germans." He told his young wife of his belief, based on the German soldiers he had encountered of late, that the Nazis were quite "exhausted and demoralized" and were unlikely to be able to "go on much longer."

Billy did not have a chance to bask in the glory of the liberation of Brussels for long. The day after he wrote to Kick, Colonel Roddy Hill ordered the 5th Coldstream to resume its advance. He directed the battalion to head northward to the villages of Beverloo and Heppen, and then on to Bourg Leopold. On September 8, the British suffered heavy casualties as they fought in torrential rain to capture Beverloo, which had functioned during the German occupation as a training camp for the maniacal 12th SS Panzer Division Hitlerjugend. Billy had emerged by this time as an inspiring leader, standing atop a tank and directing the fire against German armor, with what appeared to be no concern whatever for his own safety. In the course of the attack, his sense of calm was on magnificent display. Though under constant fire from the enemy, he was observed at one point walking to one of his sections "as calmly as if he had been in the garden at Compton Place."

After the fall of Beverloo, where approximately one hundred SS troops and recruits were taken captive, the British moved on, with the objective of clearing Heppen of the Germans. Despite the perception in Billy's September 4 letter to Kick that the Germans were drained and demoralized, the SS fought furiously. As the day waned, Billy ruefully reflected that a quarter of his company had perished. He was the last officer alive and unwounded. The heavy losses sent a chill through the remaining men, who faced having to resume the assault against Heppen the next day.

By sunrise on September 9, the downpour had stopped. The sky had brightened considerably. But overnight, the German forces in Heppen had been reinforced by large numbers of troops brought over from Bourg Leopold.

Confronted with the need to rally and inspire the men of his company anew, Billy took a page from the technique of Colonel Roddy Hill, to whom he had handed over leadership of the 5th Coldstream at the close of Operation Bluecoat. At a moment when morale was low, Hill's incongruously impeccable attire and pointedly imperturbable manner conveyed to the troops that in spite of the hell they had just been through, everything was going to be "quite all right." On the morning of the ninth, Billy appeared before his men in a white mackintosh, though it was no longer raining. As an officer, he was not required to adhere to strict battle dress, so the white mac was a clear and emphatic sign of his status. That his costume, which also included pale corduroy trousers and a beret, threatened to mark him off as a target for German snipers was precisely the point. Thusly clad, Billy projected a sense of calm indifference. On the one hand, it was as if he were impervious to the dangers that lay ahead. On the other, it was almost as if he were trying to draw fire on himself and thereby to shield his men. Since his arrival in Normandy, Billy had seen fellow officers picked off all around him, so on the present occasion he had to know that the white mac placed him in mortal danger.

At a quarter to nine, the attack on Heppen began. No. 2 and 3 companies of the 5th Coldstream received orders to go, one to the left, the other to the right. They were to clear either side of the village of Germans, then join up afterward. Within about thirty minutes' time, No. 2 Company had reached its objective. But No. 3 Company, led by Major the Marquess of Hartington, had not been so lucky. Part of his company was pinned down by the concentrated fire of some fifteen machine guns wielded by members of the elite Hermann Göring Parachute Division.

As the German guns roared, Billy seemed to have made a decision. Telling the others to stay behind, he went on ahead to reconnoiter, accompanied only by his batman. Twenty-five-year-old Corporal Bill Garnham, who viewed the scene from a protected position behind one of the village dwellings, witnessed Billy's final moments. Conspicuous in his white mac and pale corduroys, Billy, standing out in the open, was ignoring the machine gun fire and urging the platoons on when he received a fatal shot to the head.

Garnham judged that he and two other soldiers who were with him behind the house were the only Guardsmen at the moment not to have been pinned down by the gunfire. He decided, therefore, that it was up to him to avenge the death of Lord Hartington. The trio entered the house and ascended to the top floor. From their perch, they spotted a German helmet, accompanied by a sniping rifle, some fifty yards in the distance. Garnham took a shot at the sniper, who disappeared for an instant, then suddenly popped back up like a jack-in-the-box. The frustrated Guardsman again targeted the sniper with his rifle. Again the helmet briefly dropped out of sight, then popped back into view. Garnham changed over to a Bren light machine gun, but to his distress the result of his third attempt to kill the sniper appeared to be the same. This went on for about an hour, at the close of which Garnham despaired that he must be "the world's worst shot." Only later, when the British at last overtook the German position, did Garnham discover his mistake. Far from having repeatedly missed his target, he had in fact slaughtered as many as forty-five Germans: Hardly would Garnham kill one Nazi when another would pop up to replace him.

Meanwhile, as the only platoon commander had been wounded, it devolved to Company Sergeant Major Jim Cowley to lead the company on, as the British soldiers systematically cleared the houses and their environs of Germans. Before moving on to Nijmegen, where they were due to support the 82nd U.S. Airborne Division, the battalion buried Major the Marquess of Hartington, along with several other Guardsmen who fell that day, beside a tiny chapel in Heppen.

Looking back on the fight that had cost Billy his life, Major General Sir Allan Adair, commander of the Guards Armored Division, would call the capture of Heppen "the key to the whole subsequent operations." Had the men who fought and in some cases died at Heppen not succeeded in extending the bridgehead to the west, "any subsequent advances would have been extremely difficult."

A telegram addressed to the Marchioness of Hartington arrived at Compton Place on the thirteenth. At that point, the Duke and Duchess of Devonshire had not heard from Billy in almost three weeks. In Kick's absence, they read the telegram notifying the widow of Major the Marquess of Hartington's death. There were as yet no details, but at length the duke was able to learn that his son had been killed in the fighting after his battalion went through Brussels.

There was no mention of the eyewitness account of Billy's having been shot through the head. The story related to the duke and duchess was that a bullet had pierced their son through the heart. His anguished mother declared it a great weight off her mind that he had at least died instantly and had not had to suffer. Moucher Devonshire wasted no time sharing the news with Kick. She drafted an emotional letter to her daughter-in-law, informing Kick of what had happened and assuring her that she would always be cherished by her late husband's family.

"I want you never, never to forget what complete happiness you gave him," the duchess wrote to Kick. "All your life you must think that you brought complete happiness to one person. He wrote that to me when he went to the front. I want you to know this for I know what great conscientious struggles you went through before you married Billy, but I know that it will be a source of infinite consolation to you now that you decided as you did. All your life I shall love you—not only for yourself but that you gave such perfect happiness to my son whom I loved above anything in the world." The duke and duchess also sent off a cable to Kick about what had happened to Billy, but for some reason it failed to reach her.

Three days later, Kick was in New York shopping for clothes for herself and for gifts to take back with her to England at the end of the month. She was in the Bonwit Teller department store when her sister Eunice suddenly materialized, bidding her to come at once to their father's suite at the Waldorf Towers. When she arrived there, the father whose assistance she had so often sought in her dogged efforts to get back to Billy and later to find some way to marry him told her that her young husband was dead. He had gotten the news at the Waldorf, before any of the messages from the duke and duchess reached Kick. For a full week, she had gone on with her life unaware that her husband had fallen.

Kick's immediate reaction, she would later say, was to feel "numb." That evening she accompanied her family to dinner at the restaurant Le Pavillon where in typical Kennedy fashion, Billy was barely if at all mentioned. As they had done following the death of their eldest brother, Eunice and the others carried on cheerfully as though the tragedy had not really occurred.

Rose Kennedy promptly threw herself into prayers and Masses for her daughter's late husband. To Kick's mounting distress, however, there was an undertone in her mother's actions and attitude, as if Rose felt that Billy's death was punishment for the apostasy of their marriage, and even that his demise provided a chance for his widow to get right with the Catholic Church again. Rose was very soon urging Kick that the time had come "to dry our tears," though Rose's tears had yet to flow in the first place.

Kick's father also seemed to have perceived an opportunity in the tragedy. Joe Kennedy pointed out, as Kick later paraphrased it, that as it was she had had "a lot of problems that might never have been worked out and that perhaps later in life [she] might have been very unhappy." At least, the old man suggested, this new turn of events may have spared her that future discontent.

Kick initially found herself hoping against hope that the news about Billy might yet prove to have been wrong. So much of her relationship with Billy had taken place in the imagination. They had often been separated by world events and by the actions of their respective families. Through it all Kick had refused to give up on what she wanted, refused to stop pounding, and in the end she had made her way back to England and she and Billy had indeed become husband and wife. Now, in spite of what her father or anyone else told her, she found it hard to believe that she would never see Billy again. Eager to discover that there had indeed been some mistake, she reached out to Richard Wood's father at the British Embassy in Washington. It fell to Lord Halifax to inform her that the War Office in London had officially confirmed the terrible news. So there it was.

Still, by her own later account, the "realization" of Billy's death had yet to fully come to her. The great agony she would soon suffer had yet really to begin. On the telephone with Lord Halifax, Kick seemed, as noted in the British ambassador's diary, "very good and brave."

Now again, just as Kick had hesitated at the time of the death of her brother about where in light of events she belonged, whether in England or in America, vexing questions of duty and personal identity presented themselves. Initially it seemed as if she might stay with her parents and siblings at Hyannis Port. Before long, however, she had decided to return to England to be with Billy's mother, father, and sisters.

After days of holding her emotions in check in the prescribed Kennedy manner, did she long to fully pour out her grief in the company of people who would not be put off by tears? Whatever Kick's motives, Lord Halifax promptly arranged for her to fly back to England on an aircraft carrying Field Marshal Alan Brooke, chief of the Imperial General Staff, and Air Marshal Charles Portal, chief the British air staff. They had been in Quebec, where, hosted by Canadian prime minister Mackenzie King, Winston Churchill and Franklin Roosevelt had been meeting to confer about the final phase of the war.

So once again, as she had done a month earlier, Kick packed her things—including Billy's letter of July 26, 1944—and prepared to fly across the ocean, this time in the opposite direction. Arriving in Quebec City on the nineteenth of September, she was due to stay the night at the Château Frontenac, where the British chiefs of staff also had rooms. The plane, which was to carry but seven passengers including herself, was scheduled to leave early the next morning.

As she waited to return to England, she took out her diary and wrote: "So ends the story of Billy and Kick . . . I can't believe that the one thing I felt might happen should have happened—Billy is dead— . . . Life is so cruel— . . . Writing is impossible."

Also in Quebec City, she found herself rereading the letter that Billy had written to her from Giberville in the aftermath of Operation Goodwood, in which he had bidden her to face the possibility that this time, in contrast to other partings in their past, they might not be reunited after all. When she first read that letter—before the Bakewell Fair and before the tragic news about Joe and then Billy—she had focused on Billy's talk of death.

Now, it was another element of the letter that drew her attention: her late husband's "orders" as to what he would wish her to do should he indeed fail to return from the war zone. Billy wrote: "I'll just say that if anything should happen to me I shall be wanting you to try to isolate our life together, to face its finish, and to start a new one as soon as you feel you can. I hope that you will marry again, quite soon—someone good & nice."

Kick copied out Billy's words in a letter to her parents written from the Château Frontenac, adding pointedly and poignantly: "I like to think about what he said and though it makes me sad to write this I just want you both to know what B's orders were."

Ten

E ddy Devonshire was waiting for Kick when the special train from Poole Harbour arrived in London at about half past two in the afternoon on Friday, September 22, 1944.

As soon as Lord Halifax had arranged for her to travel back to England, word had been sent to the Duke of Devonshire that she would soon be en route. In the course of the flight from Quebec City, the Air Ministry kept the duke apprised of the aircraft's progress. So when a blinding mist caused the plane to alter course, landing initially at Plymouth rather than at the planned destination, Poole Harbour, the duke had been promptly notified. At Plymouth, Kick and the British chiefs of staff lingered over breakfast at the RAF mess until word arrived that the weather had cleared. Presently, they flew to Poole Harbour, where their special train awaited.

The duke wanted there to be no chance that he would fail to be there when his widowed daughter-in-law stepped off the train. In anticipation that Kick might be tearful and in need of physical comforting, he had arranged for Mrs. Bruce to accompany him. Two weeks after the death of his son and heir, the duke remained absolutely devastated. And, though of course no one knew it at the time, his state of despair was to persist for the rest of his life. He would long drink to excess, and he would chop wood in an obsessive fashion in hopes of lessening his anguish. When, in 1950, Eddy Devonshire died of a massive heart attack, a photograph of Billy would be discovered in the lid of the Russian silver cigarette box that the duke kept in his coat pocket. It was the photograph that Jean Lloyd had taken with her Brownie box camera on a sunny spring morning in her garden in Yorkshire, showing Kick and Billy in what was for the latter a moment of perfect satisfaction, as both his marriage and his return to the battlefield were finally guaranteed.

The grieving father who collected Kick at the train station and brought her back to his suite at the Mayfair Hotel to be reunited with other family members bore no trace of his former negativity about her. Nor did there seem to be any residue of the bad feeling that had previously existed about Kick's decision to fly back to the Kennedys in the U.S. when the duke and duchess perceived that her proper place was with her husband's family. For the duke and duchess, from this point on Kick served as a living reminder of their beloved son and heir, whose remains, to their further anguish, had been buried not in the graveyard at Chatsworth, but rather in Belgium, beside the graves of other Guardsmen. As Moucher Devonshire, speaking of herself and her husband, would later tell Rose Kennedy, Kick had the miraculous capacity "to bring Billy back to us more than anyone else can."

The duke and duchess's firstborn had come so close to dying in infancy that it had always somehow struck them as a miracle that he had survived. Then, in 1940, they had again feared that he was lost to them, only to again be given the gift of his return. In 1944, however, there had been no miracle, no gift of good news; and it struck Debo, who was at the Mayfair with the other family members when the duke came in with Kick, that Eddy and Moucher's hopes for the future had "died" with the loss of Billy. Both parents loved Andrew, of course, but, quite simply, the second son was not to them as Billy had been.

Debo had been visiting with Diana Mosley and her husband when she learned of Billy's death, and she had gone at once to Compton Place to be with the duke and duchess and their daughters. When she and Kick faced one another on September 22, 1944, a mere month had passed since they had stood on either side of Billy and Andrew's paternal grandmother, Duchess Evie, at the Bakewell Fair. That August day, both young Cavendish wives had been content and seemingly settled about their respective futures. Despite Andrew's lifelong jealousy of his brother, Debo had been very pleased indeed with the prospect of being the wife of a publisher and politician, a man who adored her beyond measure. A month later, Debo's life had been instantly upended by Billy's death, and by Andrew's ascendency to the long-coveted position of heir to the dukedom.

For Debo, all of this was immensely complicated by the fact that she was personally so fond of Kick, and well aware of the excitement with which both Billy and her sister-in-law had been looking forward to their future roles and responsibilities. Suddenly, it seemed, Debo was to have the life that would have been Kick's, had not fate intervened. The abrupt shift in the two young women's respective fortunes was responsible for a certain undertone of awkwardness at the time of their reunion. Nothing was said of course, but the tension was palpable.

At least as Debo would remember it, however, it all took the form of but a vague awareness on her part, for her focus at the moment was on her fears for Andrew's safety on the Italian Front. In light of Billy's death, she had asked Duke Eddy whether something might yet be done to bring Andrew home at once. But her father-in-law had replied that, having failed in his efforts to save Charlie Lansdowne, he had no hope of getting Andrew home until the war was at an end. Nancy Mitford, who saw Debo in London during this visit, thought that her sister seemed "distracted" by her concerns for her husband; and as Debo would recall many years later, indeed she had been. Not for nothing, Debo had dubbed this summer of 1944 "the summer of death." The recent deaths of Ned Fitzmaurice and Charlie Lansdowne had been almost more than she could bear. Even as she grieved for Ned and Charlie, she found herself thinking about what their deaths might foretell with regard to another set of aristocratic brothers. Would Andrew fall soon after his brother, as Charlie Lansdowne had been killed soon after his? Would the dreaded telegram arrive addressed to Debo, as previously it had come for Kick?

Of the Cavendish sisters-in-law, Kick at this point seems to have perceived the more sharply the profound alteration in their respective circumstances. Quite apart from anything to do with love, her relationship with Billy had also long been about matters of identity, ambition, and power. By 1944, she had become as never before, in Richard Wood's phrase, "very clear about what she wanted." Now, all that had fallen away from her. Now, it was Debo, not Kick, who would one day be duchess—and whose son would one day be a duke. What, then, would Kick's role be? She suddenly had no idea.

When she wrote to her parents and siblings from Compton Place soon after she returned to England, she highlighted her lost sense of identity and purpose. Prior to Billy's death, she wrote, her life had "had its purpose. I knew what it would be. Now I feel like a small cork that is tossing around." In a similar vein, she would later write to her brother Jack: "It just seems that the pattern of life for me has been destroyed. At the moment I don't fit into any design."

And there was worse: In America her young husband's death had had an air almost of unreality. At Compton Place—where she and Billy had had their honeymoon less than five months before—everything served as a trigger of memories that were at once painful and bittersweet. "The realization of Billy's death has come to me very acutely here," she wrote that first full day at Compton Place, "and I should probably have spared myself a great deal of agony if I had remained in America . . . now that I am here . . . every thing reminds me of him so much."

In New York and Hyannis Port, she had done what she could to hold her emotions in check, to mourn, as it were, in the traditional Kennedy manner. At Compton Place, by contrast, her feelings—often provoked by the countless reminders—poured out in an unstoppable torrent. Years later, Billy's sister Elizabeth would reflect that she had never in her life seen anything quite like Kick's wrenching grief. It was so overwhelming that, the duke and duchess agreed, the young widow could not possibly be left alone in her room at night. Elizabeth, the shy girl whose evening dress Ned Fitzmaurice had accidentally set afire at the November 13, 1943, party—a party that now seemed less an evocation of prewar frivolity and ease than an adumbration of the tragedy to come—had herself just lost a beloved brother. Nonetheless, with her mother's encouragement, the eighteen-year-old instantly accepted the role of devoted consoler and protector of that brother's widow. Elizabeth volunteered to sleep on the floor beside Kick's bed each night. If Kick screamed out in her sleep, or if she just needed someone to talk to, Billy's sister was determined to be there to comfort her.

On September 26, just four days after her arrival in Britain, Kick attended a Catholic Mass for Billy and young Joe, and she received Communion for the first time since her marriage. But if Kick had hoped that her Church-sanctioned return to the Communion railing would provide some solace, as religious ritual had long seemed to do for her mother, it soon became apparent that this was not to be the case—at least not now. Far from being comforted by the Catholic Church's renewed embrace, the widow reacted with slow-burning resentment to what she took to be the Church's abiding message that her marriage to Billy had been wrong. The very idea remained anathema to her.

Her mother's view, implicit in much that Rose Kennedy did and said, that Kick's relationship with Billy had indeed been sinful and that in some strange way Billy's death had been a punishment for the couple's transgressions, would contribute to a painful breach between mother and daughter that was never to be healed. The contrast between Rose's response to Kick's loss and that of Billy's mother and sisters was another

factor in Kick's increasingly fraught relations with the Kennedy matriarch. Jack Kennedy would long complain of his mother's failure, when
he was a boy, to hold him, to touch him, to give him the physical affection a child craves and requires. Kick, who early on had assumed the
lonely role of their mother's protector and defender in the family, now
found herself to be in uneasy agreement with Jack about Rose's short-
comings as a parent. In the company of the duchess, Elizabeth, and Anne,
Kick discovered, and thrived on, the emotional and physical comfort that
had been denied her in Hyannis Port. Literally as well as figuratively,
Billy's mother and sisters embraced Kick as her own mother simply had
failed to do.

There was to be a memorial service for Billy at Chatsworth on Saturday, the thirtieth of September, and Kick worried that the occasion
would only exacerbate her great sadness. The golden palace had played
such an important part in her and Billy's dreams for the future. Now it
called to mind all that was gone. For Billy's family as well, the day proved
to be extremely painful. The last major family event there before the
duke and duchess had decamped to Churchdale Hall had been Billy's
coming-of-age celebration in August of 1939. Rose Kennedy had pre-
vented Kick from attending that party, but Billy's parents and sisters each
had highly emotional memories of the day, memories that made their
return for his memorial service all the more difficult. Eddy Devonshire
perhaps suffered the most, so much so that he made a point of vowing
never to set foot in Chatsworth again. The service took place in the
church in Edensor, beside which stood the cemetery in which Billy's
mother would very much have preferred that her son be laid to rest with
other family members, had wartime conditions not precluded the return
of his remains.

For Kick, the day proved to be all that she had feared, and at intervals the tears poured down her cheeks. To make matters worse, on this
and other occasions when she encountered individuals from outside the
duke and duchess's immediate family circle, she had to endure the stares

and speculation of people who, well disposed to her though they might be, were inevitably curious about whether Billy's widow might yet produce an heir.

The question of Lady Hartington's possible pregnancy was then on many lips. Kick had been in the U.S. since the middle of August. Conceivably, at the time of her departure from Britain after her brother's death she might have been pregnant, if not yet visibly so. If there were to be a child, and if that child were to be a son, then he, not Andrew, would eventually inherit the dukedom and all that came with it. Meanwhile, in the absence of such a child, Andrew would officially become Marquess of Hartington and Debo the marchioness one year after Billy's death. Kick, known as the Dowager Marchioness of Hartington, or as Kathleen, Marchioness of Hartington, would also be called Lady Hartington; but so, under the circumstances, would Debo.

The duke and duchess, along with others who saw Kick every day at Compton Place, were aware by this point that she was not pregnant. But the world did not yet share that knowledge, and the sense that people were constantly watching and wondering was very grievous to Kick. Her close friends perceived that all the speculation upset her the more acutely because she was already distressed about her failure to have become pregnant, when so many other brides had succeeded in doing precisely that before their young husbands had had to go off to war. In separate conversations with Jean Lloyd and Fiona Gore, Kick gave the same anguished account of her less than ideal wedding night. She talked of Billy's inexperience and ineptitude that first night, and she insisted that in the end they had indeed been very happy together. Kick assured Jean and Fiona—and, to both women's perception, seemed to be reassuring herself—that had he come home after the war, there would have been plenty of children.

Briefly, there was some talk of Kick's going to Paris to help establish the Red Cross's Allied Services organization. The duchess, much as she and the duke thrived on having Kick with them, encouraged her to go over to the newly liberated city for a week to ten days. Moucher reasoned that the work would help distract Kick from morbid reflections upon her husband's death. But when it turned out that the Red Cross would require a commitment on her part to remain for at least a month, Kick said it would be impossible. She told Jack that even when she was with people she liked and knew well, before long "I just start thinking and it's no good. I'm much better down here just with the family." Strangers, no matter how solicitous, were beyond her just then. Nor had she been at all pleased by the outpouring of public sympathy for Billy's widow. Kick bristled at what she sardonically described as "the pathetic little articles about poor Lady Hartington" that she kept seeing in the pages of the British press.

For the time being, she seemed happiest poring over letters from people who had known Billy, and listening to the testimony of friends, family members, military colleagues, and the like, who might have something new and interesting to tell her about him. For the fact increasingly presented itself that, though he had been her husband, she was now living among individuals who in certain respects had known him far better than she.

During their prolonged separation, when she had been in the U.S. and he in Britain, Kick had depended on various London correspondents to report to her on aspects of Billy's life. What country house weekend had he attended? With whom had he been seen? And now again, in quest of information to which she would otherwise have had no access, she read and reread the letters that poured in about him. She was especially drawn to the testimony of those who had recently observed her husband in action in France and Belgium. The warrior and leader whose exploits they admiringly chronicled seemed somehow so very different from the "Billy" whom Kick had known. On both sides there had been a great deal of "playacting" in Kick's relations with Billy since her return from the U.S. in 1943. Billy had welcomed the opportunity to recapture with Kick something of the innocence that he had otherwise forever lost in Flanders. But there was no trace of any such innocence in the accounts of Major the Marquess of Hartington's war service that came to her now in such welcome abundance. Kick was treated to detailed descriptions of his coolly stepping in to replace Mark Howard when the latter fell in the course of Operation Epsom; of his adroit leadership during Operation Bluecoat; and of the valor during the Battle of Heppen that had cost him his life. By degrees, the widow began to understand that the identity of her young husband had been, and remained, something of a mystery to her. Hence the compulsive reading of the letters and the questioning of his fellow Guardsmen about the man Billy had at last become. The question consumed her: Who had Billy been when he died?

Compton Place, during these weeks, was filled not just with grief, but also with uncertainty about the future. Kick was hardly alone in her perplexity as to what tomorrow might hold. Billy's parents and sisters, and of course Debo as well, were dealing with uncertainty of a different kind. All were frantic about the danger to Andrew so long as he remained in Italy. For Debo and the girls, the anxiety was of a strictly personal sort. For the duke and duchess, and in particular for the former, the acute concern also had to do with the fate of the Devonshire dukedom. It was now certain that, as she had failed to produce a son of her own, Kick would soon find herself displaced. When Eddy Devonshire died, the title and all that went with it would go to Andrew—if, that is, Andrew managed to survive the war. Some people familiar with Andrew's service record with the 3rd Battalion Coldstream Guards considered that it was well nigh a miracle he had not been killed already.

Known affectionately to the soldiers under his command as "the Mad Lord," Captain Lord Andrew Cavendish had made it his firm policy to, whenever possible, risk his own life rather than the lives of his men. Andrew's brigade commander, Archer Clive, likened him in this respect to "a mother hen," so zealous had Andrew been about the safety and well-being of his men. The soldiers of Andrew's company were absolutely devoted to him as a consequence, and his superiors were much impressed with him both as a leader and as a man. Indeed, by this time he had already participated in the siege that would result in his being promoted to major and earn him the Military Cross—and, though no one yet suspected it, his family least of all, leave him traumatized for life.

On July 27, 1944, Andrew's company had been in the midst of an arduous ten-week march to Florence, a journey that had been made the more difficult by steep hills and nearly daily combat. On this particular day, Andrew had directed Sergeant John King to remain in the trench south of Strada while Andrew went over the ridge, some hundred yards in the distance, to personally reconnoiter for enemy troops. Andrew assumed that it was he himself he was exposing to danger by this order, not Sergeant King. But when he returned shortly thereafter, he discovered that Sergeant King had been blown to bits in the heavy shell fire that had begun during Andrew's absence.

The shelling, meanwhile, had thrown his weary troops into much confusion, several of the Guardsmen having been wounded almost all at once. He rallied his men and kept them going through thirty-six hours of continuous shelling, in punishing heat without food or water, until the company was at last relieved. Major Lord Andrew Cavendish was awarded the Military Cross for his leadership in the course of the ordeal. But that high honor meant little to him, for, like Jack Kennedy after the PT-109 episode, Andrew, racked with survivor's guilt, focused not on his magnificent accomplishment, but rather on his failure. He had told Sergeant King to remain in the trench, and as far as Andrew was concerned he was therefore responsible for the man's death. That Andrew had gone on, that same day, to save other men's lives struck him almost as beside the point. The memory of his role in Sergeant King's death would, in his phrase, forever "nag away" at him.

In September of 1944, Andrew and his company had just participated in the successful capture of Montecatini Alto, a village in the hills overlooking the famous Montecatini spa, when he learned of his brother's death. Debo worried that the news about Billy would cause Andrew to go "right under." She told Lady Redesdale that she feared writing to him, not knowing "what to say or how to say it." Debo was acutely aware of how sensitive Andrew was, and she suspected that his always fraught

relationship with his brother would almost certainly complicate his reaction now.

Andrew's September 22, 1944, letter to Debo therefore came as an
immense relief. It was warm, reassuring, and full of solicitude for her
and her situation at home. Andrew would later say that he had not
immediately dwelled on the prospect of inheriting the dukedom, especially since for all he knew, Kick might be pregnant. In his letter to
Debo, however, he did speak of the changes that suddenly confronted
them, and of his confidence that somehow she would make it all work
for him. "Darling, I suppose our life is going to be very different to what
we had planned. But I know that whatever life has in store, with you
beside me life has no fears." To his wife, Andrew's reference to the Military Cross with which he had recently been decorated as "most un-
deserved" seemed at the time to reflect the becoming modesty that had
long been among his most salient characteristics. In retrospect, however, Debo would have occasion to wonder whether the remark might
not also have been a hint of the terrible troubles that were to come when
Andrew—"a changed man"—returned to civilian life.

The duke's new heir had yet to come home when, late in 1944, Anne
Hunloke, Eddy Devonshire's sister, proposed the idea of taking Kick to
live with her in a borrowed flat in London's Westminster Gardens, where
a number of Conservative politicians, including Lord Cranborne, James
Stuart, and Duncan Sandys, maintained residences. Kick, when she felt
ready, would be able to return to work at the Red Cross. The duke and
duchess were themselves often in London in conjunction with their duties as Under-Secretary of State for the Colonies and director of hospitality for the Dominion soldiers, respectively. As a consequence, Billy's
parents would continue to spend a good deal of time with Kick during
the week, then take her back with them to Eastbourne on weekends.
Kick agreed to see if the arrangement might work.

First, however, Kick went off to Shropshire to spend five days as the
only "civilian" in a community of twenty Scared Heart nuns in an Elizabethan house in the Lake District known as Levens Hall. She devoted

her sojourn there to consciously seeking a way to come to terms with Billy's death, but it soon became evident that her efforts were in vain. "Now it has been four months," Kick wrote to her parents and siblings from the convent, "and although one fits back into an everyday existence it still somehow doesn't seem right. Rather like an awful dream." It galled her when fellow Catholics persisted in the claim that she had never really been married to Billy and that her union with him had been sinful. On her return to Compton Place, where she was to pack her things in anticipation of moving to London, it was Kick herself who brought up the fraught subject of the Catholic Church's ongoing disapproval of her registry office marriage. In conversation with the duchess's seventy-five-year-old uncle, Lord Hugh Cecil, known as Linky, who had come for a visit, Kick noted that in the eyes of her church she and Billy had been "living in sin." The pale, stoop-shouldered old man replied, "But so many of one's friends are nowadays." Distressed that the Anglican uncle seemed to concur with the Catholics that she and Billy had sinned, she was quick to retaliate. She repeated a story she had heard at Levens Hall to the effect that King Edward VII when he was on his deathbed had converted to Catholicism. To her delight, the assertion, so shocking to Protestant ears, caused Linky Cecil and others present almost to "jump out of their skins."

On the eve of the big move to her new flat, Kick, in a letter to the Kennedys, insisted that she was feeling much better overall. When she reached London, however, she found it difficult at first to go out in public. Even a mundane trip to the store was capable of inciting the widow's emotions and sensitivities. "I don't like to go into shops," Kick told Jean Lloyd, who saw her frequently during this period, "because I feel people are looking at me, wondering how I'm taking it." Kick as yet had no concrete plan for the future, and she could not really say why she had decided to remain in London for now even though her parents, especially her father, saw no reason why she resisted coming home at once. But where exactly was home? Kick confided to Jean that she was no longer sure of quite where she belonged.

Kick resumed work at the Red Cross, though this time in a less demanding capacity, supervising the entertainment programs at the nurses' club. After the glittering future that had seemed to open up before her when she married Billy, sharing a flat with a roommate and working at a job felt like a throwback to the life she had once had in Washington.

The duchess encouraged her to continue to make appearances and give speeches in Derbyshire as the representative of Billy and his family. Moucher maintained that because the people there persisted in their great admiration for Billy, they would be very eager indeed to see and hear his widow. Accordingly, on March 8, Kick went to Derbyshire to speak at the Women's Institute. Introduced by the mayor, she delighted the audience with her remarks on the theme "The American Housewife in Wartime." By the end of Kick's presentation, which emphasized all that women are capable of, listeners were calling out, "Give the English country housewife the recognition she deserves! More freedom for women!" Coming as it did in a locale whose mayor privately acknowledged, "We have always considered our women chattel," the audience's passionate response was very pleasing to Kick. Moreover, it amused her to consider what her traditionally minded late husband would have thought had he heard her urge female audience members on "to bigger and better things."

But Kick's success that day was also a cause for sober reflection on her part. The proceedings inevitably reminded her of her comparable triumph at the Bakewell Fair, at a time when, unlike at present, so much had seemed possible for her personally. In August of 1944, enthusiastic reports on her performance from both the duke's longtime political agent and his mother the Dowager Duchess of Devonshire had led Eddy Devonshire to exult that if Billy proved incapable of winning back the traditional family seat in Parliament, Kick could be counted on to "win it for him." Five months later, Kick clearly retained the ability—but with Andrew set to be duke someday, what at this point was all that ability of hers for? What "bigger and better things," if any, were there in store for Kick?

The duke and duchess, meanwhile, had commissioned the painter Oswald Birley, noted for his royal portraits, to produce a portrait of Billy. Kick took an interest in the gestation of the artwork, which was based largely on photographs of her late husband. The contours of Billy's face, the delicacy of his fingers and hands, the personality exuded by his characteristic half smile—all these Birley was confident he could glean from the photographic evidence. What he despaired of capturing, however, were the precise tones of the young man's skin. He therefore recruited Billy's seventeen-year-old-sister, Anne, who patiently sat for the artist. When Kick visited Birley's studio, on March 16, 1945, the sight of the as yet unfinished canvas, which showed Major the Marquess of Hartington locking eyes, as it were, with the spectator, caused his widow to explode once more in tears.

Three days after Kick's emotions had surged in this manner in the portraitist's atelier, she learned that Andrew was back from the Italian Front. The news was entirely unexpected, as Andrew had not been due to return with his battalion until later that month at the earliest. Duke Eddy, who had been in Burma to inspect the Colonial troops, had stopped off in Italy on his way home; and at the last minute Harold Macmillan had arranged for Andrew to fly to Britain with his father.

On Monday, March 19, 1945, Kick was among the family members to be reunited with Andrew in London. She expressed joy at seeing him; and in fact she was delighted that Andrew had come home alive. Still, seven years after Kick had first beheld Andrew on the staircase at Cliveden, she found that she was pained by the very sight of the second son. As far as the widow was concerned, Andrew's homecoming provided a sense of finality to her plight. "It nearly kills me to see him," Kick wrote afterward in a letter to the Kennedys, "not that he is really at all like Billy, but the whole idea of seeing Andy makes Billy's absence so much more noticeable."

To Kick's eye, Andrew, like Duke Eddy, who had brought him home, was "in terrific spirits." Andrew had not seen his adored wife since he embarked with the 3rd Battalion in November of 1943. His daughter,

Emma, had been a baby when he left. He had never yet beheld his son and heir, Peregrine, who had been born while Andrew was fighting abroad. And, though Billy had always been their mother's favorite, Andrew positively worshipped Moucher and was thrilled to fall into her arms again. Apart from his feelings for individual family members, Andrew was palpably pleased by the love that they showered upon him collectively, and by their happiness and gratitude that he had survived.

Still, Kick's sense of the surviving Cavendish brother's mood was only part of the story. At that moment, Andrew and Debo seemed to have everything, but the truth was a good deal more complicated. By Andrew's own account, happy though he was to have been reunited with his family, he felt somehow that he did not belong in this scene, that the people he really belonged with were his fellow Coldstream Guardsmen. He felt more comfortable with the men of his battalion than with anyone else, even his own family. Rejoicing as he did in his parents' immense pleasure at his safe return, Andrew strove to hide from them that much of the time his thoughts were unavoidably elsewhere—on his men, on the battles they had fought and were fighting, and above all on one soldier, Sergeant King, for whose death he continued, however irrationally, to hold himself responsible. Though Andrew was gratified that the duke and duchess were exceedingly pleased about the Military Cross with which he had been decorated, he persisted in the belief that in fact he deserved no such honor.

He felt guilty about the soldiers who were still fighting. He was ashamed to have been allowed to return to Britain with his father, ahead of his own battalion. And he was tortured by his superiors' decision to separate him from his men shortly before they reached Bologna, and to send him to a training camp in Italy where he would be out of danger for the duration—an arrangement for which he would later blame Harold Macmillan, who, acting in his capacity as minister resident, had been seeking to assuage the fears of Moucher Devonshire that her only surviving son might be killed. Andrew had been returned to his battalion in advance of its scheduled trip home, and he would never forget the sense of mortification he had experienced upon being reunited with the men he had once commanded, and the reluctance he had felt to so much as look them in the eye.

Though Andrew had long coveted Billy's position as heir to the dukedom, it pained him now to be called upon to take his fallen brother's place. Andrew was tormented by a feeling that the good things he stood to inherit one day—the title, the palace, the riches—ought to have been his brother's, and that for the rest of his life he would be acting, in his phrase, "by proxy." As he would recall many years later, seeing Kick that first day, he could not help but feel that he and Debo were about to inhabit a life that should have been been hers and Billy's.

And there was worse. Billy had always been their parents' favorite, and the second son would long be deeply unsettled by the conviction that his mother and father would have far preferred that it had been Billy who came home alive, not he. According to Andrew's sister Anne, whenever, then and later, the duke was in the presence of the second son he strove to conceal the magnitude of his grief for Billy, lest Andrew perceive himself to be less valued than his brother.

But that first day, Andrew, rather than spoil the occasion for the others, endeavored to mask and suppress the tumult of his emotions in much the same way, and for the same reasons, Kick did what she could to hide hers. She evoked her duality of mind in a letter to Jack. "Am pleased but rather agonized," she told her brother. "Seeing Andrew and all the others come home."

Since the move to Westminster Gardens, Kick, encouraged by the duke and duchess, had made it her custom to accompany Billy's family to Eastbourne at the end of her workweek. But that first weekend following Andrew's return, she chose to steer clear of it, on the explanation that she had things to do around the flat. In the weeks that followed, the duchess attributed Kick's reluctance to come to Compton Place to the fact that during March and April of the previous year Kick had spent a great deal of time there with Billy, and that as a consequence the house was "too closely connected" with him in her thoughts for her to be happy there just now.

What the duchess did not say—though Kick made it abundantly clear in her letters to her family in the U.S.—was that the presence of the second son was a no less formidable obstacle. Kick needed time to get used to seeing Andrew again and to grapple with all that his homecoming meant for her. Meanwhile, she did spend Easter with Billy's family at Compton Place, but the holiday was marred by the arrival of a telegram from the editor of *The Boston Globe* inquiring as to whether or not Kick was going to have a baby. The American newspaper's query bore directly on Andrew and Debo's prospects, of course. The telegram infuriated Kick, and otherwise provoked a good deal of embarrassment and upset all around.

If March and April had been heartbreaking for Kick, the beginning of May brought with it, in Moucher Devonshire's phrase, "the agony of her wedding anniversary." In flight from the painful memories that the sixth of May threatened to unseal, Kick spent the day as the guest of Virginia Sykes, at Sledmere. Perhaps because Billy had disliked Sledmere and the raffish set with which Lord and Lady Sykes customarily surrounded themselves there, it would be easier for Kick not to think of him and of what this day had meant to her just twelve months before.

According to the duchess, the timing of Kick's return to London on Monday, May 7, proved to be most unfortunate. Kick arrived at Westminster Gardens to find the city in jubilation over word of the Nazis' surrender. As the evening progressed, raucous festivities erupted in the streets below in anticipation of Victory in Europe Day, which was to be celebrated on the morrow. Kick had previously acknowledged that the fact that the European war seemed to be drawing to a close left her feeling somehow "rather cold." Now that Germany had indeed been vanquished, Billy's widow discovered that she was oddly ambivalent. On the one hand, she was "as thankful as any" for the Allied victory. On the other hand, she was not a little resentful about Billy's death, when so many other women's husbands had the good fortune to be coming home. As it happened, only one other young woman in her immediate circle—Hugh Fraser's sister Veronica—had lost her husband. Kick was pleased, of course, that Jean, Sissie, Debo, and the rest had their husbands back. At the same time, she found herself feeling terribly isolated and uncomfortable amidst the continuous rejoicing of friends.

Coming as it did but two days after her wedding anniversary, the mood of mass celebration that dominated London on V-E Day exacerbated Kick's painful sense of solitude. In the company of friends, she made a show of participating in the revelry. Bells tolled, fireworks exploded, bonfires blazed, and celebrants sang and danced in the streets. With Hugh Fraser and Sissie and David Ormsby-Gore, Kick stood amidst a crowd of as many as one hundred thousand cheering, screaming people in front of Buckingham Palace as King George and Queen Elizabeth emerged onto a gold-and-purple-draped balcony.

Churchill, in his victory broadcast earlier in the day, had made a particular point of reminding Britons that, while Germany had at last surrendered, the Japanese remained to be defeated. Still, there was a prevailing sense in the streets that the war was at last at an end, the postwar future about to begin. In her own case, Kick as yet had no real sense of what that future might comprise. The surge and roar of the crowds that evening seemed only to make her feel her own uncertainty and distress the more sharply.

The following evening, Kick dined alone with Billy's mother. These days, Kick and the duchess made it their habit to see one another in London, because, as the older woman understood, the memories that Compton Place held for the younger woman were still too painful and intense. The duchess anticipated that Kick would resume her regular visits to the family residence in Eastbourne sometime after June, when, Billy having by then gone abroad the previous year, it would simply be "easier" for her emotionally. In the wake of the sadness that the duchess knew the V-E Day celebrations to have caused her daughter-in-law, she made it clear to her that the time had come to face life "without the best ones," by which she meant Billy, of course. In the war years, people had had to live in "a state of flux," but now it would be necessary to "settle down & make definite plans."

But, for all of the duchess's sincere love for her daughter-in-law, and for all of the desperately needed tenderness and understanding that she provided, what exactly was on offer to Kick at this point? With the best will in the world, Billy's mother had endeavored, in her daughter Anne's phrase, to amalgamate his widow into the family and to make it her family. In all of this, the duchess was nothing if not kind. But was Kick likely to be satisfied for long with a new, all-enveloping family identity?

On the eve of the Second World War, Billy's mother had taken up Kick because she possessed the prodigious energy and vitality that would be needed to reinvigorate the stock. In 1945, was it realistic to expect that all of that energy could possibly be contained by a dowager's duties, however brilliantly performed, in representing her late husband and his family in nostalgic speeches and other public appearances?

At twenty-five years of age, was Kick likely to be content emulating that other noted dowager in the family, Billy's seventy-five-year-old paternal grandmother, Duchess Evie?

Eleven

ick begged her brother Jack for advice, but, she complained, none was forthcoming.

Should she remain in Britain? Should she return to the U.S.? What would be best for Billy's family? For the Kennedys? For her?

When Duke Eddy heard Kick mention that she might like to have a house of her own in London, he offered her one of his properties there. Shortly however, she judged that the house belonging to the duke was too small to accommodate the various Kennedy siblings when at length they visited from America, so she set about to find something larger. She anticipated that when Jack came over to cover the upcoming British general election as a reporter for the Hearst newspapers, he would look at houses with her.

Mindful that her father could not fathom why she would possibly choose to stay in that economically devastated country after the war, Kick sent assurances that of course she did not mean to make England her full-time home, but that she hoped to be able to spend part of the year in both countries. She intended to return to the U.S. for a visit in the fall, but it was evident to her English friends that she was quite keen to acquire a property in London before she left. Once Kick was back in America, her parents were likely to exert strong pressure on her to remain. If the lease of a London house were already a fait accompli, she would have the perfect excuse to return to Britain when she liked.

In the meantime, she was carefully monitoring, and reporting to Jack, the details of the postwar political reckoning that had already begun in Britain, though the Japanese, as Churchill had taken pains to point out in his V-E Day broadcast, had yet to be subdued. The watershed 1945 British general election, the first in a decade, had tremendous personal resonance for Kick. That her brother-in-law Andrew Cavendish, along with a good many of the boys in her prewar London set, such as Robert Cecil, Michael Astor, Tom Egerton, and Hugh Fraser, were standing for Parliament seemed only to highlight the fact that, to her abiding anguish, Billy's name was absent from the list.

Billy had been so passionate about postwar Britain and the part he hoped to play in the process of shaping it. It pained his widow to observe his contemporaries excitedly embark on precisely the sort of political careers that, she felt certain, would have been his had he lived.

And what role, if any, was Kick to have in all of this? There had been a time when she anticipated being constantly at Billy's side when, after the war, he returned to the political fray. There had been a time when Eddy Devonshire had predicted that she would have a brilliant political future as her husband's helpmate. Now that she was a widow, she thought of possibly assisting Andrew, who was standing for Chesterfield. Or perhaps she would canvass for Richard Wood's brother Charles, who was standing for York.

Kick wrote to Jack that none of their English friends, all of whom were of course standing as Conservatives, had any real expectation of getting in, for "a terrific swing to the Left" was anticipated. On April 26, 1945, the Tories had experienced an overwhelming defeat in a by-election held in Chelmsford. Reporting that the Conservatives were all "very shocked" by the rout, Kick went on to note that the poll numbers were of particular interest because Billy had been defeated by the Common Wealth Party by a considerably smaller majority. All of which prompted her to add: "With the war nearly at an end & doing so well this result was amazing." Like the 1944 West Derbyshire by-election, Chelmsford did not bode well for the political future of Churchill and his party after the war. The numbers in Chelmsford seemed to bear out the claim made by Common Wealth the year before that Billy's loss in West Derbyshire foretold that when Britons at last defeated the enemy, they would not be content to return to the old 1939 world.

Kick had previously argued with both her father and Jack about the postwar viability of Billy's Britain. At the time of her marriage she had in effect abandoned "the protecting walls of the convent" for the place and purpose offered to her by that Britain of old. Were that world of rank and entitlement indeed to collapse, as present political trends seemed to suggest that it was about to do in 1945, she had great difficulty perceiving a place for herself in the as yet uncharted new order that must emerge in its stead. To her brother, Kick wrote factually and objectively about the trends and the predictions, but at the same time she acknowledged that she found the massive swing to the left hard to comprehend in light of Churchill's indisputably effective conduct of the war.

When, on V-E Day, Churchill had cried out to a great crowd gathered beneath his balcony, "This is your victory!" the multitude had answered, "No, it's yours!" Then at the apex of his glory, Churchill seems to have taken it somewhat for granted that a grateful electorate would want him to remain in office, at least until the war was officially over and until the postwar territorial ambitions of Soviet Russia, still ostensibly Britain's ally, were quashed.

Though he had previously pledged that there would be a general election as soon as the Germans had been overcome, he now proposed to keep the wartime coalition intact until October. Labor, however, demanded an immediate election. Focused as he was on the Soviet threat,

Churchill seems to have underestimated many Britons' desire to start the work of building a fairer, more prosperous society as soon as possible. On May 23, 1945, he went to Buckingham Palace to tender his resignation to the King, who asked him to form an interim administration. Thereafter, Churchill stubbornly cast the British general election of 1945 as a referendum on his conduct of the war.

Churchill scoffed at what he called "those foolish people" who wished to rebuild the world after the war. Informed by a member of his circle that there were two opposing notions about him in Britain at the time—nearly universal gratitude on the one hand, and a sense that he was "not very keen on this brave new world business" on the other—Churchill riposted, "The desire for a new world is nothing like universal; the gratitude is." The crowds that came out to see Churchill in the course of his thousand-mile electoral tour suggested by their very enthusiasm that there could be no doubt about the outcome of what, in darker moments, he referred to with annoyance and anxiety as "this damned election."

Kick did ultimately manage to find a role for herself in the 1945 British general election. But instead of assisting her brother-in-law Andrew, she took up the cause of her journalist brother. Jack's presence in England at the time helped somewhat to mitigate the private pain that the election inevitably caused her. She had once anticipated working on behalf of Billy's future; now, she dedicated herself to Jack's. Ostensibly, she focused on his immediate assignment, which was to report on the election to an American audience. Kick provided Jack with important perspective and inside information, as well as with the personal introductions to interview sources, that helped him to perceive what most other American journalists simply could not.

Shortly after he arrived in mid-June, Jack warned newspaper readers in the U.S. to prepare for the unthinkable. "Britishers will go to the polls on July 5th in the first general election in almost ten years," Jack wrote, "and there is a definite possibility that Prime Minister Winston Churchill and his Conservative party may be defeated. This may come as a surprise to most Americans who feel Churchill is as indomitable at the polls as he was in war. However, Churchill is fighting a tide that is surging through Europe, washing away monarchies and conservative governments everywhere, and that tide flows powerfully in England. England is moving toward some form of socialism—if not in this election then surely at the next."

Crucially, Kick also had an eye on the political career upon which her brother hoped soon to embark in the U.S. In 1938 and 1939, Joe Junior had been the Kennedy brother who was thought to be destined for political greatness. Now Kick made certain that her English friends and family all understood that that torch had been passed on to Jack. She saw Jack's visit as an important part of his political education. Almost everywhere he and she drove together in Kick's beat-up Baby Austin automobile, they encountered lively political talk that promised to be helpful and instructive to him.

Though Kick could not possibly have known or suspected it at the time, certain of the personal relationships of Jack's that were renewed and intensified in this period—most notably his friendship with David Ormsby-Gore, who had become closer than ever to Kick after Billy's death—would impact on Kennedy's presidential policies long after his sister, who had done so much to facilitate those relationships, was dead. Without the input of Ormsby-Gore, there might never have been the 1963 partial nuclear test ban treaty with the Soviets that Kennedy himself regarded as his administration's signal achievement. In the late 1930s, David and Jack had much enjoyed each other's company, but in 1945 the "family connection" provided by Kick immeasurably deepened their bond.

When Kick brought her brother to spend the weekend at Compton Place, Jack encountered important evidence of the seismic shift that was taking place in British life. A year had passed since the Duke of Devonshire had been utterly confounded by his son's defeat in the West Derbyshire by-election. Now, however, Eddy Devonshire well understood what the wrenching loss of the family seat had meant in national terms. By degrees, he had come to see the by-election as a harbinger of

Churchill's unhappy fate in the waning days of the Second World
War. Alone among Conservatives whom Jack interviewed in this period, Kick's father-in-law forthrightly predicted "an overwhelming
victory" for Labor.

In matters of politics, Eddy Devonshire continued to be an eighteenth-
century Whig at heart. He persisted in the conviction that traditional
aristocratic governance was best by far. He never ceased to believe in
the supremacy of a social order based on the principles of enlightened
and responsible paternalism on the one side and thankful deference on
the other. By 1945, however, he also acknowledged that the time had
come to face the new reality, unpalatable though that new reality might
be. He accepted that, to a majority of the electorate, World War Two
had been fought not to preserve the traditional ways, but rather to create the new egalitarian order that the socialists were offering in the person and party of Clement Attlee.

Such was the extremity of class resentment at the time that even a
record of heroism in the war offered no shield against the angry jeers of
the crowd. This, at any rate, was Andrew Cavendish's experience when
he stood for Chesterfield. During the Italian campaign, "the Mad Lord"
had repeatedly risked his own life to protect the lives of his men. He had
been awarded a Military Cross for his bravery and selflessness. He
had earned the love of the soldiers under his command and the respect
of his superiors. But those achievements counted for nothing in Chesterfield, which had long been far from hospitable to Conservative politicians. Andrew and Debo were spat upon, and in one instance a crowd
sought to overturn their car. More often than not, the war hero was heckled and booed when he attempted to speak. In one auditorium, Andrew
heard a fellow in the rear of the house call out that he wished to shake
the candidate's hand. Gratified by what he mistakenly took for an offer
of conciliation, Andrew leapt off the platform. Hardly had he begun to
dash up the aisle, however, than an accomplice's outstretched leg caused
him to fall on his face, as the audience roared with malicious laughter.

The working class was by no means alone in seeking to break free from the old verities after the war. Some of the young aristocrats returning from battle also had begun to see the world with new eyes. Obstacles that may have seemed well nigh insurmountable before and during the war appeared a good deal less daunting now. Never perhaps was that clearer than at a picnic that Andrew and Debo hosted at Chatsworth for some of the very same members of the aristocratic cousinhood who had attended Billy's coming-of-age party there in 1939. Back then, the prospect of Catholic girls such as Kick Kennedy, Sissie Lloyd Thomas, and Veronica Fraser marrying into the great Protestant dynasties had filled the older generation with horror. Robert Cecil, for one, finally had bowed to pressure from his illustrious Tory family and ended his relationship with Veronica. In 1945, however, when Robert, too, was fighting for a hopeless seat, everything struck him as different. When he again encountered Veronica at Andrew and Debo's picnic, he asked her if she would still like to marry him. The gravely wounded war veteran explained that the religious differences just did not seem to matter anymore. Robert meant what he said, for while his relationship with Veronica never again became what it had once been, he did indeed marry another Catholic girl not long afterward.

Kick was not present at Andrew and Debo's picnic, but she did visit Chatsworth shortly thereafter to give Jack Kennedy a tour of the house that, had Billy survived the war, would one day have been hers. Also in the course of their visit to the Derbyshire countryside, Kick treated her brother to a display of the speechmaking skills that had previously made such a strong impression on the duke's political agent. Garbed in her Red Cross uniform, and accompanied once more by Billy's paternal grandmother the dowager duchess, Kick by her performance that day prompted Jack to write home—half in earnest, half in jest—that his sister was suddenly looking "like a possible candidate" to him. There was no denying that Kick was capable of charming audiences—"by looking extremely girlish and sweet," as Jack reported with perhaps a dash of brotherly condescension. But whether there would ever be an outlet for her to properly use those abilities remained an open question.

That she hoped to find such an outlet is suggested by something she did later. She proposed to her father that, when she visited her family in the early autumn, he arrange for her to deliver "some lectures" to American audiences about the work of the Red Cross in wartime Europe.

When, on Polling Day, July 5, the votes were in, policemen removed the boxes, which were to remain sealed for three weeks to allow time for the service vote to come in from overseas. On the eve of the poll, Jack had privately assured Hugh Fraser that Labor would prevail. By the time his byline next appeared in the American press, however, he was predicting a close vote that was likely to favor the Conservative Party. Churchill, meanwhile, went off to Berlin and the Potsdam Conference, where the British prime minister was eager to confront Joseph Stalin over the Soviet Union's postwar territorial ambitions in Europe. The last of the great wartime summit meetings was scheduled to take place between the seventeenth of July and the second of August.

At Potsdam on July 25, there was a forty-eight-hour intermission, during which time Churchill returned home to learn his and his party's political fate. On the aircraft to England with his daughter Mary, his mood was one of confidence that the Conservative Party would triumph and that he would soon be back at the negotiating table to face down Stalin. In London, before he retired for the evening he exulted at the news that even Labor headquarters was anticipating a Conservative victory. Just before dawn, however, Churchill was awakened by a stabbing pain, accompanied by a premonition that all was lost. By the time he joined the family and friends who had assembled to be with him as the numbers poured in, the early poll results seemed to confirm his worst fears.

The situation only grew darker as the day progressed. Eventually, it became evident that there had been a Labor landslide. Churchill himself had prevailed in his constituency Woodford, but otherwise the Conservatives were out. Clement Attlee was to be Britain's new prime minister. And it was Attlee who went on to represent Britain in his predecessor's stead during the last leg of the Potsdam Conference.

Such was the magnitude of the Labor victory—they now controlled 146 seats in the House of Commons—that it was widely believed that the party of Winston Churchill could not possibly hope to regain power for a decade at least, perhaps for an entire generation. By that estimate, Churchill, now seventy years of age, would be at least eighty before he could even hope to be prime minister again. Quite simply, the arithmetic was against him.

Kick was attending a dinner party presided over by society hostess Emerald Cunard when it was announced that Churchill had gone to Buckingham Palace to submit his resignation to the King. The Conservative rout held immense personal meaning for Kick, marking as it did the end of a world and of a way of life in which she had once invested all of her hopes, even at the risk of having to break with her family and with her church. Of the young men in Kick's circle, only Michael Astor and Hugh Fraser won their seats. Andrew Cavendish, Robert Cecil, and the rest had all been vanquished.

Nonetheless, it was at this moment that Kick gave her final answer to the lease terms that had been offered to her for a small, charming red-brick house in Smith Square, near Parliament. Before leaving for Ireland to visit Adele Astaire Cavendish, among others, Kick signed a twenty-five-year lease on the property, which she intended to decorate with, in her phrase, "Chatsworth stuff" until she managed to acquire furnishings of her own. In the early days of Kick's relationship with Billy, Adele had accompanied the couple to Lady Mountbatten's party for Sally Norton. During the war, Kick had seen a good deal of Adele when both American women worked for the Red Cross in London. Now Kick and Adele were both widows, Charlie Cavendish having died in 1944. Similarly confronted by the question of where she properly belonged, Adele viewed things in a rather different way from Kick.

When Kick visited Adele at Lismore Castle in County Waterford, she found that her forty-seven-year-old hostess was set on returning to the U.S. Now that she was alone, Adele regarded America as her home and Britain as a place to visit. Unlike Kick when she landed in London in 1938, Adele had been very much a person in her own right, when in 1923, she first appeared on the London stage with her younger brother Fred. The Astaire siblings, who had been dancing together profession-ally since she was eight and he five, were full-fledged Broadway stars. Until 1932, when she retired from the dance duo in order to marry, Adele had been the more personally popular and lavishly acclaimed member of the act by far. In later years, Adele never quite recovered from the sense of regret provoked by her loss of the limelight, as well as by the immense fame that Fred went on to achieve on his own. Kick's situation presented itself as the very opposite of Adele's. As far as Kick was con-cerned, she had not existed in her own right until she came to England on the eve of the war. In contrast to Adele, it was Britain that Kick in-tended to make her postwar home base, from which at intervals she would visit the U.S.

Meanwhile, Kick returned to London on Monday, August 13, 1945, to make the remarkable discovery that Winston and Clementine Churchill had taken up residence in the very flat above hers. Defeat had come as such a shock to Churchill that he had had no plan in place for where he would live in the event of a Labor victory. It was therefore arranged that, while his country estate Chartwell and a new London house near Hyde Park were being readied for him, Churchill moved temporarily to the Westminster Gardens quarters of his daughter and son-in-law, Di-ana and Duncan Sandys, who had offered to go elsewhere for the dura-tion. Kick, when she arrived home, observed that "at all hours of the day and night," well-wishers came and sang beneath Churchill's win-dow—and, as it happened, beneath her own.

Kick had been in Ireland when the U.S. unleashed the atomic bomb on Hiroshima and Nagasaki. On Tuesday the fourteenth, the day after she arrived in London, the Japanese surrendered unconditionally. The following morning, great crowds of people gathered round the block of flats where Kick resided, in hopes of seeing and cheering the man who had saved his country only to be hurled from power at the moment of his supreme triumph. By chance, Victory over Japan Day overlapped with the state opening of Parliament. Driven there in an open vehicle, Churchill was greeted by impassioned cries of "Churchill forever!" and "We want Churchill!" Churchill had regarded the Conservative rout as a public rebuff of his wartime leadership, so today's ovations seemed to comfort and reassure him. He responded with palpable delight to the celebrations in the streets.

By contrast, the former prime minister's downstairs neighbor, Lady Hartington, when she made her own separate trip to Parliament to hear the King's speech, found the universal jubilation "rather depressing." Naturally, she shared the people's happiness that the enemy had at last been conquered. But, lamenting as she did the passing of the old 1939 world, she emphatically failed to share their enthusiasm for what she re-garded not as the brave, but rather the bland new world that was about to come into being in England. Kick vigorously endorsed Churchill's description of his socialist successor Attlee as "a sheep in sheep's cloth-ing." Six years after Nancy Astor had welcomed her to her first English country house weekend, Kick happened to encounter Lady Astor on the day Parliament opened. Kick discovered that the older woman as well was "feeling very depressed" by events—and for reasons similar to her own.

Churchill had another reason to seem upbeat. In his new capacity as Opposition leader, he was scheduled to speak in the House of Commons the next day. He planned to lay out the new threat posed by the Sovi-ets and to urge that a postwar settlement with Moscow be aggressively pursued during the limited time that remained before other powers besides the U.S. were likely to be able to produce an atomic bomb of their own. He calculated that Stalin was far more likely to agree to a deal so long as the U.S. could threaten him with the bomb without his being able to strike back with equally deadly force. The speech was an early articulation of the ever-elusive objective of a postwar settlement in Europe that was to preoccupy the titan throughout the tumultuous last decade of his political life, and that would someday profoundly influence and inspire President John F. Kennedy.

By the time Churchill gave his landmark address, however, Kick had already fled London, feeling painfully out of sync with the prevailing holiday mood. Interestingly, it was that very same holiday spirit that would cause Churchill's speech—for all of its abundant merits, both of matter and manner—to be a good deal less than successful with the British public. Impatient to begin their peaceful, prosperous new life under the Labor government, war-weary citizens proved unreceptive to Churchill's urgent message that hardly had the enemy been overcome than a potentially even more dangerous foe had arisen in its stead, and that henceforward the Soviet menace must become the nation's priority.

On Thursday the sixteenth of August, Kick left to spend the weekend in the country as the houseguest of Michael Astor and his wife, Barbara. Michael was just taking up his duties as a member of Parliament, and Barbara was expecting another child. Jakie Astor and his wife, Chiquita, were also present during Kick's visit. In 1938, Kick's ability to participate in the political talk of Michael, Jakie, David, and Hugh had smoothed her entree into their elite set. In 1945, though the specific topics of debate and discussion had changed, Kick again found herself drawn into Michael and Jakie's animated and immensely pleasurable talk. Unlike their mother, they looked upon the convening of the new House of Commons with immense curiosity and excitement over the monumental battles that were about to be fought, both in the House and within the Conservative Party itself. Among senior Conservatives, led by Robert Cecil's father, Lord Cranborne, a movement was already afoot to oust Churchill as Opposition leader in favor of his longtime and long-suffering forty-eight-year-old heir apparent, Anthony Eden. In Michael and Jakie's company, Kick began to find the unfolding drama irresistible.

She returned to London after the weekend, in time to observe Hugh Fraser make his maiden speech in the House of Commons on the twentieth of August. The members of Kick's prewar set all had such grand hopes for Hugh, whom they had long regarded as the most promising young man of their group. The excitement attendant upon the launch of his parliamentary career did much to help Kick begin to discover a new "pattern of life," as she called it, after the war. There was never really any question of her being romantically involved with Hugh, but in 1945, as in 1938, she delighted in his invariably provocative and stimulating outlook and conversation. Kick thereafter frequented Parliament in the exuberant company of a group that, besides Hugh, included the writers Christopher Hollis (also a fledgling Conservative MP) and Evelyn Waugh.

On the night before Parliament recessed, Kick was dining at the House of Commons with her trio of Catholic cavaliers when she caught sight of Tom Driberg, a Labor MP who, in his capacity as a left-leaning journalist, had mocked Billy Hartington in print during the West Derbyshire by-election. Driberg, who had undertaken to interview the candidate touted by Conservatives as "Churchill's personal choice" in the race, had mirthfully informed readers that he soon "desisted from questioning," for the process had been "too like pulling the wings off a fly." A year and a half later, Billy's widow used the opportunity of their chance encounter in the House to insult Driberg—an experience that she afterward pronounced "very satisfactory."

Also in the waning summer of 1945, Kick took an intense personal interest in the plight of her distinguished upstairs neighbor, whose electoral defeat she was far from alone in associating with Billy's. Churchill—determined not to allow himself to be edged out as party leader; frustrated that as in the 1930s he perceived a looming danger that his countrymen foolishly refused to acknowledge; and, on the most basic level, miserable at the loss of power and prestige that had formerly allowed him to eat well when other men had to endure rationing and shortages—was mightily unhappy in these weeks. Kick, when she learned of Churchill's discontent with the lack of eggs and milk in particular, made a point of returning from a weekend in the country with a bounty of eggs for him. She went upstairs to deliver them personally, only to learn from the cook, with whom she proceeded to have "a little chat," that the former prime minister was away.

On September 9, it would be a year since Billy's death. That day, Andrew and Debo would become Marquess and Marchioness of Hartington, its having been firmly established by then that Billy and Kick had failed to produce an heir. Kick did not wish to spend the day at Compton Place. Before that, she did, however, go to Eastbourne to see Billy's family. In the course of the weekend, Andrew made a point of going off with Kick, just the two of them, to play golf. Though for different reasons, the impending anniversary, and all that it meant in terms of their respective future fortunes, was no easier for Andrew to contemplate than it was for his brother's widow. And while seeing Kick provided the duke and duchess with a welcome reminder of their late son, the same sight, triggering as it did memories of Billy, provoked in Andrew a pang of guilt. Kick herself alternated between finding it difficult to absorb the fact that her young husband had been gone for a full year and feeling, as she said, as if a hundred years had passed.

Kick arranged to be at Garrowby on September 9, in the company of Richard Wood, his mother, and several of his cousins. The following morning, she and Richard shot partridges, Kick walking for three hours, he galloping alongside on a horse, which he had learned to ride, in her phrase, "extraordinarily well." As always, Richard was kindness itself to the girl he adored, but even now he refrained from speaking to her of his feelings.

Nonetheless, rumors soon abounded in the British press that she and Richard had become engaged. On the assumption that the anniversary of her husband's death signaled Lady Hartington's reentry into the marriage market, press people rang up the duke and duchess in hopes they might comment on her supposed betrothal. Intent as they were that Kick go on serving as a living reminder of their firstborn, Eddy and Moucher were horrified and hurt by the inquiries. Their agitation was a source of distress to Kick, who found both the gossip and the assumption about her being ready to marry again hugely irritating and embarrassing.

Kick had by now given up her post at the Red Cross in anticipation of making her first postwar visit to the U.S. Initially she planned to leave

London in the latter half of September so that she might reach America in time for an address that Jack was set to give on October 5 to informally launch his political career. But the date of her departure had to be continually put off till she finally had to tell her parents that she had no choice but to miss Jack's big speech. These days, U.S.-bound ships were packed to capacity with returning soldiers, and despite her connections she found booking passage exceedingly difficult to arrange.

Traveling as part of a Red Cross contingent, Kick sailed on the liner *Queen Mary*, which reached New York Harbor on November 9, 1945. Overhead, sixteen P-47 Thunderbolt fighter planes flew in formation to welcome the more than nine thousand servicemen traveling on the British transport. That day alone in New York City, another fourteen vessels carrying an additional fourteen thousand U.S. soldiers were also due. Joe Kennedy, waiting at the West Fiftieth Street dock, made a point of informing press people that his widowed daughter intended to reside with her family in Boston. If he meant that she planned to live with them on anything like a permanent basis, the assertion would certainly have been news to Kick, who now had a permanent address of her own—4, Smith Square, London.

Nonetheless, she had been aching to see her family again. As she said, though surrounded by friends in England, there were moments when in spite of that companionship she still felt "very lonely," which was why she had been so keenly anticipating the reunion with her parents and siblings. Her inability to join them at Jack's big speech the previous month had been a considerable disappointment to her. At the time of his visit to England to cover the general election, she had been acutely conscious of acting in a way that was best for his imminent political future. To her delight, when she celebrated Thanksgiving with her family at the Cape, talk abounded of a possible run for Congress. A seat in the House of Representatives for Massachusetts' 11th Congressional District had lately opened up when its occupant, James M. Curley, became mayor of Boston. It remained only for Jack to make up his mind whether to participate in a primary, which was set to take place in June.

One element of the political table talk, however, was decidedly not to Kick's liking. Should Jack indeed enter the congressional race, Kick, because of her controversial marriage, threatened to be very much a liability among Irish Catholic voters in Boston. When Billy stood for West Derbyshire in 1944, Kick had had to be kept in the background due to her association with that figure who was so reviled in Britain, former ambassador Joseph P. Kennedy. Now again, in the event that Jack ran for Congress, it was thought best that she remain offstage as much as possible. This time, the problem was her troubling association with one of the great Protestant families of England. Any prominent participation by Lady Hartington at campaign events in Boston was likely to be political poison. In this sense at least, Kick had become as much a problematic outsider here as she had been in West Derbyshire.

Kick spent Christmas of 1945 with her family in Palm Beach. At the outset of 1946 she headed to New York, where she encountered Winston Frost, a thirty-three-year-old attorney who had served as a lieutenant commander in the Navy, and whom she had known before the war. "The Southern Gentleman," as she now dubbed him, came from an old but not wealthy Virginia family. He had attended Harvard and the University of Virginia Law School, and was said to be hunting for a rich wife. Kick, nostalgic for late nights spent at the 400 Club and other prewar London spots, was easily drawn to the tall, fair-haired, consummately charming bachelor whose principal focus was hardly his law work, but rather the dance floors of El Morocco and the Stork Club. Joe Kennedy, when he learned that his daughter had begun to see a good deal of Frost, wasted no time moving to end the relationship. He concentrated on the fact that, according to his investigations, Frost seemed to be simultaneously involved with another woman.

But, as Kick would subsequently suggest, the problem with him as a suitor really lay elsewhere. It had to do with the contrast between the life of power and politics she had been anticipating when she married Billy and the so much more limited existence of a denizen of New York cafe society. In ancient times when Kick, then a teenager, had accompanied Jack and his friends to nightclubs in New York and Palm Beach, a fellow such as Winston Frost might have seemed very suitable indeed to her. Not so now, when her experiences in England, and the particular aspirations they had generated, led her in search of something very different. Eventually, she came to look upon Winston Frost as having been "a passing fancy." She wrote of the relationship, "In the cold light of morning, after having the life I had, one doesn't waste it going from El Morocco to the Stork Club. Not if one has any sense one doesn't." Quite simply, she had outgrown that sort of existence; but where possibly was she to find something more suitable and more satisfying?

Also pursuing Kick during this period was Seymour Berry, the thirty-seven-year-old deputy chairman of *The Daily Telegraph* in London, which was owned by his father, Lord Camrose. Rich and powerful, with access to a level of British society that greatly appealed to Kick, Berry seemed a formidable candidate for her affections. After she had rejoined her family in Palm Beach, he invited her to accompany him as part of a select group set to escort Winston Churchill to the Miami Orange Bowl, where the former prime minister was to receive an honorary Doctor of Laws degree from the University of Miami. Churchill was then on holiday in Florida in anticipation of traveling to Fulton, Missouri, to deliver his game-changing Iron Curtain speech, in which he would at once warn the world of the Soviet menace and make it clear that, despite the outcome of the 1945 British general election, he had no intention of retiring. On the morning of the Orange Bowl ceremony, Kick went with Seymour Berry to collect Winston and Clementine Churchill at the private residence where they were houseguests. Later, she marched in the academic procession and sat onstage between Seymour Berry and the British Conservative politician Leslie Hore-Belisha while Churchill, resplendent in a copious scarlet gown and cap, accepted his honorary degree before an audience of eighteen thousand people. Afterward, she swam with Churchill at a private beach club and sat at the head table at the large official luncheon that was given in his honor.

Berry's newly conspicuous presence in Kick's life was not exactly welcome news at Compton Place. The duke and duchess, eager that Kick remain in the role of their son's widow but loath to interfere in her personal affairs, found themselves in a most delicate position. When at length they learned that Berry would be waiting for Kick when the SS *Queen Mary* docked in Southampton on April 30, 1946, they elected not to be there. And when Berry, in turn, discovered that Billy's parents and sisters were planning to be at the boat, he decided that it would be wisest to avoid appearing there himself. Thus, in the end neither Kick's in-laws nor her suitor were present when she emerged from the liner. There was only Berry's chauffeur. As the duke and duchess were no-where in sight, Berry's man organized a grateful Lady Hartington's extensive luggage and drove her in to town.

Twelve

Late in the afternoon of April 30, 1946, Seymour Berry's limousine pulled up in front of 4, Smith Square, just opposite the wreckage of St. John's Church, which had been hit by a German bomb in 1941.

While the chauffeur collected her bags, the tiny figure of Lady Hartington walked past the centuries-old iron fencing and through the heavy wooden front door of the Georgian house, where, at twenty-six years of age, she was about to begin life on her own. Entering a narrow hallway, she climbed two flights to the sitting room. To her immense pleasure, tea was waiting on the table, amid great quantities of flowers that, on the orders of the Duchess of Devonshire, who had herself just returned from a holiday in Monaco, were arrayed throughout.

Because of the misunderstanding on both sides that Kick professed to find most amusing, neither her in-laws nor her gentleman friend had materialized at the ship. Still, from the outset, what hencefor-ward were to exist as subtly but no less powerfully competing forces in

Kick's life—her Cavendish in-laws and those who hoped to lure her away from them—were represented in the form of the tea and flowers and myriad other welcoming niceties on the one hand and the car and driver on the other. Though Kick had chosen, much to the consternation and perplexity of the Kennedys, to live in austere postwar socialist Britain, she was unabashed in her fondness for comfort and luxury and in her attraction to those who were in a position to offer it to her.

Initially, it seemed as if, for all of her excitement about her new house, she might yet be content to sequester herself as much as possible under the warmth of the wings of the Cavendishes. Kick spent her first weekend back in Britain at Compton Place, and she gladly agreed to accompany the duke a few days hence to stay with his mother, and afterward to attend a ceremony at the University of Leeds, where he served as chancellor and where Kick would be known for the day as "Chancellor's Lady." It was obvious from the duke's invitation, and from the many others that were soon to follow, that the father who had once dreaded Kick's arrival in the Cavendish family had developed a deep emotional attachment to her. That attachment had grown more intense in the course of the five months that his daughter-in-law had just spent in the U.S. Kick's absence seemed to make the duke feel the more acutely the loss of Billy. Increasingly, it would seem as if he simply could not abide the thought of losing her as well.

So while Billy himself, in the letter written from Giberville in the aftermath of Operation Goodwood, had urged Kick to marry again soon in the event that he failed to survive the war, the duke appeared to take a very different view of what would be best for his son's widow.

On the ninth of May, Kick and the duke set off together by train for Chesterfield, in Derbyshire. Duchess Evie had taken up residence at Hardwick Hall, the Elizabethan Renaissance palace that Bess of Hardwick, ancestor of the Devonshire dukes, had built in the final decade of the sixteenth century. Seated before a fire in Duchess Evie's sitting room, Kick composed a letter to her family in the U.S. that expressed the mixture of delight and dismay with which she responded not just to

Hardwick Hall, but also, more generally, to her adopted country: "It is like an old museum, full of the most lovely furniture and pictures, but quite uncomfortable. It's odd how people in this country who possess so much have no idea about things which Americans consider quite essential to the ordinary way of life. There is no soap in one's bathroom, sugar or butter at breakfast."

By turns Kick marveled at the perfection of the old tapestries and furniture and complained of the discomfort of her "lovely, historical Elizabethan bed." To judge by her letters home, Kick's thoughts were ever darting between England and the very different life she had left behind in the U.S. In this regard, her comments on the "pageantry and color" of the traditional ceremony in which she and the duke soon participated at Leeds University are telling: "I think that this is the sort of thing I most enjoy because it is so entirely different from anything I've ever done," Kick reported to the Kennedys. "I do enjoy contrasts."

In contrast to her life with Billy's family, Kick was also fashioning a separate new existence of her own in London. As her sister-in-law Elizabeth observed, Kick, rather than persist in dwelling upon the painful past, finally "turned it off and moved on." For Kick to have done otherwise, Elizabeth judged, would have been unbearable. In June, therefore, she presided over her first dinner party, attended by a group that went on afterward to a dinner dance that Seymour Berry gave for his sister. With the help of a new cook and butler, Kick was soon hosting frequent lunches and dinners, but the focal point of her hospitality, at least when Parliament was in session, were the weekday evenings between six and eight when she was "at home" to politically minded friends.

Not long after Kick had returned from the U.S., intimates such as Jean Lloyd began to notice her habit of haphazardly stuffing one chair after another into the tiny drawing room, an odd decorating scheme that had little to do with aesthetics but everything to do with accommodating as many guests as possible, with the objective of making conversation primary. Hugh Fraser, Tony Rosslyn, William Douglas-Home, Michael Astor, Jakie Astor, David Ormsby-Gore, and other of the young men

who, to varying degrees, had been besotted with Kick in the days before Billy claimed her for his own soon established themselves as reg-
ulars at what came to be known as "Lady Hartington's salon." The
crowded drawing room, whose three windows gave pretty views of
the old square, echoed with talk of the great and controversial issues
of the day.

That spring of 1946, no subject was discussed with greater fervor in
London political circles than government efforts to desecrate and destroy
the largest of the eighteenth-century houses, which were regarded as
emblematic of the old social order. The particular edifice under official
assault was Wentworth Woodhouse in Yorkshire, the family seat of the
Fitzwilliam dynasty. That venerable Whig family had a history of vying with the Devonshire dukes over which of their noble houses possessed the greater splendor. On the first day of the Doncaster races in
1827, both the Duke of Devonshire and Earl Fitzwilliam appeared with
a coach and six, and a dozen outriders. The next day, Fitzwilliam, intent on besting his rival, famously arrived with two coaches and six, as
well as sixteen outriders.

More than a century later, as Elizabeth Cavendish recalled, no one
any longer lived at quite the level of grandeur displayed by the 8th Earl
Fitzwilliam. His father had nimbly eluded the economic devastation that
had stricken the landed classes after World War I. When the 7th Earl
Fitzwilliam's fellow aristocrats endeavored to sell off property at a steep
discount, he had been quick to claim the spoils. But whereas the father
had been known and admired for paying too little for things, the son in
turn would be much reviled for paying too much. During the Second
World War, the latter had paid eight thousand guineas for a racehorse,
the highest price then on record at Newmarket. As the 8th Earl's postwar
socialist nemesis, the Labor government's minister of fuel and power,
Manny Shinwell, scathingly pointed out in 1946, the sum had been the
equivalent of about forty years of wages of what was generally regarded
as a well-paid workman.

After the war, the coal industry, on which a good portion of the Fitzwilliam family's riches were based, was nationalized. The family remained immensely wealthy nonetheless, with broad acres and other holdings. Intent, it would seem, on making the 8th Earl, Peter Fitzwilliam, the reviled symbol of the very social and economic injustice that the socialists had pledged to eradicate, Manny Shinwell decreed that the park and gardens of the earl's family seat be mined for coal. Peter Fitzwilliam himself was hardly alone at the time in suspecting that Shinwell had issued the order not in spite of the fact that the extensive mining operation would gravely disfigure the historic property, but rather precisely because of it. The government minister had endeavored to transform the nationalization fight into a battle of personalities—and so he very much succeeded in doing.

Still, if Shinwell presumed that, in keeping with the tenor of postwar public opinion in Britain, the miners whose families had toiled in the area for generations would regard Fitzwilliam's persecutor as a hero, he miscalculated. Unlike the electors in the 1944 West Derbyshire by-election, whose votes had constituted a forceful statement against traditional aristocratic governance in general and (as Billy Hartington had perceived) against the Cavendishes in particular, the Yorkshire miners, believing themselves to have been treated fairly by earls Fitzwilliam past and present, were outspoken in their support of Peter Fitzwilliam. By that support, they seemed to ratify the Whigs' traditional view of themselves as being on the side of the people, not in conflict with them. Number 10 Downing Street, however, persisted in backing its histrionic minister of fuel and power. Fitzwilliam had returned from the Second World War a hero, whose valor had earned him a Distinguished Service Order, but, finally, that high military honor did nothing to protect him against his own government.

With dramatic flair, Manny Shinwell had endeavored to cast Peter Fitzwilliam as a villain. Still, for not a few Britons, the spectacle of the ravaging of the nobleman's magnificent park and gardens had quite the opposite effect. No matter that Fitzwilliam was an unfaithful husband, a notorious womanizer who had fathered several illegitimate children, a compulsive high-stakes gambler, and a heavy drinker. In some Conservative quarters, Fitzwilliam's impassioned defense of his property against the socialist minister's bulldozers had made him very much the hero of the hour.

In Kick's story we catch a first glimpse of Peter Fitzwilliam—"dashing and flirtatious and gay and attractive," in the words of Jean Lloyd—as he dances with Kick at a ball in honor of Britain's wartime Commandos, of which he had been a distinguished member, at the Dorchester Hotel on June 12, 1946. His oft-betrayed wife of thirteen years, Obby—once among the prettiest debs of her year, but now, as described in another context by the diarist James Lees-Milne, "rather dumpy and awkward"—is also present at the gala. Kick has chaired the event's organizing committee at the invitation of Fitzwilliam's close friends Robert and Angie Laycock, who happen to be her friends as well.

To look at, Earl Fitzwilliam and the Dowager Marchioness of Hartington make a curious couple. Peter is thirty-five years of age; Kick nearly a decade his junior. He is more than six feet tall; she is diminutive, like her mother. He is—in the phrase of Billy's sister Anne—"an astonishingly handsome man," with a history of pursuing women of exceptional beauty; Kick, to say the least, is far from beautiful. Deep creases in his forehead and faint shadows beneath his eyes project an air of dissipation; she is fresh-faced and innocent. He has the well-earned reputation of a sybarite and a seducer; she persists in regarding herself as a devout Catholic. Indeed, at the time of the Commando Ball, Kick has only recently returned from a group retreat at a nunnery organized by Hugh Fraser's sister Lady Eldon, at the conclusion of which Kick, by her own account, discovered that she was "rather sorry to leave the protecting walls of the convent."

Hardly had Kick met Fitzwilliam than her relationship with Richard Wood began to intensify. Did Richard, who had held back for so long, sense that it must be now or never? Was Kick, whom Billy had urged to marry "someone good & nice," seeking to do precisely that at a moment when a rather different option had suddenly presented itself?

All that can be known for certain is that, by Richard's own account, he had been in love with her since Washington. He had cared for her enough to selflessly support her as she made some of the most difficult decisions with regard to her future course with Billy. Kick, in turn, had come to view Richard as "the soul of honesty" and "one of the best and most understanding friends I have in all the world." She had been a frequent houseguest at Garrowby, where she existed on intimate terms not just with him, but with his parents as well. Affectionately, she had monitored Richard's progress as he mastered his artificial limbs; learned to ride again; endeavored to reemerge, nervously at first, then more confidently, in London life; and set his sights on a career as a Conservative politician.

Richard had refrained from speaking to Kick of his abiding love—until, that is, the summer of 1946, when he and she at last discussed the possibility that they might marry. In later years, he would assert that, in the end, they had decided against marriage because of the same religious differences and difficulties that had previously vexed Kick and Billy. Shortly before he died in 2002, however, Richard, known by then as Lord Holderness, would also disclose that, for Kick, there had been a far greater obstacle than religion. Longing as she did to become "a woman of influence," she required a husband who could help her to attain what she believed to be her proper sphere. Lord Holderness, while clearly concerned always to present Kick in the best light and to avoid making it seem as if it were merely grandeur and glamour she was after, acknowledged that in the end he had not been in a position to offer her anything like the life she wanted. Quite simply, Richard Wood could not match the riches of a Billy Hartington or of a Peter Fitzwilliam.

Meanwhile, Fitzwilliam—who enjoyed, in the words of one American observer, "that curious air of glamour sometimes conferred by great possessions long held and a great place in the world long maintained"—had been discreetly visiting Kick at Smith Square, as well as enlisting his friends to arrange for him to meet with her. The settings for these encounters often plunged Kick into the worlds of horse racing and gambling that Fitzwilliam, always "wonderfully easy and jolly," frequented. She went to Ascot for the Derby races, where she stayed with his friends Laura and Eric Dudley Ward, the Earl of Dudley. She accompanied Peter's wartime commander Robert Laycock and his wife, Angie, to the casino in Deauville, France, traveling there in a private aircraft provided by Fitzwilliam.

More and more, Kick found herself at dinner tables that she knew her late husband's family would have been sure to avoid. When Eddy and Moucher Devonshire, like a good many others in their social stratum, were pointedly refusing to see the Duke and Duchess of Windsor, who had come over to England for a visit, Kick accepted Eric Dudley Ward's invitation to a dinner party at Claridge's in honor of the controversial former king and his wife. Kick began to inhabit a milieu in which women, married and divorced, routinely had affairs with one or more married men. Laura Dudley Ward ran off with another member of Kick's louche new set, Gerry Koch de Gooreynd, only to return pregnant to her much older husband Eric. Laura's sister Ann, who was then married to the press lord Viscount Rothermere, carried on an affair with Ian Fleming, who subsequently became her husband. Pam Churchill, the former wife of Winston Churchill's son Randolph, resumed the affair with Averell Harriman that had previously torpedoed her marriage, this time adding the complication of a second lover, Jock Whitney.

During this time, Kick continued to live on the most intimate terms with Billy's parents, a circumstance that seems to have held no little allure for her lover. She regularly spent the weekend at Compton Place, where Eddy and Moucher continued to involve her in as many public duties as possible in her capacity as Billy's widow. She accompanied them to the Queen's Garden Party at Buckingham Palace, where she was announced as the Dowager Marchioness of Hartington. She went with Billy's sister Elizabeth to a Regency Ball in Brighton at the Pavilion of George IV, for which occasion the duchess loaned her the family diamonds. For Kick, "the most enjoyable part of the evening" proved to be the moment when a fellow guest "laid her eyes on the Devonshire diamonds on my chest. I could see she was absolutely fascinated."

In August, Kick accepted her father-in-law's invitation to shoot with him at Bolton Abbey. Despite the fact that other landowners were complaining of a general shortage of grouse that season, Eddy Devonshire insisted in advance that there would be no such problem on his estate. His remark led Kick to affectionately exclaim, "The certainty of a Duke!" Billy had often evinced the identical serene self-confidence, shading into hubris, associated with the aristocratic mystique. And, for all of the ways in which he otherwise differed emphatically from the Cavendishes, so did Peter Fitzwilliam.

But the duke's optimism proved to have been amply justified. Afterward, Kick wrote home that shooting at Bolton Abbey could scarcely have been more successful. Amazingly, "there were more grouse there than on any other moors in Yorkshire or Scotland."

At Bolton Abbey, moreover, Kick reveled in the ability of the few to live in a style that was not supposed to have survived the war. "The shooting is all done in a prewar manner with all the beaters, gamekeepers, etc.," she exulted in a letter to her parents. "It's so strange that although England is now governed by a Labor government, there still exists in this country so many remnants of the feudal past." In the mouths of most other speakers, "feudal past" would almost certainly have had a negative connotation. Kick, on the contrary, meant it not as criticism but as high praise. It is notable that elsewhere in her correspondence of this period, the phrase "prewar standards" serves as a benchmark of excellence and approbation.

When, in the autumn, her twenty-five-year-old sister Eunice was the first of the Kennedys to stay with her in Smith Square, Kick undertook to show her the remnants of that all-but-vanished prewar world. During the summer, when the dates for Eunice's impending visit were still being arranged on both sides, Kick had suggested to her parents that she and her sister might return to the U.S. together around the end of November. By the time Eunice actually appeared in London, however, Kick had drastically revised her plans. No longer prepared to leave in November, she made it clear that when her sister went home she intended to remain in England several months more. Kick attributed the change to how "interesting" London life had become for her just then. Perhaps, but in light of what followed it is not too much to suppose that by this point Kick was simply loath to break things off with Fitzwilliam. Kick's relationship with him would escalate considerably during the course of Eunice's visit, which culminated with Kick's taking the piously Catholic sister who had once denounced her marriage to a Protestant to meet the married lord with whom she was having an affair.

Eunice's sojourn in London began, however, with an opulent ball held at the Dorchester Hotel on October 4, 1946, four months after Kick first encountered Peter Fitzwilliam there. The hostess this evening was "the other Lady Hartington," as Eunice referred to Debo, who, somewhat bewilderingly, now bore the same appellation as Kick. Debo, rather to her own embarrassment at times, had lately undergone a marked personal transformation. Eddy Devonshire had insisted that she and Andrew take up residence at Edensor House, in the village overlooking Chatsworth. Billy, of course, had been in training all his life for one day becoming master of the family seat. It now fell to the second son to learn everything, and to do it so much more quickly than his brother had. From the first, Andrew's guilt about the manner in which the title and property had fallen to him made him ambivalent about his inheritance. He would not, perhaps could not, allow himself to develop the same instant emotional attachment to all that they were to one day possess that Debo evinced with regard to Chatsworth.

Whenever Jean Lloyd visited Debo during this period, the latter would propose that she and her Ogilvy cousin go over to visit Chatsworth. The routine never varied. Debo would bring with her a shooting stick whose handle unfolded to create a little seat. After the women had crossed the bridge over the River Derwent and walked on for a bit, Debo would stop suddenly, then plunge the sharpened end of her stick into the earth. From that vantage point, she would sit and gaze at Chatsworth for a long while, a woman "besotted." Each time, Debo would tell Jean the same thing—that she must arrange to reopen the house and find a way to live there.

On the night of October 4, as on other such occasions, Kick was full of praise for Debo. She applauded the magnificence of the ball, where the oysters, grouse, and champagne flowed all night. Still, Kick's affectionate words and pretty smiles did not mean that she was content to go on being a mere supporting player to Debo's new star turn. In Kick's private life, there was beginning to emerge an element of competition with her brother- and sister-in-law, a sense that though she had lost a great deal when Andrew and Debo became Marquess and Marchioness of Hartington, she might soon be in a position to have even more than they. The Fitzwilliams were richer than the Devonshires, after all, and Wentworth Woodhouse so much vaster than Chatsworth.

On Peter's side as well, there was a distinct element of competitiveness, which in his case seems to have been rooted in the long-standing rivalry between the houses of Fitzwilliam and Cavendish. Andrew Cavendish knew Peter from the racing and gambling milieux, and actually liked him personally quite a bit. Billy's brother was far from alone in noticing that Kick was hardly the sort of woman who ordinarily would have appealed to Peter. To Andrew, it was her status as the Dowager Marchioness of Hartington, as well as her intimate connection with the Duke and Duchess of Devonshire, that made her such a glittering trophy in Peter's eyes. The Fitzwilliams had a history of seizing the spoils of other great houses that had fallen into decline and decay. For Peter to claim Billy's widow for his own would be to assure and assert his family's preeminence after the Second World War. Peter's only child with the present Countess Fitzwilliam was a daughter. Complications at the time of the girl's birth were said to have precluded Obby's producing further children. Kick, who had previously been brought in to reinvigorate a ducal line, was still young enough to provide Fitzwilliam with a son and heir.

Eunice's visit, that October and November of 1946, was comprised essentially of two parts. In the first, Kick took Eunice on a tour of the settings, all of them associated with the house of Cavendish, where she and Billy would have had their life together had he survived the war. Following a stay at Compton Place, the Kennedy sisters went on to Edensor House, where they explored not only Chatsworth, but also Churchdale Hall and Hardwick Hall.

There followed a ten-day driving tour of Ireland, in the course of which they were due to inspect yet another Cavendish family–owned property, Lismore Castle. First, however, Kick and Eunice stopped at Coolattin House in County Wicklow. One of the largest private houses in Ireland, the 120-room pile was owned by Peter Fitzwilliam. If the theme of Eunice's visit to date had been "what might have been," at Coolattin House it shifted to "what yet might be." Still, Eunice could hardly be told that Kick was having an affair with their married host. There had been a time when Kick had adamantly refused to countenance the humiliations to which her father, by his womanizing, had cruelly and callously subjected her mother. Some ten years earlier, Kick had boldly protested when Joe Kennedy brought a mistress to sit at Rose's table. Now, by agreeing to visit Coolattin House at a time when Obby Fitzwilliam was in residence—indeed, by accepting the countess's hospitality—Kick had placed herself in the position of the very mistress whose presence in the Kennedy household she had once decried. Further, she had cast her unwitting sister in the role of a beard.

Kick's stay at Coolattin House marked a considerable heightening in her affair with Peter Fitzwilliam. He had brought her into one of his numerous households. He had paraded her before his wife. He had put on grand display for Kick the mode of life that would one day be hers should she become his bride—as soon as he succeeded in divorcing the present countess, that is. The particular social order embodied by the Coolattin estate—whose tenants had long been exceedingly fond of the Fitzwilliam family—was precisely the sort that Kick most admired. Coolattin suggested more than just the pre-1939 world that the new Labor government had undertaken to obliterate; it summoned vividly to life the eighteenth-century society that, before she'd even met Peter, had fired her imagination so. In this setting she saw Peter as he wished to be seen, as a true "eighteenth-century lord." Given her fondness for pageantry and color, she could not but savor the spectacle of her host, garbed in a red coat, riding off with numerous similarly habited horsemen and their many hounds—a picture she declared "one of the most lovely sights imaginable." Kick left Coolattin on the afternoon of November 3 bedazzled by much that she had seen and experienced there.

In the wake of her visit, however, she was also much troubled and perplexed. It had been difficult enough when Billy had insisted that she be the one to compromise—though in the end, having consented to Billy's stipulation about the religious upbringing of their children, Kick had finally come to believe that she had in fact done nothing sinful or wrong. What Peter was asking of her, by contrast, was so much more overwhelming to contemplate. "It was really too much for her," remembered Elizabeth Cavendish, who, unlike Eunice, knew of Kick's affair with Peter Fitzwilliam and of the wrenching decisions that confronted her. "It wasn't just that he was a Protestant. He was a married man."

Thirteen

On April 29, 1947, Kick was in a contemplative mood as the hour drew near that the liner *Queen Elizabeth*, on which she had been traveling from America, was scheduled to dock in Southampton, England. The cause of her meditations was the sight of an American teenager named Sharman Douglas who, with everything ahead of her, reminded Kick of the girl she herself had been almost a decade before. Lewis Douglas was the newly appointed U.S. ambassador to the Court of St James's, and his sprightly daughter Sharman was sailing over in the company of her mother to join him at the American Embassy.

"It made me feel rather sentimental to see the daughter age 18, going to London for the first time like I did," Kick wrote from the boat to the Kennedys, whom she had just been visiting, "although the glories I found have vanished now."

In her day, Kick had been one of London's most popular debutantes. She had swiftly and skillfully penetrated the hermetically sealed world of the aristocratic cousinhood. She had been courted by various young noblemen. She had fallen in love with the heir to a dukedom, and by sheer persistence and obstinacy she had managed to keep that love alive in the face of monumental obstacles. She had struggled with ethical and religious dilemmas and she had finally taken a decision with which she, at least, could be at peace. She had become a wife and a widow in a matter of months. She had made a glittering future for herself and she had had that future abruptly snatched away by a German sniper's bullet. She had endured and emerged from paralyzing grief. She had moved to a new home of her own and she had established a political salon there.

And now, though Kick spoke wistfully to the Kennedys of vanished glories, she perceived herself as having a chance not only to retrieve much of that glory, but perhaps even to surpass it.

One of Britain's wealthiest peers, a man whom she found incomparably attractive and whom she regarded as a hero in the great societal struggle of the postwar era, wished to marry her. This time, however, should she finally consent to become Peter Fitzwilliam's second wife, it seemed highly unlikely that she would ever discover a way, as before, to be at peace with her decision. Though Kick had defied both Hyannis Port and Rome in the past, she had never ceased to think of herself as a Catholic to whom the tenets of her faith were precious. When she married Billy Hartington, she had by no means agreed to abandon Catholicism, only to consent that any children she and he might have would be raised as Anglicans. By the time of Kick's initial plunge into the world of the aristocratic cousinhood, in 1938, Catholic principles had been long and deeply inculcated in her—and so, for all that she had experienced in the interim, they remained.

Such were the contradictions of Kick's nature that the same woman who had lately become a Whig grandee's mistress also at intervals went on retreats to convents whose "peaceful and tranquil" atmosphere, as she described it that emotionally turbulent spring of 1947, were as a balm to her. Because as a committed Roman Catholic Kick was deeply troubled by the fact that Peter was married, her excruciating conflict was not simply with her family and with her church—it was with herself. This time, nothing anyone else said or did could alter her conviction that marrying him would in fact be a sin. Thus Elizabeth Cavendish's sympathetic assessment that the dilemma was "really too much" for Kick.

In the course of her second postwar visit to the U.S., which had taken place between February and April, Kick had refrained from disclosing that dilemma to her family, who as yet knew nothing about her affair with Peter Fitzwilliam. She had, nonetheless, given signs that something might be different. Rather than wishing to rush about and see a great many people as she ordinarily would have done, she contrived to spend as much time as possible with her parents, whom she subsequently insisted she had actually "seen more of" on this trip than ever before. Kick's "new schedule this year"—in her mother's approving phrase—consisted of playing golf every afternoon with Rose, and conversing with the family at night. Whatever degree of calm she had thusly managed to attain did not last long, however. Hardly was Kick back in London when it seemed to her somehow as if she had never been away.

To an observer unaware of the tremendous decisions that faced Kick, her return to Britain in 1947 might have seemed little different from what it had been the previous year. Again, Seymour Berry's car and driver collected Lady Hartington at the dock in Southampton. Again, the charming little house in Smith Square overflowed with flowers sent over by the Duchess of Devonshire. Again, Kick spent her first weekend in the enveloping company of Billy's parents and sisters, at Compton Place. Again, the tiny drawing room in Smith Square soon echoed with the voices of her friends from prewar days.

Though the political talk still abounded with references to the nationalization of the coal industry, and to the government minister who had gone mano a mano with Peter Fitzwilliam, the mood and morale in Conservative quarters were substantially improved from the year before. Arctic weather conditions had beset Britain in the early months of 1947. Poor government planning had doomed the country to endure an inadequate supply of coal. Electrical shutdowns, business closings, mass unemployment, food and water shortages, and stalled train lines had led to broad suffering. Manny Shinwell was widely blamed for the administrative incompetence that had left Britain so woefully unprepared. The beleaguered minister of fuel and power had even had to be put under police protection on account of the myriad anonymous threats that had been made against him.

Beyond the mass resentment of Shinwell, there had occurred a diminution of public confidence in the Labor government overall, a development that Conservatives viewed as a matchless political gift. Previous predictions based on the 1945 Labor landslide had suggested that the party of Winston Churchill would have to wait two five-year election cycles at the very least before it could hope to be returned to power. The coal crisis scrambled all such calculations. Suddenly, the pundits were saying that the socialists could be vulnerable as early as the next general election. Churchill or, should the ongoing efforts to oust him as party leader prove successful, Anthony Eden could become Britain's next prime minister a good deal sooner than anyone in the party had dared to dream.

Kick had not been back in England for long when she encountered Eden at a dinner party given by Margaret Biddle in London. She had previously met the Conservative crown prince, who was tall, slim, and debonair, with ice blue eyes and a well-tended gray mustache, in October of 1946. At the time, she had been seated between Eden and the Duke of Windsor at the Earl of Dudley's dinner party for the Windsors. Emerald Cunard had been Eden's other dinner partner, and in the course of the evening she had encouraged him to take a romantic interest in Kick. "Anthony, don't you think Kick is pretty?" she asked. "Kick, don't you think Anthony is wonderful?" Eden was then hoping to repair his broken marriage to the mother of his three sons, Beatrice Eden, with whom he was about to leave for a holiday in the Caribbean. So, though he and Kick had chatted happily about politics, by evening's end Lady Cunard's matchmaking efforts appeared to have been in vain.

Everything seemed very different, however, when Eden met Lady

Hartington again six months later. His attempt to reconcile with Beatrice had come to naught. While Kick had been in the U.S., he had returned to England without his wife, who had refused to accompany him. He swiftly emerged as a conspicuous presence in Kick's life. This was in sharp contrast to the secrecy that continued to characterize her overlapping relationship with Peter Fitzwilliam, who, to Kick's anguish, persisted in regularly appearing in public with his wife. In retrospect, some of Kick's friends wondered whether, coming as it did at a time when she was struggling with the issues that Fitzwilliam's offer of marriage presented, the relationship with Eden—who was pursuing other women at the time as well—was an effort on her part to discover an appealing alternative.

If she longed to become a woman of influence, it could not but count hugely with her that Eden was in line to be his party's next leader. If she dreamed of seeing the Conservatives returned to power, it was no small factor that he might soon reside at Number 10 Downing Street. When, that June of 1947, she sat beside Eden as he took the salute in his private box at the Royal Tournament, the world's largest military tattoo, at the Olympia, she reveled in the "tremendous ovation" he received from the crowds. She was impressed when, after lingering with her at the 400 Club until five in the morning, he went on the next day to open the debate for the Opposition on foreign affairs in the House of Commons— an address that, she had it directly from no less an authority than Hugh Fraser, had been "first class." Kick found Eden fascinating to talk with about subjects ranging from Churchill's vagaries to the mysterious goings-on backstage at Stalin's Kremlin. Eden was pleasing to look at, consummately charming, and hugely entertaining. Yet for all of his abundant attractions, he lacked, at least for Kick, the sexual magnetism that continued to draw her to Fitzwilliam.

It certainly did not help Eden's chances with Kick that his London residence was, to her eye, "a rather squalid little house with very few comforts." Peter Fitzwilliam, on the other hand, had "the largest house in England." Wentworth Woodhouse was larger even than Chatsworth, which was located but twenty miles away. Peter seemed to be upping the ante when he invited her to stay at Wentworth, along with other houseguests including the film producer Alexander Korda and the Conservative politician Oliver Stanley, during the last weekend of July in 1947. The Whig palace had three hundred and sixty-five rooms (supposedly one for each day of the year), a thousand windows covering some two hundred and fifty thousand square feet, and the longest country house facade in all of Europe. The roof alone stretched for some two and a half acres. If one wished to walk completely around the house, one needed at least half an hour to do it, perhaps more.

For Kick, no less affecting than Wentworth's splendor was the spectacle of the depredations to which the Labor government had subjected that splendor. For all of the gaiety and grandeur that prevailed at Peter Fitzwilliam's dinner table, the incongruous scene outside assured that this was to be no idyllic country house weekend. "The gardens have all been dug up and taken over by the government for coal," Kick reported afterward to the Kennedys. "I've never seen anything so awful as the machinery is right outside one's window and these valuable old trees have all been uprooted and it will never be the same."

When that August of 1947 Kick wrote to her family of her visit to Wentworth, she pointedly, and quite uncharacteristically, omitted any reference to the name of her host. The following month, Jack would be the first Kennedy family member with whom she broached the subject of her affair. Newly elected to represent the 11th District in the House of Representatives—a campaign that Kick had followed from afar with intense interest and enthusiasm—Jack Kennedy was in Britain on a congressional fact-finding mission. In the course of his visit, he joined Kick at a house party that she had arranged at Lismore Castle. Among her guests was Anthony Eden, with whom she had been eager that Jack have the benefit of, in her phrase, "an exchange of ideas." Despite the conspicuous presence of Eden, however, it was Peter Fitzwilliam of whom she spoke confidentially to her brother in Ireland. She told Jack that she was in love with Peter, whom she compared to Rhett Butler in

Gone With the Wind; and she urged her brother not to say anything of the affair to their parents until she had had a chance to speak to them herself.

More and more, however, other people—people whom Kick would have preferred at this stage to believe that if she was romantically interested in anyone, it was in Eden—were beginning to discover her secret. Indeed, it was not long after Kick returned to London following the house party that Jean Lloyd accidentally found out about Fitzwilliam.

Jean and Kick were alone at Smith Square of an evening when the telephone rang during dinner. Kick left the room to take the call. When she returned she said casually, "That was Peter."

"Is that Peter Cazalet?" said Jean, referring to one of the young men from their prewar set.

"No," said Kick. "Peter Fitzwilliam."

Jean—who had come to know Fitzwilliam during the war, when he had been staying at the same hotel in Scotland as she and her husband while the latter pursued a two-month gunnery training program—was appalled. Now, nearly a decade after Nancy Astor had assigned her to "look after" Kick, Jean still felt bound by that charge, still felt hugely protective of her friend. But whereas the Little American Girl had been eager to be guided in matters she admittedly did not understand, Lady Hartington had seemingly earned the right to make her own distinctions. Jean therefore struggled to remain silent, though she would always feel that Kick could not but have perceived her alarm upon hearing Fitzwilliam's name.

The next time she saw Kick, the meeting took place by chance. Happening upon her at Wilson's, a bar where some of the younger aristocrats liked to have lunch, Jean ruefully remarked that Kick appeared to have "gone in a different direction," an allusion—but no more than that—to her relationship with Fitzwilliam.

Sadly and softly, Kick insisted that she had not.

Yet even Kick could hardly deny that the affair had begun to open a breach between her and some of her old friends. Notably, David Ormsby-

Gore, when he spoke to Kick of his concerns, proved a good deal more plainspoken than Jean had been. David passionately maintained that she could never be happy with a man as dissolute and self-indulgent as Fitz-william. With equal ardor, she countered that David simply did not know Peter as she did. As far as Kick was concerned, because of the public stand that Peter had taken against Shinwell and the socialists, her argument had the force of truth.

Even if her old friends failed to see him that way, she really had managed to cast him, at least to herself, in a most flattering light. Jean, David, and others in their circle regarded this as self-deception on Kick's part. They judged that her passion for Fitzwilliam was as blinding as it was all-consuming.

Most complicated, perhaps, was the attitude taken by Billy's sister Elizabeth. Like the others, she doubted that in the end any marriage to a man of Peter Fitzwilliam's habits and propensities could possibly last. He had been willing to destroy his first wife; why would he not be prepared to do the same to her successor, should it suit him? Still, when late in 1947 Kick finally decided to accept Fitzwilliam's marriage proposal, Elizabeth agreed to accompany her to the U.S. "for moral support" when she told Rose and Joe the news. Elizabeth could see that Kick was "absolutely terrified" of facing the Kennedys. In 1944, Elizabeth, rather than leave her recently widowed sister-in-law alone, had slept on the floor beside Kick's bed night after night at Compton Place. Now, three years later, she was equally intent that Kick always have a loyal friend nearby in the difficult days to come. The plan was for Kick to fly to the U.S. in February 1948, rather than travel by boat. Elizabeth would join her there at the beginning of March.

At this point, Kick's parents had no idea that the impending visit was to be anything other than routine. If her letters home had given the Kennedys reason to worry, it would have been about her relationship with Anthony Eden, of whom she spoke openly and warmly. She wrote of visits to Eden's country house in Chichester and of the political talk she had heard there. She threw out tantalizing bits of gossip about the

Conservative Party's internecine power struggles, and she suggested that when she arrived home presently she would have a good deal more to tell. She expressed the hope that her father was prepared to sit at home every night in Palm Beach listening to her talk her "great big head off." She suggested that her theme would be postwar British politics, though she well knew what the true subject of those conversations must inevitably be.

In the meantime, at Christmas of 1947 Kick arrived at Churchdale Hall fresh from a stay with Eden in the country. She was to celebrate the holiday with "just the family"—by which she meant Billy's family, with, as it happened, the curious addition of Debo's mother, Lady Redesdale, and sister Unity. Eight years after the notorious Unity Mitford had attempted suicide in the wake of Britain's declaration of war against Nazi Germany, she persisted in declaring herself a fascist. Kick judged Unity to be "slightly more sane" than the year before, but unhinged nonetheless. When Unity told the family circle of her latest plan, to enter a convent, one of the guests suggested that if she did that, she might go mad. "But I am mad," Unity replied, with a look of utter seriousness upon her face.

Unity and her mother were staying in Edensor with the Hartingtons. Debo and Andrew had just returned from South Africa, where, as part of the heir's ongoing apprenticeship, Eddy Devonshire had sent him to explore investment opportunities. Andrew was proving to be an apt pupil, but there were grave problems as well. Far from diminishing over time, the aftereffects of the trauma that Debo knew him to have experienced in Italy seemed only to have become the more deeply ingrained.

Andrew had always had a taste for alcohol, but these days he drank even more, apparently to dull his excruciating guilt over the soldier, Sergeant King, for whose death he still held himself responsible. He felt guilty as well for the life he had inherited—stolen, as far as he was concerned—from his brother, and he insisted repeatedly that it was he who ought to have died rather than Billy. This twofold instances of survivor's guilt disastrously fed into each other. By turns Andrew was depressed, irritable, explosive.

He and Debo, who had once been so ineffably happy together, saw their marriage begin to unravel. At moments, the sweet, loving, sensitive man Debo had married would reemerge, only to sink without explanation into the mists of distant unreachability. The darkness that pervaded Andrew had exacerbated the couple's anguish when, within a year, Debo lost two babies, one by miscarriage and the other a few hours after birth. By Debo's own account, at a certain point early on she concluded that in order to protect her living children she must "choose" them over Andrew, always putting their needs before those of the erratic, self-flagellating husband whom she had never ceased to adore.

At the same time, as Lord Holderness would point out many years afterward, through the decades Debo, in countless ways the stronger spouse, did much to shape Andrew, to help make it possible for him to play the public part that fate had assigned him. Lord Holderness further reflected that had Billy survived the war, Kick, like Debo the stronger partner, would no doubt have done the same for her husband. Kick's miscalculation, her friend sadly went on, was to assume that she would be able to accomplish anything like that with the already fully formed and exceedingly strong-willed Earl Fitzwilliam.

That Christmas of 1947, Andrew sorely wanted to warn Kick about the folly she was about to commit were she to marry Fitzwilliam. However, he worried that it might seem as if he were acting not out of sincere concern for her well-being, but rather out of familial loyalty to Billy. So, to Andrew's immense frustration, in the end he chose to say nothing.

Kick also initially found herself quite unable to confront the inevitable, when, shortly, she was reunited with her parents in Palm Beach. Her visit to the U.S. was scheduled to last for two months, so again and again she found herself putting off any announcement to her family of her wedding plans. In the meantime, she and Elizabeth enjoyed a visit to Washington, where Jack and Eunice were sharing a house in George-town that seemed to be constantly filled with people, popular music, and—most of all, Elizabeth remembered—joyous laughter. Since last Kick had seen Jack, at Lismore Castle, he had fallen gravely ill in London, been diagnosed with Addison's disease, been given no more than a year to live, and received the last rites of the Roman Catholic Church. Remembering his and Kick's high spirits in Washington that year, it seemed inconceivable to Elizabeth that Kick could have had any particular knowledge of his recent ordeal.

Here, as in Florida, Kick and her sister-in-law shared a bedroom, and at night they delighted in the sound of pebbles being thrown at Eunice's window from the street by a young man named Sargent Shriver, who was then courting her. Also during this time, Kick took Elizabeth to meet her bohemian friend and colleague from her *Times Herald* days, John White, who still lived and entertained amid piles of books in "the cave." When Kick told him the story of her affair with Peter Fitzwilliam, John White, ever the egoist, saw the liaison as the culmination of his own long-ago efforts to awaken and enlighten her sexually. Though it was another man who had succeeded in breaking down her defenses, White exulted that Kick was liberated from her parents' values and views at long last.

But was she really? For all of her outward air of worldliness, certain of those inculcated beliefs, notably the prohibitions against divorce and against marrying a divorced man, remained as intrinsic to how Lady Hartington, aged twenty-eight, viewed the world as they had been to Kick Kennedy's perspective five years before. In advance of Kick's showdown with her parents, it was not any decline in her powers of retort that seemed to worry her. It was that, however much she wanted this marriage to take place, she could not help but regard it as wrong. In spite of herself, everything in her training and background led her to see it that way. When, previously, David Ormsby-Gore had raised the character issue with her, Kick had been able to argue with conviction that David simply misperceived Peter Fitzwilliam. With her mother, however, the ground was certain to shift to Peter's status as a married man. Anything Kick said on that count was likely to put her in a false position.

Kick was booked to return to England on the liner *Queen Elizabeth* from New York City on April 22, 1948. Shortly before her departure, she joined Joe and Rose on the occasion of the reopening of the Greenbrier Hotel in White Sulphur Springs, West Virginia, where they had had their honeymoon thirty-four years ago. On the present occasion, Kick postponed the disclosure of her wedding plans until the final night of their stay there. Immediately, there were hot words between her mother and herself. Rose Kennedy stipulated that if Kick committed the sin of marrying a divorced man, she would promptly be cut off from the family—not just from her parents, but from her siblings as well. The threat, whether or not Rose would be able to carry it out in its entirety, left Kick reeling. To her further anguish, her father, also in the room at the time, appeared by his silence to agree with Rose, both about the marriage and the banishment.

When Kick returned to London without having agreed to break off with Fitzwilliam, Rose did not resort to intermediaries, or retreat to a hospital bed, as she had done when she frantically sought to prevent her daughter's marriage to Billy Hartington. This time, the indignant matriarch pursued Kick, all the way to Smith Square, where the women battled on for four days. In the unlikely event that Kick had forgotten either point, Rose laid out yet again the Church's position on divorce and renewed her threats of expulsion from the Kennedy family circle. She demanded that Kick give up her life in London and accompany her to the U.S. at once. Still, when their war of words had died down, the mother had not succeeded in swaying the daughter from her purpose.

Nor had Rose extinguished Kick's hope that there was something old Joe might yet do on her and her lover's behalf. However much Kick had changed and grown through the years, she had never ceased to believe in the powers of "Darling Daddy" to make everything right.

Soon, the news that Joe Kennedy planned to be in Paris in May seemed to provide an opening. Kick and Peter were due to be in Cannes around that same time, and she asked the old man if they might come to see him. Her father agreed to have lunch with her and her lover at the Ritz Paris hotel on Saturday, the fifteenth. During Kick's convent school years, Joe had often been willing to influence the nuns to bend the rules in her favor by offering them a film screening or some other gift. Now, half in earnest and half in jest, Peter Fitzwilliam declared that in the event her father persisted in his opposition to the marriage, Peter would himself travel to the Vatican and propose to the Pope that he build the Catholics a new church. One way or another, Peter was determined to marry Kick as soon as he could divorce his wife.

Two days before they were to see Joe at the Ritz, Kick and Peter were en route to Cannes on a chartered ten-seat de Havilland Dove plane when they stopped at Le Bourget airfield, near Paris, to refuel. On an impulse, Peter called some racing world friends in Paris and invited them for lunch on the Champs-Elysées. When he and Kick returned to the aircraft some two and a half hours later, the pilot insisted that turbulent weather conditions ahead made it unsafe to take off; any attempt to reach Cannes would require flying directly into a massive thunderstorm. Peter, however, simply would not hear of postponing the flight until the danger had passed. In defiance of the elements, he angrily demanded that the aircraft take off without delay. At twenty minutes past three in the afternoon, the plane, carrying Kick, Peter, and a two-man crew, departed for Cannes.

Jean Lloyd was asleep when the telephone rang very early Friday morning. She had gone to bed late because Andrew and Debo were staying with her and her husband in London. Between children and adults, the small house in Chelsea was packed to overflowing, but no one seemed to mind very much. On the contrary, the difficulties presented when four adults sought to bathe and prepare for the evening, with but one bathroom available to them, had proven to be a source of mirth to both couples. The previous day's visit had been a happy one, at the end of which Debo had been assigned a bed in an upstairs room, while Andrew had been shown to a cot in David's tiny dressing room.

In later years, Jean remembered being confused about who might be calling at this hour. Shaking herself awake, she picked up the phone and heard the familiar voice of Tom Egerton, Andrew's closest friend. Tom explained that Kick had been killed in a plane crash in France with Peter Fitzwilliam. Before Jean had had a chance to register quite what Tom had said, he asked her to awaken Andrew and tell him what had happened.

Jean rushed to the dressing room and stood before the door behind which Andrew lay asleep. All she could think of then—she recalled long afterward—was Kick as she had looked that first evening at Cliveden in 1938, all aglow and full of energy and expectation, as Andrew bounded wildly up the staircase to greet her. Jean's reverie lasted for no more than a few moments, but at the time she felt as though she were frozen in place "for an eternity." Finally, she managed to lift her hand and knock at the door.

Andrew's reaction to the news was immediate. There had been no need for Tom Egerton or anyone else to tell him what he must do; Andrew seemed to know instinctively. He pulled on his clothes and left the house before dawn in anticipation of making the rounds of newspaper proprietors in London. His aim was to ensure that both Kick and her late husband's family were shielded against any mention in the press of her affair with a married man. Thanks to Andrew's intervention, it was generally written only that Lady Hartington and Earl Fitzwilliam had been passengers on the same ill-fated aircraft. Kick was reported to have been en route to Cannes when, in Paris, she had a chance encounter with Peter Fitzwilliam, who, also on his way there, offered her a ride in his private plane.

Meanwhile, Joe Kennedy, in Paris when he learned of the accident, had set off at once for the town of Privas, some ten miles from where the plane had crashed in the midst of a thunderstorm. At the time of his arrival, the bodies were still in the process of being transported to Privas in an oxcart. Kick, whose corpse had been discovered on the sodden ground not far from the shattered aircraft, had been identified with the aid of her American passport. Still, it remained for Joe Kennedy to make the final definitive identification of the daughter he had long designated, in Rose's words to Nancy Astor, his "favorite of all the children." Until he actually saw her, old Joe yet retained a faint hope that there might be some mistake. But when, on Friday night, the four bodies—Kick's, Peter's, the pilot's, and the radioman's—were brought in at last to the town hall in Privas, Joe acknowledged that the young woman with the broken jaw and the deep laceration on the right side of her face was indeed his child.

In Washington, when a reporter telephoned the Georgetown house shared by Congressman Kennedy and his sister with the news that "Lady Hartington" had died in a plane crash, Eunice, who took the call, initially seized on the fact that there were actually two women in Britain who bore that name. To Eunice's horror, she found herself wishing momentarily that it was Debo who had been killed rather than Kick. The newsman quashed that possibility by noting that the deceased woman's passport bore the name "Kathleen." Jack thereupon joined his mother and other family members in Hyannis Port. At that point, old Joe seems to have assumed that Jack was arranging to have Kick buried in the U.S. But when, on the fifteenth of May, Joe telegraphed his son to learn the details of the burial arrangements, to the patriarch's frustration none were forthcoming.

Only weeks before, when she'd gone to London, Rose Kennedy had urged Kick to come back with her to the U.S. at once. Now, no one on the American end seemed to be in any great hurry to bring back Kick's remains. When it became agonizingly apparent that the Kennedys were making no move, the Duchess of Devonshire intervened. Billy's mother offered to bury Kick in the family plot in Edensor village, near Chatsworth. The duchess promised, moreover, to do everything in strict accordance with the requirements of the Roman Catholic Church. She made it clear that every detail of the Requiem Mass at the Farm Street Church in Mayfair, London, and of the burial service that followed, would be precisely as Kick's mother might have wished.

In light of the paralysis and disarray in the Kennedy camp, Joe Kennedy agreed to the plan. Rose refused to travel to England to see her daughter buried. Nor did any other Kennedy fly over from the U.S. Even Jack, though he said he would be there, failed to materialize in the end. He, Rose, and the others held their own memorial service in Hyannis Port. Joe, meanwhile, was the sole family member to attend the Requiem Mass. While Joe was in London, his palpable and monumental sadness did not, however, restrain him from making a pass at Billy's twenty-two-year-old-sister, Elizabeth.

Friends from every period and facet of Kick's life in England crowded the Farm Street Church on Thursday, May 20. The young aristocrats with whom she had frolicked at Cliveden, Hatfield, Cortachy, and other great houses before the war; guests at the legendary party she had co-hosted in London in 1943, where not a few of the uniformed young men were soon to die; habitués of the Conservative political salon she had established in Westminster after the war; members of the louche London set she had been cultivating of late—all these and many more came to the Requiem Mass. Collectively, they had endured war, death, trauma, social and political cataclysm—and now this. Some onlookers wept and others fought back tears when Sissie Ormsby-Gore fell to her knees before the casket, placed her head sideways on the lid, and began to wail.

Following the Mass, a good many of the mourners proceeded to a special train that had been made available to them by the duke. When the large party arrived in Derbyshire, Chatsworth employees and tenants lined the road to the old churchyard of St. Peter's Church in Edensor, where a Roman Catholic priest was set to officiate. Standing at Kick's graveside were two old men for whom her death amounted almost to a mortal blow. Both men had battled long and arduously to bar Kick from

Chatsworth, yet both were here today to see her laid to rest in the cemetery, where the grass around the centuries-old headstones was trimmed by grazing sheep. Eddy Devonshire had once regarded Kick as an evil influence who deployed her powers to insinuate herself into his family. He had later come to view her as the one person who might help his eldest son and heir to retrieve the family's power. And finally, she had become the person who could best help assuage the duke's anguish at the death of that son.

Like the duke, who had seen his glory snatched away by Derbyshire electors on the one hand and by a Nazi bullet on the other, Joe Kennedy cut a devastated and diminished figure at the graveyard. He who had enjoyed such immense popularity and influence when he first arrived in Britain had since become an outcast, many of whose confident assumptions and predictions had, like Eddy Devonshire's, been disproven in the fullness of time. Joe also shared with Eddy the loss of a much-worshipped eldest son, and now of Kick. In 1938, Joe, the most proactive of parents, had presented England to Kick as a gift like all the others it had afforded him such pleasure to lavish upon her in the past. In 1948, all he could do was passively consent to allow another family to bury her there.

At last, the fraught and much-contested matter of Kick's identity was settled not by her own efforts, but by the duchess's. The very fact of her burial in the Cavendish plot; the inscription memorializing her as the widow of Major the Marquess of Hartington; and the various Cavendishes, Cecils, and other members of the tribe who collected at the graveside—all of these elements conspired to enfold her, both for those present and for posterity, in her late husband's family, even though at the time of her death she had been about to marry into a rival dynasty.

By interring her in this place and in this manner, the duchess—who, ten years before, had claimed Kick for her son Billy because of the energy and life force with which, it was hoped, she would reinvigorate the stock—claimed her for him in death as well.

• • •

It was very late that night when the old duke finished his tale.

Billy's younger brother, "the boy who couldn't wait to grow up," was a fragile figure as he sat hunched over in his leather chair in the golden palace that Kick had once dreamed would be hers. Earlier in the evening, he had sent me on with introductions to other members of the aristocratic cousinhood who would fill out Kick's story for me, but he had been determined to tell his part first.

The house was still and dark when we finally said good night. As I closed the door of the library, he remained behind, alone with the ghost of the Little American Girl who had become for him and the aristocratic cousinhood the emblem of the world they'd lost.

ACKNOWLEDGMENTS

Kick's story is also the story of a vanished world. It is a story based most crucially on the memories, letters, diaries, and annotated scrapbooks of the major players themselves. By chance, as Debo Devonshire often reminded me, I was fortunate to begin my journey into this story and the world of the aristocratic cousinhood at a moment when a number of the key players were still alive and willing and able to share their memories, insights, and questions—for their questions were also important. Had I come to the story now, it would have been too late.

I could not have written this book without the two people on the stairs with Kick at Cliveden that long-ago Easter weekend of 1938. Jean Lloyd not only decoded the rules and personalities of the cousinhood for Kick in those years, but she then did the same for me in marathon conversations over the course of months and months. At Clouds Hill, she fed me "pickup lunches" and explained a world that was to her simply nature but that was to me as utterly foreign as it had once been to Kick. She took me to Hatfield House; she introduced me to Fiona and insisted

I come with her to one of their lunches at Pimlico House, where Kick and Billy used to escape together during the war, to listen in while the two spoke with the intimacy that lifelong friends do of the Little American Girl and her dreams and ambitions. And when Jean found her daily diaries of the period, she went through them with me day by day, explaining the entries, detailing the personalities involved, answering my questions. It was, needless to say, the sort of gift for which a biographer lives.

Andrew Devonshire, the 11th Duke of Devonshire, invited me to Chatsworth and gave me the inspiration for not one, but two books— this one and what became a book about Winston Churchill. I hope that in some small way I have been able to convey the significance of some of the things he told me. He was a remarkable man, the last of his kind. As Jean, who adored her cousin Andrew, liked to laugh: "He wanted to be an eighteenth-century rake." Perhaps he was—but he was also much more: a man of enormous intelligence, an extraordinary conversationalist, and a deeply complicated human being.

Debo Devonshire, Andrew's duchess, was not at Cliveden that first weekend when Kick appeared, but she was a central figure in my research for this story. No one has ever been more generous with a writer than Debo was with me—not just on this book, but on my biography of Kick's brother Jack and then on my book about Winston Churchill. Debo had long been a celebrated duchess when I met her, but as I came to know her, I came to understand that although it was never as painful for her as it was for Andrew to live his brother's life, it was not without pain for Debo to share what might have been Kick's. Debo was also later a great friend of Kick's brother when he was president, and from Jack she had crucial understandings of Kennedy family dynamics that she shared with me.

If these three are the people to whom my debt is greatest, there are others without whose help the research for this story would have been impossible. Most important among them were Kick's sisters-in-law Anne Tree and Elizabeth Cavendish, both of whom were endlessly generous and helped me in innumerable ways to understand not only Kick, but also the dynamics of the Cavendish family. Lord Holderness, the inspirational war hero who became not merely one of Kick's most trusted friends and confidants, but who very clearly loved her until the day he died, spoke to me of her with a frankness, thoughtfulness, and extreme care that made me understand aspects of Kick I might otherwise never have been able to grasp. Fiona Arran was revelatory about both Billy and Kick, and about Kick's relationship to the strange new world in which she found herself.

Betty Coxe Spalding was not just Kick's roommate in Washington and the one who came up with the plan for the Red Cross that finally allowed Kick to return to Billy—she also knew Kick at Hyannis before that, and along with her husband spent weekends of the Kennedy presidency with JFK and was privy to some of his most important thoughts about his sister, his parents, and the rest of the family. We had marathon talks over many months about Kick and the Kennedys, about Jack and the parents.

I also owe thanks to numerous other people who have talked to me about either Kick herself or other pivotal players in her story and the story of this world. Lord Carrington listened to my questions about Andrew and gave me answers that proved invaluable as I attempted to understand this very complicated man. Lady Soames, Debo's cousin, shared her fascinating perspective on Debo, and also provoked from Debo herself some utterly unexpected comments. Lord Salisbury and Hugh Cecil talked to me about the Cecil family during my research on the Churchill book. I also wish to thank Andrew Parker Bowles, who was Billy's godson; Lady Kennard; and Sir Nicholas Henderson.

Through the years, so many people have talked to me about the Kennedy family and its various members as I wrote books about or involving them that there are far too many names to list, but I am grateful to them all. I would also like to express my gratitude to all of the archivists and librarians who facilitated my research in Boston, New York, Washington, London, Oxford, Derbyshire, and other locations: the

National Archives at Kew; the Bodleian Library at Oxford; the British Library; Chatsworth; the JFK Library; the Library of Congress; the University of Reading; the FDR Library; Eton Library; Cambridge University Library; the University of Rhode Island; the Sterling Library, Yale; and the Beinecke Library, Yale.

I want to thank Sally Richardson, Thomas Dunne, Peter Joseph, and Melanie Fried at St. Martin's Press. And at the Helen Brann Agency, I would like to express my gratitude to my agent, Helen Brann, and to her assistant, Carol White.

It is beyond my capacity to even begin to express how great my debt is to my husband, David Packman. This book and my life have been enriched by him in ways that I can never begin to explain or thank him for properly.

SOURCE NOTES

One

2 "I fancied her. I wanted to claim her for myself": Andrew Devonshire (formerly Andrew Cavendish) to BL, author interview.

2 it was exclusively the friends: Jean Lloyd (formerly Jean Ogilvy) to BL, author interview. Also, Cliveden visitors' book, University of Reading (hereafter UR). Also, Jean Ogilvy's diary.

2 He had spotted something: Andrew Devonshire to BL, author interview.

2 he should not even have been included: Anne Tree (formerly Anne Cavendish) to BL, author interview.

2 "the boy who couldn't wait to grow up": Jean Lloyd to BL, author interview.

3 A year earlier . . . : Anne Tree to BL, author interview.

3 "constipated older brother": Jakie Astor quoted by Debo Devonshire (formerly Debo Mitford) to BL, author interview.

3 frequently made miserable: Jean Lloyd to BL, author interview. Also, Anne Tree to BL, author interview.

3 not to his taste: Jean Lloyd to BL, author interview.

3 "mousy brown": Jean Lloyd to BL, author interview.

3   set much too high: Debo Devonshire to BL, author interview.

3   "on the lumpy side": Jean Lloyd to BL, author interview.

3   British girls much envied: Debo Devonshire to BL, author interview.

3   obsessed with the conviction: Jean Lloyd to BL, author interview.

3   Andrew would long remember: Andrew Devonshire to BL, author interview.

3   "such vitality": Andrew Devonshire to BL, author interview.

3   Andrew had realized by this time: Andrew Devonshire to BL, author interview.

4   unprecedented blast: Debo Devonshire to BL, author interview.

5   liked to take care of compatriots: Jean Lloyd to BL, author interview.

5   "I've got this little American girl . . .": Nancy Astor quoted by Jean Lloyd to BL, author interview.

5   "rather lost": Jean Lloyd to BL, author interview.

5   "didn't need any looking after!": Jean Lloyd to BL, author interview.

5   a long series of treats: Joseph P. Kennedy's generosity toward his daughter is apparent in Kathleen Kennedy's early correspondence with her parents, John F. Kennedy Library, Boston (hereafter JFKL).

6   "unshakable self-confidence": Jean Lloyd to BL, author interview.

6   Kick appeared to sense: Jean Lloyd to BL, author interview.

6   For a long moment: Jean Lloyd to BL, author interview.

7   To her the aristocratic cousinhood: Debo Devonshire to BL, author interview.

7   who was himself not always quite certain: Andrew Devonshire to BL, author interview.

7   Andrew realized . . . : Andrew Devonshire to BL, author interview.

7   a major crush: Jean Lloyd to BL, author interview. Also, Debo Devonshire to BL, author interview.

7   virtually as a brother: Andrew Devonshire to BL, author interview.

8   "the essence of charm": Andrew Devonshire to BL, author interview.

9   "country-member bad boys": Andrew Devonshire to BL, author interview.

10   matchlessly endearing and entertaining: Andrew Devonshire, author interview.

10   chatter: Jean Lloyd to BL, author interview.

10   acted as though: Jean Lloyd to BL, author interview.

10   arrival: Hugh Fraser's arrival is registered in the Cliveden visitors' book, UR.

11   "a decadent, degenerate Britain": Winston S. Churchill, *The Second World War, Volume I, The Gathering Storm* (Boston: Houghton Mifflin Company, 1985), p. 71.

11   "foolish boys": Winston S. Churchill, *The Gathering Storm*, p. 71.

11   "ever-shameful": Winston S. Churchill, *The Gathering Storm*, p. 71.

12   "entitled": Andrew Devonshire to BL, author interview.

12   "excuse": Andrew Devonshire to BL, author interview.

13   Jean explained to her: Jean Lloyd to BL, author interview.

13   "nose-to-nose": Jean Lloyd to BL, author interview.

13   "the next dance . . .": Jean Lloyd to BL, author interview.

13   eagerness to listen: Jean Lloyd to BL, author interview. Also, Andrew Devonshire to BL, author interview.

13   "decadent": Kathleen Kennedy to John F. Kennedy, February 13, 1942, JFKL.

14   "the best thing that ever happened to me": Kathleen Kennedy to Nancy Astor, April 19, 1938, UR.

14   shut down: Jean Lloyd to BL, author interview.

14   a matter of etiquette: Jean Lloyd to BL, author interview.

15   "I've got my dad, too": Kathleen Kennedy quoted by Jean Lloyd to BL, author interview.

Two

16   "over and over": Jean Lloyd to BL, author interview.

17   "the lunch of the two Joes": Jean Lloyd to BL, author interview.

17   Jean could not but be struck: Jean Lloyd to BL, author interview.

17   "twinkle": Jean Lloyd to BL, author interview.

17   "coarseness": Jean Lloyd to BL, author interview.

18   "a little backward": Kathleen Kennedy quoted by Jean Lloyd to BL, author interview.

18   launched herself far more successfully: Debo Devonshire to BL, author interview.

18   include her in lunches with leading debs: Jean Lloyd to BL, author interview. Also, Jean Ogilvy's diary. Also, Debo Devonshire to BL, author interview.

18   "frightfully beautiful": Jean Lloyd to BL, author interview.

19   her diary entry: Kathleen Kennedy, diary entry, May 11, 1938, JFKL.

19   her visit three days later: Kathleen Kennedy, diary entry, May 14, 1938, JFKL.

19   "drunken youths from Oxford": Kathleen Kennedy, diary entry, May 14, 1938, JFKL.

19   Because of Robert's prodigious drinking: Jean Lloyd to BL, author interview.

20   exceptionally strict with her daughters: Debo Devonshire to BL, author interview.

20   On one particular evening: Jean Lloyd to BL, author interview.

20   took her along with him to Oxford: Kathleen Kennedy, diary entry, May 20, 1938, JFKL.

20   Ciro's: Kathleen Kennedy, diary entry, May 26, 1938, JFKL.

21   "to her English contemporaries . . .": Deborah Devonshire, *Wait for Me!: Memoirs of the Youngest Mitford Sister* (London: John Murray, 2010), p. 98.

22   "petty jealousies": Kathleen Kennedy, diary entry, June 2, 1938, JFKL.

22   seemed taken anew: Jean Lloyd to BL, author interview.

22   the Cecils: See David Cecil, *The Cecils of Hatfield House: An English Ruling Family* (Boston: Houghton Mifflin Company, 1973).

23   when she arrived at Hatfield House: Kathleen Kennedy, diary entry, June 17, 1938, JFKL.

23   secret egress via a closet: Veronica Maclean, *Past Forgetting: A Memoir of Heroes, Adventure and Love* (London: Headline Publishing, 2002), p. 88.

23   intervened: Debo Devonshire to BL, author interview.

23   conniving Catholic girls: Jean Lloyd to BL, author interview.

23   a good deal of trouble: Kathleen Kennedy, diary entry, June 17, 1938, JFKL.

24   "John Stanley got rather rough": Kathleen Kennedy, diary entry, June 18, 1938, JFKL.

24   short-sheeted as a prank: Kathleen Kennedy, diary entry, June 18, 1938, JFKL.

24   Tony Loughborough helped: Kathleen Kennedy, diary entry, June 18, 1938, JFKL.

25   his grandmother who had suggested: Kathleen Kennedy, diary entry, June 18, 1938, JFKL.

25   made a vivid impression: Jean Lloyd to BL, author interview. Also, Andrew Devonshire to BL, author interview.

25   a reputation for being tough: Jean Lloyd to BL, author interview. Also, Andrew Devonshire to BL, author interview.

25   tennis matches at Wimbledon: Kathleen Kennedy, diary entry, June 14, 1938, JFKL.

25   dinner party hosted by Lord and Lady Airlie: Kathleen Kennedy, diary entry, June 24, 1938, JFKL.

26   half smile: Jean Lloyd to BL, author interview.

26   "rather sleepy": Jean Lloyd to BL, author interview.

26   "I can't be bothered to drink it": Billy Hartington quoted by Jean Lloyd to BL, author interview.

26 jealous of Andrew's greater ease: Debo Devonshire to BL, author interview.

26 "a good talk": Billy Hartington and Lady Alice Salisbury quoted by Jean Lloyd to BL, author interview.

26 absorbed in each other: Jean Lloyd to BL, author interview.

26 visibly distressed: Jean Lloyd to BL, author interview.

27 "forced": Kathleen Kennedy, diary entry, June 24, 1938, JFKL.

27 David Ormsby-Gore rescued: Jean Lloyd to BL, author interview.

27 "It was difficult for each to imagine . . .": Andrew Devonshire to BL, author interview.

27 This evening, her consummate disappointment . . . : Deborah Devonshire, *Wait for Me! Memoirs of the Youngest Mitford Sister,* p. 98.

27 spent as much time as possible: Jean Lloyd to BL, author interview.

27 "romantic": Kathleen Kennedy, diary entry, June 24, 1938, JFKL.

28 in the scrapbook she maintained: Kathleen Kennedy's scrapbook, JFKL.

28 As a consequence of their nearly having lost him: Jean Lloyd to BL, author interview.

29 "more than ordinary affection": Harold Macmillan, diary entry, September 24, 1944, *War Diaries* (London: Macmillan, 1984), p. 530.

29 Andrew further resented: Anne Tree to BL, author interview.

29 A lifetime of fraught personal relations: Jean Lloyd to BL, author interview.

29 two oft-spoken-of episodes: Jean Lloyd to BL, author interview.

29 "outdo": Jean Lloyd to BL, author interview.

30 "heresy": Kathleen Kennedy quoted by Betty Coxe Spalding to BL, author interview.

30 "favorite of all the children": Rose F. Kennedy to Nancy Astor, June 14, 1948, UR.

30 "the Big One": Fiona Arran (formerly Fiona Gore) to BL, author interview.

31 "gravitas": Hugh Fraser, oral history, JFKL.

31 roughness and aggressiveness: Fiona Arran to BL, author interview. Also, Jean Lloyd to BL, author interview.

31 "I would not be surprised . . .": Lady Redesdale quoted by Debo Devonshire to BL, author interview.

32 accompanied by his aunt: Kathleen Kennedy, diary entry, July 13, 1938, JFKL.

33 Rose Kennedy had her reservations: Debo Devonshire to BL, author interview.

33 "favorite": Anne Tree to BL, author interview.

33 acquiesced to his brother's claim: Andrew Devonshire to BL, author interview.

35   "We listened to the radio for news flashes . . .": Kathleen Kennedy, diary en-
      try, September 19, 1938, JFKL.

Three

36   September 21, 1938: Dates based on Jean Ogilvy's diary.

36   two chairs remained conspicuously empty: Jean Lloyd to BL, author interview.

36   Jean perceived that Kick: Jean Lloyd to BL, author interview.

37   Lady Airlie was the parent: Debo Devonshire to BL, author interview.

37   tended to be good-humored: Debo Devonshire to BL, author interview.

37   he was instructed to tell: Jean Lloyd to BL, author interview.

37   As the girls understood: Jean Lloyd to BL, author interview.

39   "All you can hear or talk about . . .": Kathleen Kennedy to Lem Billings, Sep-
      tember 23, 1938, JFKL.

39   "You are all dangerous . . .": Lord Airlie quoted by Jean Lloyd to BL, author
      interview.

39   Accompanying them now: Debo Devonshire, author interview.

40   The duchess privately preferred: Debo Devonshire to BL, author interview.

40   even in this romantic setting: Debo Devonshire to BL, author interview.

40   The determined silliness and laughter: Debo Devonshire to BL, author inter-
      view.

41   Ivar Colquhoun sprayed: Kathleen Kennedy, diary entry, September 19,
      1938, JFKL.

41   Jakie Astor: Jean Lloyd to BL, author interview. Also, Kathleen Kennedy,
      diary entry, September 19, 1938, JFKL.

41   she listened to: Kathleen Kennedy, diary entry, September 19, 1938, JFKL.

42   "I have never seen such happiness": Kathleen Kennedy, diary entry, Septem-
      ber 26, 1938, JFKL.

42   Munich and the war were the only topics of conversation: Jean Lloyd to BL,
      author interview.

42   "to find peace and everyone deliriously happy": Kathleen Kennedy, diary en-
      try, September 26, 1938, JFKL.

42   went to stay at Churchdale Hall: Kathleen Kennedy, diary entry, October 3,
      1938, JFKL.

43   talked for hours every night: Kathleen Kennedy, diary entry, October 3,
      1938, JFKL.

43   One speech: Andrew Devonshire to BL, author interview.

43 "Peace he certainly . . .": *Hansard*, House of Commons Debate, European Situation, October 4, 1938, vol. 339, cc 169–308 UK Parliament.

43 "These precedents do not justify . . .": Hansard.

44 Andrew would darkly reflect: Andrew Devonshire to BL, author interview.

45 Kick had a good deal more freedom: Debo Devonshire to BL, author interview.

45 travel to Cambridge in the company of Jane Kenyon-Slaney: Kathleen Kennedy, diary entry, October 27, 1938, JFKL.

46 "All Billy's relatives . . .": Kathleen Kennedy, diary entry, November 23, 1938, JFKL.

46 To the duchess's perception: Jean Lloyd to BL, author interview. Also, Anne Tree to BL, author interview.

46 "normally reticent": Jean Lloyd to BL, author interview.

46 she had no intention of giving in: Anne Tree to BL, author interview.

47 to Billy's right: Kathleen Kennedy, diary entry, December 9, 1938, JFKL.

47 a tacit acknowledgment: Jean Lloyd to BL, author interview.

47 "dirty looks": Kathleen Kennedy, diary entry, December 9, 1938, JFKL.

47 at the 400 Club: Kathleen Kennedy, diary entry, December 9, 1938, JFKL.

47 "mad games . . .": Kathleen Kennedy, diary entry, December 10, 1938, JFKL.

47 the better part of the evening: Kathleen Kennedy, diary entry, December 13, 1938, JFKL.

47 breaks a previously arranged date: Kathleen Kennedy, diary entry, December 14, 1938, JFKL.

47 several long lunches: Jean Ogilvy's diary.

47 went on to Ciro's: Kathleen Kennedy, diary entry, December 21, 1938, JFKL.

48 she confessed: Jean Lloyd to BL, author interview.

48 Rose had exhibited: Debo Devonshire to BL, author interview.

49 she dreaded the explosion: Jean Lloyd to BL, author interview.

49 Kick had indignantly objected: Betty Coxe Spalding to BL, author interview.

49 "acted as if . . .": Arthur Krock, transcript of interview by Joan and Clay Blair Jr., Massachusetts Historical Society, Boston (hereafter MHS).

50 "Such is Kick! . . .": Kathleen Kennedy's scrapbook, JFKL.

50 the cousins remarked: Jean Lloyd to BL, author interview.

51 forcefully confronted with the duties: Jean Lloyd to BL, author interview.

51 he felt he would be: Anne Tree to BL, author interview.

52 would not have been permitted: Kathleen Kennedy, diary entry, February 14, 1939, JFKL.

53 Billy had become absorbed: Anne Tree to BL, author interview.

53   a model for the influential figure: Anne Tree to BL, author interview. Also, Richard Holderness to BL, author interview.

53   "The Prime Minister . . .": The Duke of Devonshire quoted in Robert Kee, *The World We Left Behind* (London: Weidenfeld, 1990), p. 144.

54   more than a thousand spectators: Julian Amery, *Approach March: A Venture in Autobiography* (London: Hutchinson and Co., 1973), p. 115.

55   undertook to make Kick understand: Andrew Devonshire to BL, author interview.

56   showed them a movie: The scene of the film screening is based on interviews with Fiona Arran and Jean Lloyd.

57   "grow up more quickly": Jean Lloyd to BL, author interview.

57   "not to waste a minute": Jean Lloyd to BL, author interview.

57   "I have seen much . . .": Robert Rhodes James, ed., *Chips: The Diaries of Sir Henry Channon* (London: Phoenix, 1996), p. 204.

58   He thereupon spoke: Anne Tree to BL, author interview.

58   out of the question: Anne Tree to BL, author interview.

58   forbade her: Debo Devonshire to BL, author interview.

58   more than 2,500 guests: Debo Devonshire's scrapbook.

58   the more conspicuous by her absence: Jean Lloyd to BL, author interview.

58   did persist in talking about her: Jean Lloyd to BL, author interview.

59   "These Catholic girls are a menace!": Lord Dick Cavendish quoted by Jean Lloyd to BL, author interview.

59   the Duchess of Richmond's ball: Andrew Devonshire, *Accidents of Fortune* (Norwich; Michael Russell, 2004), p. 26.

59   officially entered the Coldstream Guards: Public Records Office, Kew (hereafter PRO).

59   "Some day—somehow": Kathleen Kennedy to Rose F. Kennedy, July 6, 1944, JFKL.

Four

61   "like a beautiful dream": Kathleen Kennedy to Joseph P. Kennedy, September 18, 1939, JFKL.

61   "Thanks a lot . . .": Kathleen Kennedy to Joseph P. Kennedy, September 18, 1939, JFKL.

62   "killing time": Kathleen Kennedy quoted in Peter Collier and David Horowitz, *The Kennedys: An American Drama* (New York: Summit, 1984), p. 131.

62 "a castle and not . . .": Amanda Smith, ed., *Hostage to Fortune: The Letters of Joseph P. Kennedy* (New York: Viking, 2011), p. 517.

62 "a person . . .": Lem Billings quoted in Doris Kearns Goodwin, *The Kennedys and the Fitzgeralds* (New York: Simon & Schuster, 1987), p. 703.

63 Jean Ogilvy sent word: Jean Lloyd to BL, author interview.

63 "He is . . .": Robert Rhodes James, ed., *Chips: The Diaries of Sir Henry Channon*, p. 22.

63 "They bemoaned your absence . . .": Nancy Astor to Kathleen Kennedy, n.d., UR.

63 where her real life and real friends: Jean Lloyd to BL, author interview.

65 a sealed private message: Nancy Astor to Philip Lothian, November 27, 1939, UR.

65 "scandalous": Nancy Astor to Joseph P. Kennedy Jr., February 2, 1940, UR.

65 shown no such reluctance: Philip Lothian to Nancy Astor, December 2, 1939, UR.

68 the ambassador wrote to notify: Joseph P. Kennedy to Rose F. Kennedy, April 5, 1940, JFKL.

68 "without America taking credit for it": Joseph P. Kennedy to Rose F. Kennedy, April 5, 1940, JFKL.

69 "shuttled off to war": Joseph P. Kennedy to Rose F. Kennedy, April 16, 1940, quoted in David Nasaw, *The Patriarch: The Remarkable Life and Turbulent Times of Joseph P. Kennedy* (New York: Penguin Press, 2012), p. 438.

70 "a psychological tonic": *New York Times*, May 11, 1940.

71 "I still keep . . .": Kathleen Kennedy to Joseph P. Kennedy, May 21, 1940, quoted in Doris Kearns Goodwin, *The Kennedys and the Fitzgeralds*, p. 704.

71 "nothing but a miracle": Field Marshal Lord Alanbrooke, *War Diaries, 1939–1945* (London, Weidenfeld & Nicolson, 2001), p. 67.

73 "and the next time . . .": *New York Times*, June 2, 1940.

73 "drawn, miserable": Nancy Astor to Philip Lothian, June 10, 1940, UR.

74 hoping that good news: Nancy Astor to Philip Lothian, June 16, 1940, UR.

74 struggling desperately: Jean Lloyd to BL, author interview.

75 "They just attacked and attacked": Billy Hartington quoted by Jean Lloyd to BL, author interview.

75 strategy of terror: on the terror tactics of the Germans, see Sinclair McKay, *Dunkirk: From Disaster to Deliverance* (London: Aurum Press, 2014), p. 114.

77 their talk that first day: Jean Lloyd to BL, author interview.

Five

79   "calling the huddle": Charles Spalding, oral history, JFKL.

79   "The big difficulty . . .": Joseph P. Kennedy to Rose F. Kennedy, August 2, 1940, JFKL.

79   "I wish . . .": Kathleen Kennedy to Joseph P. Kennedy, August 6, 1940, JFKL.

81   shipped off to live with Nancy Astor: Debo Devonshire to BL, author interview.

81   Jean traveled daily: Jean Lloyd to BL, author interview.

81   Joe Airlie had: Jean Lloyd to BL, author interview.

82   Foreign Office documents: FO 371/24251, PRO.

84   interview with *The Boston Globe*: FO 371/2451, PRO.

84   address to film industry figures: E. A. Cleugh to Richard Ford, November 22, 1940, FO 371/2451, PRO. Also, Fairbanks to Roosevelt, November 19, 1940, Franklin D. Roosevelt Library, Hyde Park.

85   "Hope the New Year . . .": Amanda Smith, ed., *Hostage to Fortune: The Letters of Joseph P. Kennedy*, p. 517.

85   Soon, Nancy Astor was signaling: Nancy Astor to Kathleen Kennedy, February 22, 1941, UR.

85   "Every few days . . .": Tony Rosslyn to John F. Kennedy, October 27, 1940, JFKL.

86   "over the dead bodies . . .": Tony Rosslyn to John F. Kennedy, January 6, 1941, JFKL.

86   "pals": Debo Devonshire to BL, author interview.

87   when he told the story afterward to his brother: Andrew Devonshire to BL, author interview.

87   Even he had been heard to exclaim: Jean Lloyd to BL, author interview.

87   the arrangement appeared to work out no better: Debo Devonshire to BL, author interview.

88   "It was a . . .": Billy Hartington quoted by Kathleen Kennedy in letter to Joseph P. Kennedy, October 22, 1941, JFKL.

88   to be living more in Belgium and France: Jean Lloyd to BL, author interview.

88   "temporarily": Andrew Devonshire to BL, author interview.

89   "my Billy": Sally Norton quoted by Debo Devonshire to BL, author interview.

89   "after Billy": Debo Devonshire to BL, author interview.

89   "should have to make do with second best": Billy Hartington to Rose F. Kennedy, April 30, 1944, JFKL.

89   she would later acknowledge: Betty Coxe Spalding to BL, author interview.

90 "hang around": Frank Waldrop, transcript of interview by Joan and Clay Blair Jr., MHS.

90 "and even if . . .": Kathleen Kennedy to Joseph P. Kennedy, October 3, 1941, JFKL.

92 "I am nearly going mad" Kathleen Kennedy to Joseph P. Kennedy, October 20, 1941, JFKL.

92 "Rather sad . . .": Kathleen Kennedy to Joseph P. Kennedy, October 22, 1941, JFKL.

Six

93 "usual childhood illnesses": John F. Kennedy's naval records, JFKL.

93 cling to her collective Kennedy identity: Betty Coxe Spalding to BL, author interview.

94 the Kennedy Kids: Betty Coxe Spalding to BL, author interview.

94 as Kick later recalled: Kathleen Kennedy to John F. Kennedy, July 29, 1943, JFKL.

94 "quick victory": JFK notes on dinner at Mrs. Patterson's, JFKL.

95 sit up late with him: Betty Coxe Spalding to BL, author interview.

96 "the devil's position": John White, transcript of interview by Nigel Hamilton, MHS.

97 "Tonight for the first time . . .": John White's diary quoted in Doris Kearns Goodwin, *The Fitzgeralds and the Kennedys*, p. 727.

97 viewed himself as a beneficent presence in her life: Betty Coxe Spalding to BL, author interview.

98 "Frivolous, but harmless": John White, transcript of interview by Nigel Hamilton, MHS.

98 "in the way": John White, transcript of interview by Nigel Hamilton, MHS.

99 But whereas John White: John White, transcript of interview of Joan and Clay Blair, Jr., MHS.

99 "Jack's Future": Betty Coxe Spalding to BL, author interview.

100 "He had the charm . . .": Inga Arvad's unpublished memoir, MHS.

100 "I have gooey . . .": John White, transcript of interview by Joan and Clay Blair Jr., MHS.

100 "motherly": Betty Coxe Spalding to BL, author interview.

101 "a boy with a future": Inga Arvad, *Washington Times Herald*, November 27, 1941.

101 "big bag of wind": Kathleen Kennedy quoted in Lynne McTaggart, *Kathleen Kennedy: Her Life and Times* (New York: Dial, 1983), p. 97.

101 "ignorant, thick headed Mick": John White quoted in Lynne McTaggart, *Kathleen Kennedy: Her Life and Times*, p. 99.

102 lunch at a local restaurant: John White, transcript of interview by Nigel Hamilton, MHS.

103 "arranged": Cissy Patterson quoted in Ralph G. Martin, *Cissy* (New York: Simon & Schuster, 1979), p. 418.

104 intensive monitoring operation: memorandum for the attorney general, Re: Mrs. Paul Fejos, nee Inga Arvad, Espionage, Internal Security, January 21, 1942, FBI.

104 "getting ready to . . .": John White, transcript of interview by Joan and Clay Blair Jr., MHS.

104 bequeathed to Kick: Betty Coxe Spalding to BL, author interview.

104 Kick's personal photographs: Betty Coxe Spalding to BL, author interview.

105 broken off with Sally Norton: Nancy Astor to Kathleen Kennedy, December 24, 1941, JFKL.

105 a prime mover in the breakup: Anne Tree to BL, author interview.

105 seemed to affect Billy profoundly: Anne Tree to BL, author interview.

105 "I long to . . .": Kathleen Kennedy to Nancy Astor, UR.

105 "definitely": Kathleen Kennedy to Nancy Astor, n.d., UR.

105 to ask her brother whether he still believed: Kathleen Kennedy to John F. Kennedy, February 13, 1942, JFKL.

106 By Kick's calculations: Betty Coxe Spalding to BL, author interview.

106 "I would advise strongly against . . .": John F. Kennedy to Kathleen Kennedy, March 10, 1942, JFKL.

107 When Lem Billings visited: Lem Billings to John F. Kennedy, n.d., JFKL.

107 The agency bugged: report, Re: Mrs. Paul Fejos, with aliases, Espionage—G, February 23, 1943, FBI.

108 "but 18 summers . . .": Inga Arvad quoted in Nigel Hamilton, *JFK: Reckless Youth* (New York: Random House, 1992), p. 478.

108 she told her parents: Kathleen Kennedy to Joseph P. Kennedy and Rose F. Kennedy, March 20, 1942, JFKL.

108 made the rounds: Kathleen Kennedy to John F. Kennedy, July 8, 1942, JFKL.

108 at her personal expense: FBI 6/24/42.

109 "too happy to do": Kathleen Kennedy to John F. Kennedy, July 8, 1942, JFKL.

109 At bedtime: Betty Coxe Spalding to BL, author interview.

109 "You're late!": John White, transcript of interview by Nigel Hamilton, MHS.

110 she conspired with: Kathleen Kennedy to Rose F. Kennedy, November 23, 1942, JFKL.

110 approached the publisher: Kathleen Kennedy to Rose F. Kennedy, February 1, 1943.

110 Betty Coxe proposed: Betty Coxe Spalding to BL, author interview.

110 she expressed confidence: Betty Coxe Spalding to BL, author interview.

111 "desperate" to be with Billy again: Richard Holderness (formerly Richard Wood) to BL, author interview.

111 As he would recall: Richard Holderness to BL, author interview.

112 he was, by his own subsequent account: Richard Holderness to BL, author interview.

112 he would reflect that it was Kick: Richard Holderness to BL, author interview.

114 viewed the job as an expedient: Betty Coxe Spalding to BL, author interview.

114 she complained: Kathleen Kennedy round-robin letter to her family, June 27, 1943, JFKL.

Seven

117 Kick had not told: Debo Devonshire to BL, author interview.

118 she was unhappy: Jean Lloyd to BL, author interview.

118 Eager to see: Anne Tree to BL, author interview.

118 "As far as . . .": Tony Rosslyn to John F. Kennedy, July 25, 1943, JFKL.

118 Kick wrote home: Kathleen Kennedy's round-robin letter to her family, September 23, 1943, JFKL.

119 "a tough situation": Kathleen Kennedy's round-robin letter to her family, September 23, 1943, JFKL.

119 "quite unchanged": Kathleen Kennedy to John F. Kennedy, July 3, 1943, JFKL.

119 "not obvious": Kathleen Kennedy to John F. Kennedy, July 3, 1943, JFKL.

120 "film star handsome": Debo Devonshire to BL, author interview.

120 "suddenly so attractive": Jean Lloyd to BL, author interview.

120 more physically imposing: Jean Lloyd to BL, author interview.

120 "put their heads together": Kathleen Kennedy's round-robin letter to her family, July 14, 1943, JFKL.

120 "heavy betting": Kathleen Kennedy's round-robin letter to her family, July 14, 1943, JFKL.

120 At his request: Anne Tree to BL, author interview.

120 "For twenty four hours . . .": Kathleen Kennedy to John F. Kennedy, July 29, 1943, JFKL.

121 "a return to innocence": Andrew Devonshire to BL, author interview.

121 He welcomed the opportunity: Andrew Devonshire to BL, author interview.

121 She saw him: Andrew Devonshire to BL, author interview.

121 "There wasn't a . . .": Kathleen Kennedy's round-robin letter to her family, August 24, 1943.

122 he was displeased: Jean Lloyd to BL, author interview.

122 "racy": Jean Lloyd to BL, author interview.

122 "liked to experiment": Jean Lloyd to BL, author interview.

122 preferred that the setting: Jean Lloyd to BL, author interview.

122 pass the night in a sleeping bag: Fiona Arran to BL, author interview.

123 "more like a bed": Kathleen Kennedy quoted by Fiona Aran to BL, author interview.

123 "childlike": Fiona Arran to BL, author interview.

123 Though when he was: Andrew Devonshire to BL, author interview.

123 he knew that he could never: Anne Tree to BL, author interview.

124 As Billy later explained: Billy Hartington to Rose F. Kennedy, April 30, 1944, JFKL.

124 On the present occasion: Jean Lloyd to BL, author interview.

124 "It should be me": Billy Hartington quoted by Jean Lloyd to BL, author interview.

125 Somehow Billy seemed terrified: Jean Lloyd to BL, author interview.

125 had already attempted to ensure: Duke of Devonshire to the Dowager Duchess of Devonshire, November 13, 1944, Chatsworth.

125 "Things you can't imagine": Billy Hartington quoted by Jean Lloyd to BL, author interview.

125 their immense sadness: Kathleen Kennedy's round-robin letter to her family, November 11, 1943, JFKL.

125 Kick billed the event: Kathleen Kennedy's round-robin letter to her family, November 17, 1943, JFKL.

126 her old friends: Debo Devonshire to BL, author interview.

128 Eddy anticipated: Andrew Devonshire to BL, author interview.

130 his mother had arranged: Anne Tree to BL, author interview.

131 Kick's presence: Anne Tree to BL, author interview.

132 "so holy and good": Billy Hartington to Rose F. Kennedy, April 30, 1944, JFKL.

132 He asked Kick: Anne Tree to BL, author interview.

Eight

133 "jump out . . .": Kathleen Kennedy's round-robin letter to her family, July 14, 1943, JFKL.

134 "a strange episode": Lord Harlech (formerly David Ormsby-Gore), oral history devoted to Robert F. Kennedy, JFKL.

134 "was putting unnecessary pressure on Kick": Lord Harlech, oral history devoted to Robert F. Kennedy, JFKL.

134 "hurt": Lord Harlech, oral history devoted to Robert F. Kennedy, JFKL.

134 to make Kick feel: Anne Tree to BL, author interview.

135 wrote of Billy's candidature: Kathleen Kennedy's round-robin letter to her family, January 20, 1944, JFKL.

135 wooden legs: Kathleen Kennedy's round-robin letter to her family, February 22, 1944, JFKL.

135 Mindful as always of her feelings for Billy: Richard Holderness (formerly Richard Wood) to BL, author interview.

135 She talked a good deal: Richard Holderness to BL, author interview.

136 "a woman of influence": Kathleen Kennedy quoted by Richard Holderness to BL, author interview.

136 "very ambitious": Richard Holderness to BL, author interview.

136 "very clear on what she wanted": Richard Holderness to BL, author interview.

136 "a great political hostess": Richard Holderness to BL, author interview.

136 "power and authority": Richard Holderness to BL, author interview.

137 "the goods and chattel": Quoted in Debo Devonshire's scrapbook.

137 "the worst and dirtiest": Duchess of Devonshire to John F. Kennedy, October 19, 1944, JFKL.

138 "So am I . . .": Quoted in Debo Devonshire's scrapbook.

138 instructed Eddy Devonshire: Debo Cavendish to Diana Mosley, September 21, 1943, Charlotte Mosley, ed., *The Mitfords: Letters Between Six Sisters* (New York: Harper, 2007), p. 190.

138 Churchill was heard from: Churchill's letter to Billy Hartington quoted in John Pearson, *The Serpent and the Stag* (New York: Holt, Rinehart and Winston, 1983), p. 277.

139 "the straw in the wind": Debo Devonshire to BL, author interview.

139 her presence had to be downplayed: Elizabeth Cavendish to BL, author interview.

140 "the most overwhelming impact": Kathleen Kennedy quoted by Richard Holderness to BL, author interview.

140   "I don't know . . .": Duke of Devonshire quoted in Kathleen Kennedy's round-robin letter to her family, February 22, 1944, JFKL.

140   "I do . . .": Billy Hartington quoted in Kathleen Kennedy's round-robin letter to her family, February 22, 1944, JFKL.

140   "Britain will not be content . . .": Quoted in Debo Devonshire's scrapbook.

140   "It has been . . .": Quoted in Debo Devonshire's scrapbook.

140   Debo, standing in the crowd: Deborah Devonshire, *Wait for Me!: Memoirs of the Youngest Mitford Sister*, p. 129.

141   there was no longer any doubt: Richard Holderness to BL, author interview.

141   "Frankly I do . . .": Rose F. Kennedy to Kathleen Kennedy, February 24, 1944, JFKL.

142   Kick countered: Kathleen Kennedy to Joseph P. Kennedy and Rose F. Kennedy, March 22, 1944, JFKL.

142   never been more lucid: Richard Holderness to BL, author interview.

143   "Poor Billy . . .": Kathleen Kennedy to Joseph P. Kennedy and Rose F. Kennedy, March 22, 1944, JFKL.

144   "What are you doing?": Kathleen Kennedy quoted by Jean Lloyd to BL, author interview.

145   found herself bristling: Jean Lloyd to BL, author interview.

145   "We're off!": Billy Hartington quoted by Jean Lloyd to BL, author interview.

146   "fantastic": Kathleen Kennedy's round-robin letter to her family, April 24, 1944, JFKL.

146   "how easily": Kathleen Kennedy's round-robin letter to her family, April 24, 1944, JFKL.

146   At daybreak: Jean Lloyd to BL, author interview.

146   Kick excitedly informed: Jean Lloyd to BL, author interview.

147   "the protecting . . .": Kathleen Kennedy Hartington to Joseph P. Kennedy and Rose F. Kennedy, June 9, 1946, JFKL.

148   As Jean understood: Jean Lloyd to BL, author interview.

148   "I have definitely . . .": Kathleen Kennedy to Joseph P. Kennedy and Rose F. Kennedy, April 24, 1944, JFKL.

149   recorded in her diary: Amanda Smith, ed., *Hostage to Fortune: The Letters of Joseph P. Kennedy*, p. 584.

150   "the dearest . . .": Kathleen Kennedy to Rose F. Kennedy, July 6, 1944, JFKL.

150   Kick scoffed: Anne Tree to BL, author interview.

150   by this point Kick: Anne Tree to BL, author interview.

151   To his vast disappointment: Jean Lloyd to BL, author interview.

152 "very shaken . . .": Lord Harlech, oral history devoted to Robert F. Kennedy, JFKL.

152 "The best is . . .": Joseph P. Kennedy to Kathleen Kennedy, September 8, 1943, JFKL.

153 Kick and Billy took turns: Jean Lloyd to BL, author interview.

154 entered the bedroom: The account of the wedding night is based on the author's interviews with Fiona Arran and Jean Lloyd, to both of whom Kick related the identical story.

155 she responded to say: Kathleen Kennedy Hartington to Joseph P. Kennedy, May 8, 1944, JFKL.

155 Kick wrote to her mother: Kathleen Kennedy Hartington to Rose F. Kennedy, May 9 and May 10, 1944, JFKL.

156 "figured out how to do it": Kathleen Kennedy Hartington quoted by Fiona Arran and Jean Lloyd to BL, author interviews.

156 "the eye": Kathleen Kennedy Hartington's round-robin letter to her family, May 18, 1944, JFKL.

157 "This way . . .": Quoted in Kathleen Kennedy Hartington's round-robin letter to her family, May 23, 1944, JFKL.

157 "I am . . .": Kathleen Kennedy Hartington's round-robin letter to her family, May 23, 1944, JFKL.

158 "This love seems . . .": Billy Hartington quoted in Doris Kearns Goodwin, *The Fitzgeralds and the Kennedys*, p. 789.

Nine

159 5th Coldstream Battalion: For the activities of the 5th Coldstream Battalion in this period, see Julian Paget, *Second to None: The History of the Coldstream Guards* (Yorkshire: Pen and Sword, 2000).

160 "the summer of death": Debo Devonshire to BL, author interview.

160 Word that Mark Howard had fallen: Debo Devonshire to BL, author interview.

160 Many years afterward: Anne Tree to BL, author interview.

160 heightened anxieties at Compton Place: Anne Tree to BL, author interview.

161 helped persuade her: Anne Tree to BL, author interview.

161 found the V-1s terrifying: Joseph P. Kennedy Jr. to Joseph P. Kennedy Sr., August 4, 1944, JFKL.

162 "I have been . . .": Billy Hartington to Kathleen Kennedy Hartington, July 26, 1944, JFKL.

162   Billy knew by this time: Andrew Devonshire to BL, author interview.

163   Not that Debo minded: Debo Devonshire to BL, author interview.

163   professed to loathe: Debo Cavendish to Nancy Mitford, June 22, 1944, Charlotte Mosley, ed., *The Mitfords: Letters Between Six Sisters*, p. 201.

163   liked Kick personally very much: Debo Devonshire to BL, author interview.

163   At this point: Debo Devonshire to BL, author interview.

163   What had mattered: Debo Devonshire to BL, author interview.

164   exacerbated her fears: Debo Devonshire to BL, author interview.

164   "a sort of evil influence": Kathleen Kennedy Hartington's round-robin letter to her family, May 18, 1944, JFKL.

164   "ferociously anti-Catholic": James Lees-Milne, *Prophesying Peace* (London: Faber and Faber, 1984), p. 93.

164   "I am . . .": James Lees-Milne, *Prophesying Peace*, p. 93.

165   "looked askance": James Lees-Milne, *Prophesying Peace*, p. 93.

165   "over a period . . .": Kathleen Kennedy Hartington's round-robin letter to her family, May 18, 1944, JFKL.

165   Bakewell Fair: Debo Devonshire's scrapbook.

166   "Billy was magnificent . . .": Kathleen Kennedy Hartington's round-robin letter to her family, September 23, 1944, JFKL.

166   At the dowager's behest: Anne Tree to BL, author interview.

167   It was in the midst: Anne Tree to BL, author interview.

167   might yet match: Joseph P. Kennedy Jr. to John F. Kennedy, August 10, 1944, JFKL.

167   "I am afraid . . .": Duke of Devonshire to Joseph P. Kennedy, August 14, 1944, JFKL.

167   he assumed that Kick: Anne Tree to BL, author interview.

168   stunned the duke and duchess: Debo Devonshire to BL, author interview.

168   There was some feeling: Debo Devonshire to BL, author interview. Also, Jean Lloyd to BL, author interview. Also, Anne Tree to BL, author interview.

169   "even shone through her sadness": John F. Kennedy to the Duchess of Devonshire, September 21, 1944, Chatsworth.

169   "was so manifest and so infectious . . .": John F. Kennedy to the Duchess of Devonshire, September 21, 1944, Chatsworth.

170   it was Billy: Kathleen Kennedy Hartington to Rose F. Kennedy and Joseph P. Kennedy, September 20, 1944, JFKL.

170   "he was always . . .": Duchess of Devonshire to Kathleen Kennedy Hartington, September 13, 1944, Amanda Smith, ed., *Hostage to Fortune: The Letters of Joseph P. Kennedy*, p. 600.

170   word of the August 20 death: Debo Devonshire to BL, author interview.

171   To Kick's perception: Jean Lloyd to BL, author interview.

172   "We have advanced . . .": Billy Hartington to Kathleen Kennedy Hartington, September 4, 1944, quoted in Doris Kearns Goodwin, *The Fitzgeralds and the Kennedys*, p. 803.

173   September 9: The account of the events of September 9 draws from the author's interviews with Andrew Devonshire, Debo Devonshire, Anne Tree, Elizabeth Cavendish, and Jean Lloyd. Also, the scrapbooks of Debo Devonshire and Jean Lloyd. Also, Julian Paget, *Second to None: The History of the Coldstream Guards*.

175   Looking back: Address by Major General Sir Allan Adair at the 5th Battalion Coldstream Guards Farewell Parade, Cologne Stadium, July 1945.

176   the duke was able to learn: Anne Tree to BL, author interview.

176   "I want you . . .": Duchess of Devonshire to Kathleen Kennedy Hartington, September 13, 1944, Amanda Smith, ed., *Hostage to Fortune: The Letters of Joseph P. Kennedy*, p. 600.

177   "numb": Kathleen Kennedy Hartington's round-robin letter to her family, September 23, 1944, JFKL.

177   "to dry our tears": Rose F. Kennedy to Kathleen Kennedy Hartington, September 25, 1944, JFKL.

177   "a lot of problems . . .": Kathleen Kennedy Hartington's round-robin letter to her family, September 23, 1944.

177   "I like to think . . .": Kathleen Kennedy Hartington to Rose F. Kennedy and Joseph P. Kennedy, September 10, 1944, JFKL.

Ten

180   Poole Harbour: Field Marshal Lord Alanbrooke, *War Diaries, 1939–1945*, p. 597.

180   The duke wanted: Debo Devonshire to BL, author interview.

180   In anticipation: Anne Tree to BL, author interview.

181   his state of despair was to persist: Jean Lloyd to BL, author interview.

181   a photograph of Billy: Jean Lloyd to BL, author interview.

181   For the duke and duchess: Debo Devonshire to BL, author interview.

181   "to bring Billy back . . .": Duchess of Devonshire to Rose F. Kennedy, May 15, 1945, JFKL.

181   struck them as a miracle: Jean Lloyd to BL, author interview.

181   "died": Debo Devonshire to BL, author interview.

182   she had gone at once: Debo Devonshire to BL, author interview.

182   the tension was palpable: Debo Devonshire to BL, author interview.

182   a vague awareness on her part: Debo Devonshire to BL, author interview.

182   she had asked Duke Eddy: Debo Devonshire to BL, author interview.

182   "distracted": Nancy Mitford to Lady Redesdale, September 24, 1944, Char-
      lotte Mosley, ed., *Love from Nancy: The Letters of Nancy Mitford* (Boston:
      Houghton Mifflin, 1993), p. 130.

182   indeed she had been: Debo Devonshire to BL, author interview.

183   almost more than she could bear: Debo Devonshire to BL, author interview.

183   she found herself thinking: Debo Devonshire to BL, author interview.

183   "very clear about what she wanted": Richard Holderness (formerly Richard
      Wood) to BL, author interview.

183   "had its purpose . . .": Kathleen Kennedy Hartington's round-robin letter to
      her family, December 23, 1944, JFKL.

184   she had never in her life: Elizabeth Cavendish to BL, author interview.

184   the duke and duchess agreed: Elizabeth Cavendish to BL, author interview.

184   Elizabeth volunteered: Elizabeth Cavendish to BL, author interview.

184   a painful breach: Debo Devonshire to BL, author interview. Also, Jean Lloyd
      to BL, author interview.

185   his mother's failure: Debo Devonshire to BL, author interview.

185   Kick worried: Kathleen Kennedy Hartington's round-robin letter to her
      family, September 23, 1944, JFKL.

185   Now it called to mind: Debo Devonshire to BL, author interview.

185   For Billy's family as well: Anne Tree to BL, author interview.

185   made a point of vowing: Jean Lloyd to BL, author interview.

185   would very much have preferred: Anne Tree to BL, author interview.

185   poured down her cheeks: Anne Tree to BL, author interview.

185   stares and speculation: Jean Lloyd to BL, author interview.

185   were aware by this point: Debo Devonshire to BL, author interview.

186   Her close friends perceived: Jean Lloyd to BL, author interview.

186   In separate conversations: Jean Lloyd to BL, author interview. Also, Fiona
      Arran to BL, author interview.

187   "I just start . . .": Kathleen Kennedy Hartington to John F. Kennedy, Octo-
      ber 31, 1944, JFKL.

187   "playacting": Andrew Devonshire to BL, author interview.

188   By degrees: Jean Lloyd to BL, author interview.

188 uncertainty about the future: Anne Tree to BL, author interview.

188 Known affectionately: Duke of Devonshire to the Dowager Duchess of Devonshire, November 13, 1944, Chatsworth.

188 "mother hen": Duke of Devonshire to the Dowager Duchess of Devonshire, November 13, 1944, Chatsworth.

189 "nag away": Andrew Devonshire to BL, author interview.

189 "right under": Deborah Devonshire, *Wait for Me!: Memoirs of the Youngest Mitford Sister,* p. 130.

189 she suspected that: Debo Devonshire to BL, author interview.

190 "Darling, I suppose . . .": Quoted in Deborah Devonshire, *Wait for Me!: Memoirs of the Youngest Mitford Sister,* p. 131.

190 In retrospect: Debo Devonshire to BL, author interview.

191 "Now it has been . . .": Kathleen Kennedy Hartington's round-robin letter to her family, January 13, 1945, JFKL.

191 In conversation with: Kathleen Kennedy Hartington's round-robin letter to her family, January 21, 1945, JFKL.

191 feeling much better: Kathleen Kennedy Hartington's round-robin letter to her family, January 21, 1945, JFKL.

191 "I don't like . . .": Kathleen Kennedy Hartington quoted by Jean Lloyd to BL, author interview.

191 Kick confided: Jean Lloyd to BL, author interview.

192 like a throwback: Kathleen Kennedy Hartington to John F. Kennedy, January 25, 1945, JFKL.

192 very eager indeed: Kathleen Kennedy Hartington's round-robin letters to her family, February 11 and February 17, 1945, JFKL.

192 amused her to consider: Kathleen Kennedy Hartington's round-robin letter to her family, March 10, 1945, JFKL.

193 "It nearly kills me . . .": Kathleen Kennedy Hartington's round-robin letter to her family, March 24, 1945, JFKL.

193 "in terrific spirits": Kathleen Kennedy Hartington's round-robin letter to her family, March 24, 1945, JFKL.

194 By Andrew's own account: Andrew Devonshire to BL, author interview.

194 Andrew strove to hide: Andrew Devonshire to BL, author interview.

195 it pained him now: Andrew Devonshire to BL, author interview.

195 Andrew was tormented: Andrew Devonshire to BL, author interview.

195 he could not help but feel: Andrew Devonshire to BL, author interview.

195 he strove to conceal: Anne Tree to BL, author interview.

195   endeavored to mask: Andrew Devonshire to BL, author interview.

195   "Am pleased . . .": Kathleen Kennedy Hartington to John F. Kennedy, April 1, 1945, JFKL.

196   "too closely connected": Duchess of Devonshire to Rose F. Kennedy, April 15, 1945, JFKL.

196   the arrival of a telegram: Kathleen Kennedy Hartington's round-robin letter to her family, April 3, 1945, JFKL.

196   "the agony . . .": Duchess of Devonshire to Rose F. Kennedy, May 15, 1945, JFKL.

196   unfortunate: Duchess of Devonshire to Rose F. Kennedy, May 15, 1945, JFKL.

196   "rather cold": Kathleen Kennedy Hartington's round-robin letter to her family, April 3, 1945, JFKL.

197   one other young woman: Kathleen Kennedy Hartington to John F. Kennedy, April 1, 1945, JFKL.

197   "easier": Duchess of Devonshire to Rose F. Kennedy, May 15, 1945, JFKL.

197   "without the best ones": Kathleen Kennedy Hartington's round-robin letter to her family, May 12, 1945.

Eleven

199   she complained: Kathleen Kennedy Hartington to John F. Kennedy, April 1, 1945, JFKL.

199   too small: Kathleen Kennedy Hartington's round-robin letter to her family, May 27, 1945, JFKL.

199   Mindful that her father: Debo Devonshire to BL, author interview.

200   it was evident to her English friends: Jean Lloyd to BL, author interview.

200   It pained his widow: Jean Lloyd to BL, author interview.

200   possibly assisting Andrew: Kathleen Kennedy Hartington's round-robin letter to her family, May 27, 1945, JFKL.

200   canvass for Richard Wood's brother: Kathleen Kennedy Hartington's round-robin letter to her family, June 20, 1945, JFKL.

200   "a terrific swing to the Left": Kathleen Kennedy Hartington to John F. Kennedy, April 28, 1945, JFKL.

201   "very shocked": Kathleen Kennedy Hartington to John F. Kennedy, April 28, 1945, JFKL.

201   "With the war . . .": Kathleen Kennedy Hartington to John F. Kennedy, April 28, 1945, JFKL.

202   "those foolish people": Lord Moran, Churchill: *Taken from the Diaries of Lord Moran: The Struggle for Survival, 1940–1965* (Boston: Houghton Mifflin, 1966), p. 271.

202   "not very keen . . .": Lord Moran, *Churchill: Taken from the Diaries of Lord Moran: The Struggle for Survival, 1940–1965*, p. 269.

202   "The desire for . . .": Lord Moran, *Churchill: Taken from the Diaries of Lord Moran: The Struggle for Survival, 1940–1965*, p. 270.

202   "Britishers will go . . .": John F. Kennedy, *New York Journal-American*, June 24, 1945.

204   spat upon: Andrew Devonshire, *Accidents of Fortune*, p. 61.

204   In one auditorium: Deborah Devonshire, *Wait for Me!: Memoirs of the Youngest Mitford Sister*, p. 145.

205   he asked her: Veronica Maclean, *Past Forgetting: A Memoir of Heroes, Adventure and Love*, p. 169.

205   "like a possible candidate": John F. Kennedy to his family, July 15, 1945, JFKL.

205   "by looking extremely . . .": John F. Kennedy to his family, July 15, 1945, JFKL.

206   "some lectures": Kathleen Kennedy Hartington's round-robin letter to her family, August 1, 1945.

206   On the aircraft: Mary Soames to BL, author interview.

207   "Chatsworth stuff": Kathleen Kennedy Hartington's round-robin letter to her family, July 22, 1945, JFKL.

207   returning to the U.S.: Kathleen Kennedy Hartington's round-robin letter to her family, August 1, 1945, JFKL.

208   In later years: Hermes Pan to BL, author interview.

208   the very flat above hers: Kathleen Kennedy Hartington's round-robin letter to her family, August 18, 1945, JFKL.

208   "at all hours": Kathleen Kennedy Hartington's round-robin letter to her family, August 18, 1945, JFKL.

209   "rather depressing": Kathleen Kennedy Hartington's round-robin letter to her family, August 18, 1945, JFKL.

209   "feeling very depressed": Kathleen Kennedy Hartington's round-robin letter to her family, August 18, 1945, JFKL.

210   as the houseguest of Michael Astor: Kathleen Kennedy Hartington's round-robin letter to her family, August 18, 1945, JFKL.

211   "very satisfactory": Kathleen Kennedy Hartington to Joseph P. Kennedy and Rose F. Kennedy, August 24, 1945, JFKL.

211   "a little chat": Kathleen Kennedy Hartingtom's round-robin letter to her family, September 2, 1945, JFKL.

212   as if a hundred: Kathleen Kennedy Hartington's round-robin letter to her family, September 10, 1945, JFKL.

212   "extraordinarily well": Kathleen Kennedy Hartington's round-robin letter to her family, September 10, 1945, JFKL.

212   engaged: Kathleen Kennedy Hartington's round-robin letter to her family, October 1, 1945, JFKL.

212   horrified and hurt: Anne Tree to BL, author interview.

213   the latter half: Kathleen Kennedy Hartington's round-robin letter to her family, August 24, 1945, JFKL.

213   "very lonely": Kathleen Kennedy Hartington's round-robin letter to her family, September 10, 1945, JFKL.

215   "a passing fancy": Kathleen Kennedy Hartington to Joseph P. Kennedy, July 2, 1947, JFKL.

216   Berry's man: Kathleen Kennedy Hartington's round-robin letter to her family, May 4, 1946, JFKL.

Twelve

217   flowers: Kathleen Kennedy Hartington's round-robin letter to her family, May 4, 1946, JFKL.

218   deep emotional attachment: Jean Lloyd to BL, author interview.

218   grown the more intense: Jean Lloyd to BL, author interview.

219   "lovely, historical . . .": Kathleen Kennedy Hartington's round-robin letter to her family, May 10, 1946, JFKL.

219   "I think . . .": Kathleen Kennedy Hartington's round-robin letter to her family, May 10, 1946, JFKL.

219   "turned it off and moved on": Elizabeth Cavendish to BL, author interview.

219   unbearable: Elizabeth Cavendish to BL, author interview.

219   dinner party: Kathleen Kennedy Hartington's round-robin letter to her family, June 30, 1946, JFKL.

219   her habit of haphazardly: Jean Lloyd to BL, author interview.

220   echoed with talk: Jean Lloyd to BL, author interview.

220   no subject was discussed with greater fervor: Andrew Devonshire to BL, author interview.

220   a history of vying: Andrew Devonshire to BL, author interview.

220   On the first day: E. A. Smith, *Whig Principles and Party Politics: Earl Fitzwilliam and the Whig Party, 1748–1833* (Manchester: Manchester University Press, 1975), p. 33.

220   no one any longer: Elizabeth Cavendish to BL, author interview.

220   quick to claim the spoils: Andrew Devonshire to BL, author interview.

220   the sum had been the equivalent: Catherine Bailey, *Black Diamonds: The Rise and Fall of an English Dynasty* (London: Penguin Books, 2007), p. 388.

221   was hardly alone at the time: Andrew Devonshire to BL, author interview.

221   they seemed to ratify: Andrew Devonshire to BL, author interview.

221   quite the opposite effect: Andrew Devonshire to BL, author interview.

221   fathered several illegitimate children: Catherine Bailey, *Black Diamonds: The Rise and Fall of an English Dynasty*, p. 284.

222   very much the hero of the hour: Andrew Devonshire to BL, author interview.

222   "dashing and flirtatious and gay and attractive": Jean Lloyd to BL, author interview.

222   "rather dumpy and awkward": James Lees-Milne, *Caves of Ice* (London: Chatto & Windus, 1983), p. 53.

222   "an astonishingly handsome man": Anne Tree to BL, author interview.

222   "rather sorry to leave . . .": Kathleen Kennedy Hartington to Joseph P. Kennedy and Rose F. Kennedy, June 9, 1946, JFKL.

222   began to intensify: Richard Holderness to BL, author interview.

223   he had been in love: Richard Holderness to BL, author interview.

223   "the soul of . . .": Kathleen Kennedy Hartington's round-robin letter to her family, May 18, 1944, JFKL.

223   refrained from speaking: Richard Holderness to BL, author interview.

223   she required a husband: Richard Holderness to BL, author interview.

223   "that curious air of glamour . . .": Joseph W. Alsop, *"I've Seen the Best of It"*: *Memoirs* (New York: W. W. Norton & Company, 1992), p. 408.

223   discreetly visiting: Andrew Devonshire to BL, author interview.

223   plunged Kick into the worlds of horse racing and gambling: Andrew Devonshire to BL, author interview.

224   "wonderfully easy and jolly": Joseph W. Alsop, *"I've Seen the Best of It"*: *Memoirs*, p. 408.

224   More and more: Anne Tree to BL, author interview.

224   accepted Eric Dudley Ward's invitation: Kathleen Kennedy Hartington's round-robin letter to her family, October 18, 1946, JFKL.

224   continued to live: Andrew Devonshire to BL, author interview.

224 "the most enjoyable . . .": Kathleen Kennedy Hartington's round-robin letter to her family, August 26, 1946, JFKL.

225 "The certainty of a Duke!": Kathleen Kennedy Hartington's round-robin letter to her family, August 11, 1946, JFKL.

225 "there were more grouse . . .": Kathleen Kennedy Hartington's round-robin letter to her family, August 26, 1946, JFKL.

225 "The shooting is . . .": Kathleen Kennedy Hartington's round-robin letter to her family, August 26, 1946, JFKL.

225 "prewar standards": Kathleen Kennedy Hartington's round-robin letter to her family, August 1, 1946, JFKL.

226 "interesting": Kathleen Kennedy Hartington to Joseph P. Kennedy and Rose F. Kennedy, October 3, 1946, JFKL.

226 "the other Lady . . .": Debo Devonshire to BL, author interview.

226 rather to her own embarrassment: Debo Devonshire to BL, author interview.

226 Debo would bring with her: Jean Lloyd to BL, author interview.

227 "besotted": Jean Lloyd to BL, author interview.

227 that she must arrange: Jean Lloyd to BL, author interview.

227 applauded the magnificence of the ball: Kathleen Kennedy Hartington to Joseph P. Kennedy and Rose F. Kennedy, October 28, 1946, JFKL.

227 an element of competition: Jean Lloyd to BL, author interview.

227 On Peter's side as well: Andrew Devonshire to BL, author interview.

227 liked him personally: Andrew Devonshire to BL, author interview.

227 For Peter to claim: Andrew Devonshire to BL, author interview.

229 "eighteenth-century lord": Jean Lloyd to BL, author interview.

229 "one of the . . .": Kathleen Kennedy Hartington's round-robin letter to her family, November 8, 1946, JFKL.

229 "It was really . . .": Elizabeth Cavendish to BL, author interview.

Thirteen

230 "It made me . . .": Kathleen Kennedy Hartington's round-robin letter to her family, April 29, 1947, JFKL.

231 "peaceful and tranquil": Kathleen Kennedy Hartington to Rose F. Kennedy, June 1, 1947, JFKL.

232 "really too much": Elizabeth Cavendish to BL, author interview.

232 "seen more of": Kathleen Kennedy Hartington's round-robin letter to her family, April 29, 1947, JFKL.

232 "new schedule . . .": Rose F. Kennedy's round-robin letter to her children, March 6, 1947, JFKL.

232 never been away: Kathleen Kennedy Hartington's round-robin letter to her family, April 29, 1947.

232 the mood and morale: Andrew Devonshire to BL, author interview.

233 dinner party for the Windsors: Kathleen Kennedy Hartington's round-robin letter to her family, October 18, 1946, JFKL.

234 "tremendous ovation": Kathleen Kennedy Hartington's round-robin letter to her family, June 22, 1947, JFKL.

234 "first class": Kathleen Kennedy Hartington's round-robin letter to her family, June 22, 1947, JFKL.

234 he lacked: Jean Lloyd to BL, author interview.

234 "a rather squalid . . .": Kathleen Kennedy Hartington's round-robin letter to her family, June 22, 1947, JFKL.

234 "the largest . . .": Kathleen Kennedy Hartington's round-robin letter to her family, August 3, 1947, JFKL.

235 "The gardens have . . .": Kathleen Kennedy Hartington's round-robin letter to her family, August 3, 1947, JFKL.

235 "an exchange of . . .": Kathleen Kennedy Hartington to Joseph P. Kennedy, August 24, 1947, JFKL.

236 Jean Lloyd accidentally: Jean Lloyd to BL, author interview.

236 Sadly and softly: Jean Lloyd to BL, author interview.

237 she countered that David: Jean Lloyd to BL, author interview.

237 They judged that: Jean Lloyd to BL, author interview.

237 she doubted that: Elizabeth Cavendish to BL, author interview.

237 "moral support": Elizabeth Cavendish to BL, author interview.

237 "absolutely terrified": Elizabeth Cavendish to BL, author interview.

237 she was equally intent: Elizabeth Cavendish to BL, author interview.

237 Elizabeth would join: Kathleen Kennedy Hartington's round-robin letter to her family, December 19, 1947, JFKL.

238 "great big head off": Kathleen Kennedy Hartington's round-robin letter to her family, January 21, 1948, JFKL.

238 "just the family": Kathleen Kennedy Hartington's round-robin letter to her family, December 16, 1947, JFKL.

238 "slightly more sane": Kathleen Kennedy Hartington's round-robin letter to her family, December 16, 1947, JFKL.

238 "But I am mad": Unity Mitford quoted in Kathleen Kennedy Hartington's round-robin letter to her family, December 16, 1947, JFKL.

238   the more deeply ingrained: Deborah Devonshire to BL, author interview.

238   stolen: Andrew Devonshire to BL, author interview.

239   By turns: Jean Lloyd to BL, author interview.

239   At moments: Jean Lloyd to BL, author interview.

239   "choose": Debo Devonshire to BL, author interview.

239   did much to shape Andrew: Richard Holderness to BL, author interview.

239   had Billy survived: Richard Holderness to BL, author interview.

239   Kick's miscalculation: Richard Holderness to BL, author interview.

239   wanted to warn: Andrew Devonshire to BL, author interview.

239   he worried: Andrew Devonshire to BL, author interview.

239   in the end he chose: Andrew Devonshire to BL, author interview.

239   she and Elizabeth: Elizabeth Cavendish to BL, author interview.

240   it seemed inconceivable: Elizabeth Cavendish to BL, author interview.

240   at night they delighted: Elizabeth Cavendish to BL, author interview.

241   she had never ceased: Debo Devonshire to BL, author interview.

243   Jean remembered: Jean Lloyd to BL, author interview.

243   All she could think of: Jean Lloyd to BL, author interview.

243   "for an eternity": Jean Lloyd to BL, author interview.

243   His aim was: Jean Lloyd to BL, author interview.

244   "favorite of all the children": Rose F. Kennedy to Nancy Astor, June 14, 1948, UR.

244   found herself wishing: Debo Devonshire to BL, author interview.

244   telegraphed his son: Joseph P. Kennedy to John F. Kennedy, May 15, 1948, JFKL.

245   a pass at Billy's twenty-two-year-old sister: Elizabeth Cavendish to BL, author interview.

245   Some onlookers wept: Jean Lloyd to BL, author interview.

246   cut a devastated: Debo Devonshire to BL, author interview.

INDEX

Harriman, Averell, 224

Hartington, Kathleen, Marchioness of
("Kick") (formerly Kathleen
Kennedy)
    Berry's courtship of, 215–16, 217,
        219, 232
    burial place of, 244–46
    Cavendish's courtship of, 1–3,
        6–10, 21, 33–34
    death of, 242–46
    Eden's courtship of, 233–38
    education of, 62, 89
    father's relationship with, 4–6, 14,
        30, 55–56, 61, 98, 148–58,
        152–53, 199–200, 213–14,
        237–38, 239–46, 254n5
    Fitzwilliam's courtship of, 222–29,
        231–42
    Frost's courtship of, 214–15
    Hartington's courtship of, 25–30,
        32–34, 36–59, 62–63, 80, 86–92,
        93, 96–97, 105–15, 116–32,
        133–53
    husband's death and, 174–79, 180–98
    journalistic ambitions of, 89–110
    Kennedy, Jack, relationship with,
        8–9, 62, 79, 93–95, 98–107, 120,
        152, 183, 187, 199–200, 202,
        214–15, 235–36, 240, 244–45
    Kennedy, Joe Jr., death and,
        167–70, 184
    Kennedy, Joe Jr., relationship with,
        9, 30, 151–54
    Lloyd, Jean, friendship with, 5–7,
        14–15, 16–18, 21–22, 25, 34–35,
        36–42, 47–49, 63, 89, 144–48,
        153, 155–56, 186, 191, 219,
        236–37

    marriage of, 153–58, 159–79, 218,
        229, 231
    mother's relationship with, 8–9,
        48–49, 58, 141–42, 150–55,
        170–71, 184–85, 237, 239–41,
        244–45
    physical characteristics of, 3, 37
    political ambition of, 135–36,
        139–41, 163–65, 182–83,
        191–92, 198, 200–203, 205–6,
        214–16, 223, 239, 246
    Red Cross service by, 110, 113–14,
        116–32, 144, 153, 160, 163, 168,
        186–87, 190, 192, 205–6, 207,
        212–13
    religious observation by, 8–9,
        45–53, 58–59, 66–67, 113, 120,
        123–24, 131–32, 133–34,
        141–44, 147–53, 155–56,
        171, 177, 184–85, 190–91, 229,
        231
    societal debut of, 4, 18–19, 21–22
    speeches given by, 162–65, 166,
        182, 192
    White's courtship of, 95–110, 113,
        131, 154, 240
    Wood's relationship with, 111–13,
        127, 135–36, 140, 142, 177, 183,
        200, 212, 222–23, 239
Hartington, William Cavendish,
    Marquess of ("Billy") (formerly
    Earl of Burlington), 21, 23
    death of, 128, 174–79, 180–98,
        246
    Kick's courtship by, 25–30,
        32–34, 36–59, 62–63, 80,
        86–92, 93, 96–97, 105–15,
        116–32, 133–53

SS Panzer Division Hitlerjugend, 12th
    Unit of, 173. *See also* Germany/
    Nazis
Stalin, Joseph, 206, 209–10, 215
Stanley, Lord John, 21, 22, 24
Stanley, Oliver, 235
Stratheden, Lord, 158, 161
Stuart, James, 129, 190
Stuart, Rachel, 129
Sykes, Lady Virginia Gilliat, 122, 196
Sykes, Sir Richard, 122, 196

Talbot, Edward Keble, 142
Thomas, Sissie Lloyd. *See* Ormsby-
    Gore, Sissie Lloyd Thomas
Trafford, Ann de, 52
Twilight War, 64. *See also* World
    War II

United Kingdom (UK)
    appeasement policy in, 11–14,
        18–19, 34–35, 37–45, 53–56, 59,
        65, 78, 94, 130, 169
    armed forces of, 19, 37–38, 59,
        69–76, 87, 125, 128–29, 153,
        158–62, 165–66, 171–76,
        187–90, 193–95, 204, 221,
        269n159
    political/cultural shifts in, 129–30,
        134–41, 199–211, 220–22, 225,
        228–29, 232–35, 238, 247
    primogeniture in, 28, 30
    V-E Day in, 196–97, 200
    World War II entrance by, 53–59
United States (U.S.)
    partial nuclear test ban treaty of
        1963 by, 203
    Pearl Harbor bombing in, 102–3

war participation by, 65–71, 79–80,
    82–84, 94, 102–3, 114, 116–17
United States Navy
    Kennedy, Jack, in, 93, 104, 109,
        121–22, 167, 168–69, 171, 189
    Kennedy, Joe Jr., in, 126, 167
    Navy Cross decoration in, 167
University of Leeds, 218–19
U.S. Airborne Division, 82nd, 175

V-1 buzz bombs (doodlebugs), 160–61
the Vatican, 141, 144, 242
Victoria, Queen (of UK), 22–23, 44
Victory in Europe Day (V-E Day),
    196–97, 200

Waldrop, Frank, 90, 96, 102–3
Ward, Eric (Earl of Dudley), 224,
    233
Ward, Laura, 224
Washington (cruise liner), 60–61
Washington Times Herald, 90, 95,
    100–103, 106, 110, 240
Waugh, Evelyn, 211
Wentworth Woodhouse, 220–22, 227,
    234–35
Wernher, Gina, 18, 31, 81
West Derbyshire by-election of 1944
    (UK), 128–30, 134–41, 201, 203,
    211, 214, 221
Whig Party (UK), 204, 220, 221
White, Alderman Charles, 129–30,
    136–41
White, John, 95–110, 113, 131, 154,
    240
Whitney, Jock, 224
Why England Slept (Kennedy), 78, 94,
    99